'Full of exhilaration and hope ... the most sustained indictment of the Blair administration yet published' *London Review of Books*

'A superb account of one of the most scandalous tales of modern times ... a frightening and convincing story of one of the most audacious business strategies ever unleashed' *Management Today*

'Whatever you think of George Monbiot's political views, he writes like an angel' Frances Cairncross, *Nature*

'It's a wonderful book' Gitta Sereny, *Start the Week*

'Grim, accessible and sometimes darkly hilarious ... in the US it might have won a Pulitzer prize for its reportage ... It is chilling' John Vidal, *Ecologist*

'This important piece of investigative journalism reveals how far we have all succumbed to the corporative culture' *New Scientist*

'This is a closely argued book which should make most executives and managers think a little more carefully about what they are doing, and what they think they are achieving. Monbiot isn't some political fanatic who can be safely ignored, but a distinguished writer and journalist who has looked inside the agencies of government and commerce, and doesn't like what he sees' *Ambassador*

'George Orwell once said that all writing is worthless unless it provokes action. *Captive State* ought to inspire a revolution' *Red Pepper*

CAPTIVE STATE
THE CORPORATE
TAKEOVER OF BRITAIN

George Monbiot has been named by the *Evening Standard* as one of the twenty-five most influential people in Britain and by the *Independent on Sunday* as one of the forty international prophets of the twenty-first century. He is the author of the investigative travel books *Poisoned Arrows*, *Amazon Watershed* and *No Man's Land*. He writes a column for the *Guardian* and is Honorary Professor at the Department of Philosophy, University of Keele, and Visiting Professor at the Department of Environmental Science, University of East London. From 1993 to 1995, he was a Visiting Fellow of Green College Oxford and, from 1999 to 2000, he was Visiting Professor at the Department of Philosophy, University of Bristol. In 1995, Nelson Mandela presented him with a United Nations Global 500 Award for outstanding environmental achievement. He has also won a Lloyds National Screenwriting Prize for his screenplay *The Norwegian*, a Sony Award for radio production and the One World National Press Award.

Also by George Monbiot

Poisoned Arrows

Amazon Watershed

No Man's Land

CAPTIVE STATE
THE CORPORATE
TAKEOVER OF BRITAIN

GEORGE MONBIOT

PAN BOOKS

First published 2000 by Macmillan

This edition published 2001 by Pan Books
an imprint of Pan Macmillan Ltd
Pan Macmillan, 20 New Wharf Road, London N1 9RR
Basingstoke and Oxford
Associated companies throughout the world
www.panmacmillan.com

ISBN-13: 978-0-330-36943-5
ISBN-10: 0-330-36943-1

11 13 15 17 19 18 16 14 12

A CIP catalogue record for this book is available from
the British Library.

Typeset by SetSystems Ltd, Saffron Walden, Essex
Printed and bound in Great Britain by
Mackays of Chatham plc, Chatham, Kent

Acknowledgements

I am greatly indebted to my assistant Sandy Kennedy and my researchers Greg Muttitt, Chris Grimshaw and Andrew Wood; also to Antony Harwood, Mari Evans, Tanya Stobbs, Nicholas Blake, Tim Lang, Jean Shaoul, Janet Griffin, Chris Baker, Ian Milton, Wolfgang Müller, Alan Simpson, Sean Geoghegan, John Verrall, Richard Wolfson, Charles Woolfson, Dave Whyte, Steve Tombs and Tim Murphy.

Thank you too to my friends for putting up with me throughout the stressful and exhausting three years this book has taken to research and write, to Zoë Bicât, Adrian Arbib, Hannah Scrase, Susan Hawley, John Vidal, Zoe Broughton, Hugh Warwick, John French, Paula Casal, Caspar Henderson, Mark Lynas, Oliver Tickell, Sir Crispin Tickell, Jay Griffiths, Simon Fairlie, Michael Zair, George Marshall, Guy Horton, Eka Morgan, Darrell Posey, Laura Rival, Crispin Jackson, Kate Geary, Matt Grainger, Nick and Natalie Bicât, my mother and father and many others.

A note on the text

Where I have used the present tense, this indicates the most up-to-date information available at the time of writing. Some of the details may have changed between completion of the final draft and publication. Throughout the text, money is as valued in the year given, unless I specify 'real terms'.

Contents

CONTENTS

CAPTIVE STATE
THE CORPORATE
TAKEOVER OF BRITAIN

Introduction

The Christmas Liberation Front first struck in December 1997. Manchester's celebrations had been sponsored that year by Renault, and the generous donor, in a surfeit of seasonal spirit, had attached its own logo to the top of the municipal Christmas tree. In the dead of night a person or persons unknown climbed the tree, removed the Renault diamond and replaced it with a gold star. Christmas, their organization declared, had been restored to the people.

Manchester's seditious guardians of the public realm are not alone in their efforts to prevent Christmas from becoming a corporate acquisition. In 1998, Westminster City Council sought to prevent the Regent Street Association from using Britain's most celebrated display of Christmas lights to reveal that this was 'The season to be Tango'd': a soft drinks manufacturer had paid for the display. But, the council realized, the association had applied for planning permission so late that if this exhibition were banned there would be no lights on Regent Street at all. The following year, in the hope of averting similar manifestations of excessive generosity, the council helped pay for the lights

1

itself. The authority could scarcely claim to be impervious to the persuasions of the corporate pound, however: at the time of writing it is planning to invite a sponsor to attach its name to the 'Welcome to Westminster' signs beside major approach roads, in return for a 'seven-figure contribution' to the council's new promotional scheme.[1]

There is, it seems, hardly an emblem of public life in Britain which has not been rebranded. A firm called Mediasign, whose sister company rejoices in the name of Bribex, puts local authorities in touch with businesses prepared to sponsor their street signs. The companies replace signs which are damaged or missing, and pay a fee to the council. In return, their logo appears beside the name of the street. Derby, Redcar, Walsall and Birmingham are among the early beneficiaries.[2]

Following an act of parliament passed in 1996, the police have been permitted to 'accept gifts of money, and gifts or loans of other property, on such terms as appear to the authority to be appropriate'.[3] Several forces have responded to the new dispensation. The saddles used by the City of London's mounted police now bear the logo of HSBC, after the bank helped to save the division from closure by meeting some of its costs.[4] Crime prevention in Cleveland is sponsored by General Accident Insurance and a company called Modern Security.[5] In Avon and Somerset law and order was, until recently, underwritten by the drinks chain Threshers.[6] A firm of solicitors called Caesar and Howie has paid for the acquisition by Lothian and Borders Police of a motorbike for long-distance patrols.[7] Villains apprehended by its rider will need look no further for legal assistance than the advertisement on the fairing.

Britain's millennium celebrations testified to a peculiar

vision of nationhood. The national beacon, lit by the Queen to kindle a 'chain of flame' from London to Aberdeen, was a gigantic crucible on which 'British Gas' was scored in words eleven metres long, beneath a crown consisting of eighteen BG logos. The Millennium Dome exhibits the work of some of our most cherished national institutions: the American companies Manpower, Ford and McDonald's. Its Body Zone was sponsored by the chemist chain Boots, its Mind Zone by the weapons manufacturer British Aerospace and its Learning Zone by the supermarket Tesco. The 'Our Town' stage, where 'the diversity of local culture is celebrated',[8] was financed by that guardian of diversity, McDonald's. British Airways and the British Airports Authority used the Dome's Journey Zone to explain to visitors the many advantages of Heathrow Airport's proposed Terminal 5, in which they both have a certain interest. Regrettably, they forgot to represent the concerns of local residents, who have been campaigning to stop the development on the grounds that the extra noise, pollution and congestion would ruin their lives.

At the 1999 Labour Party Conference, Tony Blair told delegates that he would 'set the people free' by creating 'a model twenty-first century nation, based ... on the equal worth of all'.[9] But some attendees at the conference were worth rather more than others. To reach the speeches, delegates had to fight their way past sixty-two corporate stalls: some complained that it looked more like a trade fair than a political gathering.

The conference's fringe meeting on 'Social Justice in a Global Economy' was sponsored by the Swiss company ABB. ABB built the turbines for the Three Gorges Dam in China, which is displacing over one million people from their land.[10] The meeting on 'Holding Government and Companies to Account' was sponsored by the lottery company Camelot. In 1998, the Virgin boss Richard Branson successfully defended himself against an action for libel. He had claimed that the Chairman of G-Tech, then part of the Camelot Consortium, had tried to bribe him not to bid against Camelot for the lottery contract. The meeting on 'Renewing Democracy, Rebuilding Communities' was financed by Tesco, widely blamed for shattering communities by building out-of-town superstores. When Lord Whitty, a minister at the Department of the Environment, was asked by the BBC whether the exhibitors at the conference were buying access to ministers, he replied, 'You don't buy access to ministers. You buy access to the whole party.'[11] I think he was trying to reassure us.

*

These are just the outward signs of the corporate takeover of Britain, the crude and generally trivial manifestations of a far deeper problem. Corporations, the contraptions we invented to serve us, are overthrowing us. They are seizing powers previously invested in government, and using them to distort public life to suit their own ends. *Captive State* tells the story of this coup d'état.

It demonstrates that the provision of hospitals, roads and prisons in Britain has been deliberately tailored to meet corporate demands rather than public need. It shows how urban regeneration programmes have been subverted to serve the interests of private companies, how planning permission is offered for sale to the highest bidder, and how the Department of the Environment, Transport and the Regions has fallen prey to a perilous conflict of interest. It examines the means by which the superstores have achieved their pre-eminence in Britain, closing down competing shops and controlling their suppliers. It documents some of the curious discrepancies between the duties of business people appointed to government posts and their former activities.

It shows how biotechnology companies have sought to turn the food chain into a controllable commodity and details the extraordinary web of influence linking them to government ministers and government agencies. It investigates the corporate takeover of British universities, and the resulting distortions of the research and teaching agendas. More briefly, it examines the corporate takeover of schools, the neglect of health and safety enforcement and the deregulation of business, coupled with the increasing regulation of the citizen. *Captive State* shows how corporations have come to govern key decision-making processes within the European Union and, with the British government's blessing, begun to develop a transatlantic single market, controlled and run by corporate chief executives. In conclusion, it suggests some of the means by which corporate power might be contained and accountable, democratic government protected from its excesses.

Many of the stories I have to tell have never been told before. Some of them raise serious constitutional questions. Some, I believe, are – or should be – resigning matters. But others suggest a process far deeper and broader than any brokered by a single administration – the corporate control of the means of government, as well as its implementation. *Captive State* details the institutional corruption of a nation which has long enjoyed a reputation for integrity.

Researching and writing this book has not been easy. Working in the absence of freedom of information laws is rather like trying to draw a star map on a cloudy night. Occasional breaks in the cloud enable you to see the odd star and to start charting its relationship to its neighbours, before the sky closes up again. When the cloud breaks once more, the stars have moved a little way across the sky, and you have to revise the map accordingly. I know that I will never be able to chart a complete, or even moderately well-furnished map: this account remains full of black holes and empty spaces. Far from facilitating attempts to examine the influence of corporations, the government has, perhaps understandably, helped to frustrate them. The Department of Trade and Industry's booklet *Protecting Business Information* advises executives to 'reduce the risk of damage to your company's reputation' by protecting sensitive information. Staff should be gagged ('ensure a confidentiality agreement is signed') and all sensitive documents should be destroyed 'by approved cross-cut shredding, pulverising, burning or pulping'. Among those from whom material should be hidden are 'investigative journalists' seeking 'to obtain newsworthy information'.[12]

*

This is not the first time that corporate power has threatened democracy. Gladstone's efforts to regulate the rail industry, for example, were obstructed by the 132 MPs who held directorships in railway companies. Abraham Lincoln wrote: 'I see in the near future a crisis approaching that unnerves me and causes me to tremble for the safety of my country . . . corporations have been enthroned and an era of corruption in high places will follow.'[13]

These powers have re-emerged, yet the government shows few signs of trembling for the safety of its country.

New Labour, its leaders often remind us, is 'the party of business', which aims to establish 'the most business friendly environment in the world'.[14] There is, Tony Blair told the Confederation of British Industry, 'great commitment and enthusiasm, right across the government, for forging links with the business community'.[15] 'We want a society,' the cabinet minister Peter Mandelson announced, 'that celebrates and values its business heroes as much as it does pop stars and footballers.'[16]

Parliamentary opposition to the corporate takeover of Britain is muted. The Conservatives, who initiated many of the intrigues to which the Labour Party has succumbed, call only for the needs of business to be better served. Some Liberal Democrat MPs have spoken out against the corporate threat to parliamentary sovereignty, but they have, for the most part, been ignored. Though many Labour backbenchers are apprehensive of the implications for democracy, most have been stifled and silenced.

This is not to suggest, however, that the appeasement of corporations by the British government is either consistent or comprehensive. Some ministers, such as David Clark, Nigel Griffiths and Michael Meacher, have sought to resist the delegation of their powers to unelected business people. As Secretary of State for Trade and Industry, Margaret Beckett established a reputation, only partly deserved, of treating applications for takeovers and mergers with caution. Most of the resisters have, however, been sacked, in Clark and Griffiths's case for the cardinal sin of keeping the promises in Labour's manifesto.

Some policies have been approved which displease corporations: the introduction of a minimum wage, for example, of energy taxes, limited working hours and the

7

recognition of trades unions. But in every case, the impact of the new legislation has been cushioned until it meets only the minimum demands of the unions, or the minimum standards required by European Union directives or international treaties.

The trades unions were dismayed when their members failed to secure a right to bargain collectively with employers. They found the minimum wage levels disappointing, especially as a lower band was established for eighteen-to-twenty-one-year-olds. The government's energy tax proposals have twice been downgraded to allow major rebates for the most energy-intensive industries. In January 2000, the government dropped its plans for a code of practice for part-time workers. There is, it has assured corporations, no more to come. The new employment legislation, Tony Blair insists, 'seeks to draw a line under the issue of industrial relations law ... Even after the changes we propose, Britain will have the most lightly regulated labour market of any leading economy in the world.'[17]

*

It is not hard to see why corporations might wish to infiltrate government. Their demands and those of the electorate are frequently in conflict. By bypassing the electoral process, communicating directly with ministers and officials, they can pre-empt legislation which might be popular, but could restrict their ability to make money. Many businesses see government as an opportunity as well as a problem. It has long been a source of funds: relocation and development grants, research money and training costs, for example. It also controls that part of the economy which some firms have identified as their means of future growth. In the 1980s, corporations lobbied for, and secured, a widespread privatization or part-privatization of state-owned assets. It continues, through the Private Finance Initiative, to this day.

Opportunities for privatization are now more limited than they were in the mid-1980s, however, as the most accessible possessions of the state have already been procured, and public resistance impedes more ambitious schemes. Now many of the world's biggest companies have chosen a new route to growth: consolidation. By engineering a single, 'harmonized' global market, in which they can sell the same product under the same conditions anywhere on earth, they are hoping to extract formidable economies of scale. They are seizing, in other words, those parts of the global economy still controlled by small and medium-sized businesses.

To succeed, big business has to push government out of the way. It must extract politics from the national domain and into the international sphere, where the electorate, faced with the falling health, safety and environmental protection standards which accompany harmonization, cannot intervene. A compliant state, willing to assist in its own redundancy, is an indispensable asset.

At first sight, it is harder to see why a government should wish to allow the corporations to usurp it. I believe there may be several reasons.

The first, and most obvious, is that the simplest means of obtaining power is to appease those who possess it already. The Conservative administration, whose links with big business could fairly be described as organic, built up the power of the corporations in Britain, placing their representatives on official committees or even in the Cabinet, handing over control of key sectors of the economy, deregulating business practices and harnessing the civil service to their advancement. International bodies such as the World Trade Organization and some sections of the European Commission have also succumbed to corporate control. Confronting big business now means confronting all the institutions it has captured and co-opted.

Consolidation in the print and broadcast media industries has also enabled a few well-placed conglomerates to exert a prodigious influence over public opinion. They have used it, unsurprisingly, to campaign for increasing freedom for business (and, incidentally, reduced freedoms for everyone else). Globalization, moreover, has enabled companies to hold a gun to government's head: if it refuses to meet their demands, they threaten to disinvest, move their plant to Thailand, and damage its credibility by making thousands of workers redundant. The sheer size of the new transnational corporations also enables them to swing an unprecedented weight.

The Labour Party, in other words, like left-of-centre parties all over the world, was presented with a brutal choice. It could continue to oppose the massively increased forces of corporate Britain, with the result that it would face a hard and painful struggle to be elected, and the possibility, if it failed, of the final disappearance of the party. Or it could bend to the power of business, promising that it would deliver not only what the corporations wanted, but also, in the absence of an official anti-corporate opposition, a pliant parliament and a discouraged electorate.

The problem with appeasement, of course, is that it makes the appeased more powerful, which makes the need to appease them still greater. As the Labour government has been confident of winning a second term in office, it appears to have worried less about the electorate than about business, which seems more likely to switch its allegiance back to the Conservatives.

Finally, not all the opportunities provided for corporations are provided deliberately. Their ability to exploit every ambiguity and uncertainty offered by legislation borders, sometimes, on genius. I find I cannot blame them: enterprising companies will always seek to maximize their opportunities. But a government which allows them to do so at public expense is a government which has surely lost its way.

*

The corporation is an ingenious device for acquiring rights and shedding responsibilities. This was not, however, how the institution was conceived. The solicitor Daniel Bennett has written a brief history of corporate emancipation.[18] He notes that the first corporations in Britain were charitable institutions, churches, schools and hospitals for example, which used incorporation to avoid the legal and financial problems – such as death duties – encountered by a body which outlived its founders. These organizations were licensed by the Crown, which determined what they could and could not do. Engaging in profitable commercial activities was forbidden.

By the end of the sixteenth century, the monarch began to award 'charters of incorporation' to trade associations. The associations were granted a royal monopoly in certain economic sectors, but did not buy and sell in their own right. Businesses had to join an association in order to trade. This closely regulated system began to break down after a trade association called the East India Company was chartered. It slowly and unlawfully transformed itself into a profit-making company of shareholders, jointly owning the stock previously belonging to its member businesses.

Other trade associations swiftly followed suit, and soon the Crown and then parliament began to license them as commercial corporations. They were stifled after the bursting of the South Sea Bubble in 1720, but began to re-emerge towards the end of that century. Gradually they acquired many of the legal rights hitherto granted only to humans. Governments lost the ability to destroy them if they exceeded their powers.

Throughout the twentieth century, companies learnt new means of discarding their obligations: establishing subsidiaries, often based offshore and in possession of no significant assets, for example, to handle contentious operations. In 1998, a leaked letter from the Lord Chancellor's office revealed that the government was planning to protect British-based multinationals from legal claims made against them by workers in the Third World.[19] In 1999, the Court of Appeal forbade 3,000 South Africans suffering asbestos poisoning to sue Cape plc, the corporation alleged to be responsible, in the British courts, even though Cape is a British company. While they appear to be able to exempt themselves from national law, multinational companies also remain immune from international human rights law, which applies only to states. At the same time, however, corporations in Britain are able to sue for libel, to call the police if their property is threatened, to take out injunctions against protesters or workers. They may use the law as if they were human beings, in other words, but in key respects they are no longer subject to it.

*

Defenders of corporate power have argued that the companies' freedom of action is crucial to the survival of a competitive economy. If their operations were restricted, they would leave the country, moving to places in which they could trade more freely. The result would be widespread unemployment and a collapsing tax base. Business, some argue, being more efficient and better organized than the state, is better placed to manage public life than government.

It is true that some companies might leave the country if the climate for investment became less favourable, though the threat has often been exaggerated. There is no question that greater corporate freedom worldwide puts pressure on every nation to undercut its neighbours by relaxing its standards. But it is important to determine precisely which conditions are required to encourage corporations to stay, and which gifts are superfluous, the withdrawal of which would be met with grumbling but no action. More importantly, as nation states negotiate international treaties, they should surely seek to arrest the race to the bottom that some of these compacts appear to encourage. The World Trade Agreement, for example, sets maximum standards for the protection of workers, consumers and the environment, but not minimum standards. Were states to negotiate higher global standards, they would be able to protect their citizens without fearing the loss of capital and jobs.

It is also true that many corporations are efficient and well managed. But they are, by definition, managed in interests at variance with those of the public. Their directors have a 'fiduciary duty' towards the shareholders: they must place their concerns above all others. The state, by contrast, has a duty towards all members of the public, and must strive to achieve a balance between their competing interests. Interestingly, Peter Mandelson, the minister regarded by many as the most amenable to corporate power, appears to recognize this conflict. 'It is not practical or desirable,' he wrote in 1996, 'for company boards to . . . represent different stakeholder interests. Boards should be accountable to shareholders.'[20] 'The government of an exclusive company of merchants,' Adam Smith observed, 'is, perhaps, the worst of all governments for any country whatever.'[21]

*

We hear plenty about the economics of scale, but there is a politics of scale as well: the bigger business becomes, the more we, as consumers and citizens, shrink by comparison. If, for example, the bakery at the bottom of my street decided to alter the way it baked its bread and I complained, threatening to take my custom elsewhere, the owners would be mortified. If half a dozen customers complained, they would return to the old way of baking immediately. I have power in this marketplace, because they are no bigger than I am. If I make a similar complaint to a supermarket, I will doubtless be treated with respect, and perhaps even asked to fill in a form, but when I have gone, the staff will tap their heads. The superstores are big enough not to have to worry about me, unless I am joined by tens of thousands of others. As businesses grow, their customers' power becomes blunt and diffuse.

The diffusion of consumer power makes markets less responsive to demand. They may be sensitive to price, for example, but they are likely to be less able to respond to narrower requirements. This is why, when people who work outdoors want a pair of boots or trousers that will last for years, they don't go to the outdoor shop in the high street, but to the army surplus store, whose products will give them three or four times the use. This is because, inefficient as it is, the initial purchaser, the Ministry of Defence, wields power in the marketplace. Big enough to be heard by the supplier, it can fine-tune its demand until it obtains precisely what it wants.

Nor is it always true that prices will fall as businesses consolidate. While the companies may reap significant economies of scale, they may experience less pressure, as they grow, to pass them onto consumers. This appears to have been the experience, for example, of Britain's superstores. Vertical integration and de facto cartels in some sectors are likely to make the market less competitive.

Most importantly, however, big business means big politics. The bigger companies become, the more power they accumulate. As they grow, their concerns become ever further removed from those of the citizens they dwarf, until the world is run not for the benefit of its six billion poor or merely comfortable inhabitants, but for that of a handful of remote billionaires.

In Britain, small business in some sectors appears to be threatened with extinction. Independent butchers, bakers, fishmongers and greengrocers have all but disappeared from many high streets. Small farms are swiftly being absorbed by larger units, many of which are run by city-based management companies and investment firms. Car dealerships, filling stations, hotels and restaurants, breweries, local newspapers, television companies and publishers are concentrating in ever fewer hands. Even the Internet, which spawned thousands of small companies in the 1990s, now appears to be consolidating.

The death of small business is accompanied by the emergence of giga-corporations: companies whose shares are valued in the many billions of dollars. Though the value of mergers and acquisitions in Europe broke all records in 1998, in 1999, according to the *Financial Times*, it doubled again.[22] The United Kingdom is the most acquisitive nation in Europe, responsible for US$386bn worth of takeovers in 1999, by comparison to the second-placed Germany's total of $261bn.[23] The corporations appeared determined to beat their own record within the first few months of 2000. The Royal Bank of Scotland overcame National Westminster Bank's resistance and bought it for £21bn. The drugs companies SmithKline Beecham and Glaxo-Wellcome – themselves, as their names suggest, the products of recent mergers – agreed a union which would create a single, £114bn company. Vodafone Airtouch seized the German mobile phone company Mannesman for £113bn. In America, TimeWarner and the Internet company AOL concluded the biggest corporate deal in history, worth, according to some estimates, almost $300bn.

One result of this consolidation is that we are faced with a profusion of minor choices and a dearth of major choices. We can enter a superstore and choose between twenty different brands of margarine, but many of us have no choice but to enter the superstore. Were we to tell the corporations dominating some sectors that, dissatisfied with their services, we shall take our custom elsewhere, they would ask us which planet we had in mind. Employees blessed with certain skills and qualifications have more management opportunities to grasp than ever before, with the promise of vast bonuses and share options for the most fortunate. But the opportunities to enter business on your own account are, in many sectors, limited. The opportunities to drop out altogether and survive, for example, as a small farmer or craftsman, have been all but eradicated.

*

The struggle between people and corporations will be the defining battle of the twenty-first century. If the corporations win, liberal democracy will come to an end. The great social democratic institutions which have defended the weak against the strong – equality before the law, representative government, democratic accountability and the sovereignty of parliament – will be toppled. If, on the other hand, the corporate attempt on public life is beaten back, then democracy may re-emerge the stronger for its conquest. But this victory cannot be brokered by our representatives. Democracy will survive only if the people in whose name they govern rescue the state from its captivity.

CHAPTER ONE

The Skye Bridge Mystery

Robbie the Pict is a man of the kind a country produces just once in a generation. Large and hairy, with a broad ginger beard and hands like shovels, he looks like a champion caber tosser. He is famous, however, not for brute force, but for a cunning and pedantic regard for the law. Though an amateur, he has become, some people claim, one of Scotland's foremost constitutional experts. He is the bane of police, crown prosecutors and government ministers.

The Pict is credited by some Scots with the return to Scotland of the ancient throne of the northern kingdom, the Stone of Scone. In his book *The Cludgie Stane of Destiny*, Robbie argues that the stone Edward I stole from the Scots and placed beneath the throne in Westminster Abbey is not, in truth, the real Stone of Destiny, but a toilet lid, cannily substituted for the genuine article before the English army arrived at Scone.[1] Nevertheless, the Pict insists, it is a Scottish toilet lid which, thanks to the constitutional importance it acquired while languishing under the English throne, had become the cornerstone of Scottish sovereignty. Having reported the stone stolen to the Chief Constable of Perthshire in 1993, with a description of the property and eye-witness accounts of the theft, he launched a private prosecution of the Dean of Westminster Abbey for handling stolen goods. When the Dean protested that it was not he, but the Crown, which claimed to own the stone, the Pict instead sued the British government. After three years preparing the case, his final demand landed on the desk of the Home Office Constitutional Unit. Twenty-four hours later, John Major announced that the stone would be sent back to Scotland.

But it is for his engagement in another campaign that Robbie the Pict is best known. For several years ago, the island on which he lives became the laboratory for a novel and controversial experiment.

Skye, as everyone knows, lies over the sea. This topographical distinction delights the tourists following the flight of Bonnie Prince Charlie. But by the end of the 1980s it was becoming something of a nuisance to the residents. The car ferries which connected the island to the mainland kept breaking down, with the result that people often had to queue for two or three hours. Busy people with jobs on the mainland and traders with produce in need of delivery began to find that the romantic detachment of their island home was incompatible with the demands of the twenty-four-hour economy. While some residents, concerned about damage to the environment and the loss of Skye's special character, wanted to sustain their separation from the mainland, others began calling for a bridge. The strait, or kyle, that separated Skye from the mainland, they argued, was scarcely a mile wide at its narrowest point. English islands close to the mainland coast were served by roads; was it not time, they suggested, for Skye too to be connected to the national network?

The Scottish Office, a department of what was then the Conservative government, agreed. Road building was, at the time, a central component of the government's economic programme: wherever feasible, everyone in Great Britain, it maintained, should have access to the trunk road network. There was, it told the people of Skye, just one problem: it had no money. Public funds spent on building a bridge would be public funds not spent on the island's health and education. Rather than be defeated by this constraint, however, it had devised an innovative and remarkable solution.

The people of Skye would get their bridge, but it would be financed not by the government but by a private company. The company would build the structure at its own expense, then recoup the money by charging a toll. The Skye Bridge would, in other words, be the first project built under something called 'The Private Finance Initiative'. The initiative, started by the Conservatives and developed by Labour, has become the means by which many, even most, of the new roads, bridges, rail links, schools, hospitals and prisons in Britain are now built. Private finance, both governments have argued, mobilizes money which wouldn't otherwise be available. The government has to borrow less than it would otherwise have to, schemes are built faster and (thanks to the efficiencies of the private sector) more cheaply than they would be if left to the government.

The people of Skye, accustomed as they were to the wiles of unscrupulous Sassenachs and mainlanders, were suspicious. They didn't see why, when the bridges connecting English islands to the mainland were free, they should have to pay tolls. But the government assured them the bridge would offer excellent value, and the islanders would be able to take pride in participating in an original and exciting new venture.

By the time the bridge was completed, in October 1995, the residents of Skye had discovered that the deal was rather less advantageous than they had been led to believe. In the week the bridge opened, the government-run ferry service across the kyle was stopped: thenceforward the only efficient means of getting to Skye was the bridge. This might have been uncontroversial, had the toll the private companies levied not been the highest, per metre of road, in the world. At the time of writing, the one-mile crossing costs £5.70 each way.

The islanders, curious to discover how this extraordinary situation had come to pass, began to investigate. The story they uncovered, which is revealed in this chapter, is one of the murkiest and most disturbing tales of official collusion, mendacity and incompetence ever disclosed in Britain, a scandal which has more in common with the development of hydroelectric dams in Brazil than with the scrupulous detachment we have chosen to believe surrounds infrastructure projects in Britain.

While the bridge was commissioned and built by the Conservative administration, the islanders charge that the Labour government, far from addressing the irregularities, has compounded them. Moreover, problems similar to those underpinning the Skye Bridge fiasco have begun to emerge among the other Private Finance Initiative projects which the Labour government now pursues with enthusiasm. Schemes designed to serve the public interest have been distorted until their primary objectives become the welfare of the private sector. The Private Finance Initiative has become the means to a new and inescapable form of corporate control.

*

I met Robbie the Pict playing football around the toll booth on the Skye Bridge. The Pict had discovered that Hamilton Park, the land on which the booth and the approach road had been built, had been established with a deed which only a compulsory purchase order could repeal. In its hurry to get the bridge built, the Scottish Office had initiated compulsory purchase proceedings but forgotten to complete them. Legally, therefore, the land remained a designated recreation area, and Robbie and his friends were lawfully entitled to play football there, and use the toll barrier as a goal. 'They don't want to arrest us for this one,' he told me, 'as they don't want the issue raised in court. We could mount a legal challenge to the existence of the toll booths.'

It was another of Robbie's many legal discoveries which had first convinced the people of Skye that the tolls were worth fighting. The toll regime, Robbie believed, breached Article 18 of the Act of Union, which forbids the Crown to levy a tax in Scotland in circumstances not encountered in England. As there was no sole road crossing to an inshore island which was tolled in England, and as the Scottish Office had told the European Union that the tolls should be classified as a tax, the charges looked to Robbie like a straightforward violation of the act. Convinced that they had a constitutional as well as a moral case, the islanders began one of the biggest and most sustained campaigns of civil disobedience in Scotland since the Lewis Risings of 1919.

The campaign began with a petition, circulated by the *West Highland Free Press*. Though Skye has only 10,000 inhabitants, within a few weeks 7,000 people had signed up, demanding a free crossing rather than a toll bridge. They were ignored. So, when the bridge opened, many of the islanders simply refused to pay. Six hundred people, respectable crofters, shop keepers, doctors, factory workers and engineers, most of whom had never been in trouble before, were arrested. Some collected dozens of charges: Robbie the Pict was arraigned on 129. The Highlands police and judicial systems nearly collapsed beneath the load. The islanders launched a series of legal counter-suits. Every month they organized a major demonstration, every week they found a new angle for the media to exploit. Though prominent, Robbie the Pict is just one among the many hard-working and inventive people who have sustained Britain's longest-running insurrection. When I arrived in the summer of 1998, the Skye Revolt was, if anything, even fiercer than when the bridge opened, almost three years before.

*

An old man in an oilskin, with the crimson complexion of someone who has spent his life in the wind, hauled a dinghy out of the water and up the shingle to a hut surrounded by lobster pots. He stopped to watch a flock of oystercatchers flicker past like the scratches on an old film, then crunched away over the stones.

The oystercatchers landed beside the water, where they ran to and fro like a crowd at the scene of a catastrophe. A herring boat passed in a cloud of gulls, and beyond it the currents of the kyle spilt into the sea, streaked by lanes of foam and scars of clear, stretched water.

On the green above the beach at Kyleakin, a swarm of children ran up and down with a football. A woman stopped her bicycle. 'Colin, I want Jamie back by nine. Do you hear me? Colin? Colin!' The baskets of flowers hanging from the lampstands tugged at their chains, petals bouncing away on the wind. Above the houses and the green neon of the Castle Moil Bar, two fangs of ruined fort, held together by a steel brace, scored a crude H on the sky. Beyond them the hills disappeared into the mist, receding in ever paler shades of grey.

Hanging across this intimate scene, as incongruous against its tweed and heather colours and companionable scale as a Chieftain tank at a vicarage fete, was a band of concrete, slung across the sky. One great hoofed foot was planted on the island where Gavin Maxwell wrote *Ring of Bright Water*. A redundant lighthouse nestled beneath its hip. This simple Modernist arch spanned a scandal of Rococo complexity.

*

In a room at the back of the Royal Hotel, Portree, John Campbell lined up a battery of documents. For the last two years he and some of the other islanders had spent every hour between working and sleeping in seeking to uncover the terms on which the bridge had been built. Beneath his eyes were the olive thumbprints of prolonged exhaustion. His hands fluttered as he rolled a cigarette. He looked up, and the crow's feet bunched around his steady brown eyes.

'They thought we were *teuchers* – ignorant highlanders. But I think you'll find we've done a more thorough job than they have.'

The islanders' investigations had progressed slowly until Robbie the Pict placed an advertisement in the local newspaper, offering a reward to anyone who could deliver the secret reports they needed. A few weeks later, a parcel was left on the postmaster's doorstep. It was two feet high, wrapped in brown paper, unmarked and unaddressed. It contained a stack of internal, confidential papers from the Scottish Office: almost every document the islanders had requested but had been refused. Among them was the draft concession agreement for the Skye Bridge, the consultants' reports, feasibility studies and partial accounts. Slowly, meticulously, John Campbell and the other islanders began to tell the story that lay behind the bridge.

Their discoveries have shown how laws and procedures were bent or broken by the government to enable private corporations to extract a staggering profit from the people of Skye. Their findings were passed to the National Audit Office and the House of Commons Public Accounts Committee. These bodies conducted their own investigations. The Public Accounts Committee published, in 1998, one of the most damning reports it has ever produced.[2] Even so, as the islanders were later to discover, the committee merely scratched the surface of the scandal. And, far from responding to Parliament's concerns, the Labour government had worked as hard as its predecessor to cover the tracks of the deal.

During the years leading up to the decision to build the bridge, the government-owned ferry service which ran people from Skye to the mainland and back began falling apart. New boats were promised but never arrived, and the old ones broke down repeatedly, leading to endless delays and, at peak season, to queues three hours long. The ferry operators announced that they would no longer be able to run a twenty-four-hour service: the boats couldn't take the strain. As the ferries floundered, public pressure for the bridge built up. The Highland Regional Council, despairing at the economic damage Skye was suffering, agreed with the government that a road crossing should be developed as soon as possible, and if that meant building a privately owned toll bridge, then that was the way it would have to be. Soon after construction began, at the beginning of 1992, when it was too late to prevent the tolls from being levied, two beautiful new boats arrived, the twenty-four-hour service resumed and the queues all but disappeared. The islanders were not slow to conclude that the delays and disasters which had beset the ferry service had been engineered by the government, to ensure that its proposals won popular support.

Similar suspicions surrounded the cost of the ferry crossing. The tolls on the bridge were to be based on the fares the boats charged. These, when the bridge was first mooted, were steep, but not outrageous. From then onwards, however, the price of the ferry tickets rose astronomically, until, in 1995, the kyle crossing was making £1m in profit every year. Again, the islanders surmised that the ferry fees had risen so steeply in order to present the tolls, once the bridge opened, as a good deal, being marginally cheaper than the prices the boats charged.

On the week in which the bridge was completed, the ferry service was terminated by order of the government. The consortium which ran the bridge had been granted a private monopoly.

It is a lucrative monopoly. When the bridge opened, cars were charged £4.30 each way to make the one-mile crossing. By the time I arrived on Skye, the toll had risen to £5.60. The Forth Bridge, by contrast, several times longer than the

Skye Bridge, costs 80p to cross in one direction, and nothing on the way back. Following massive public pressure and several broken promises, the Labour government has allowed the residents of the island a discount, but only if they buy tickets in non-transferable books of twenty. As many of the islanders visit the mainland only once or twice a year, the books are useless to them. Visitors continue to pay the full fee.

When the ferries ran, foot passengers travelled for free. Today the buses crossing the Kyle take longer than the ferries did and charge for the service. They have to: buses, full or empty, must pay £15.90 every time they use the bridge.

These are just the direct costs the tolls impose on the islanders, who are among the poorest people in Britain. The local enterprise company calculated that removing the tolls would boost the economy of Skye by £1.5m a year, with a net gain of ninety-seven jobs. Every time a tourist crosses the bridge, £11.20 that he or she might have spent on the island disappears. Still more money is lost when the tourists turn away: the islanders' surveys suggest that some fifty cars a day turn back from the bridge when they see how much they have to pay.

Were tolls of this size required to meet the developers' costs, they could, conceivably, be justified. But the taxpayer has already provided most of the money the bridge would have cost to build, had it been funded by the government.

The bridge and its surrounding infrastructure cost, according to one of the companies which constructed it, a total of £25m to build.[3] Rushing to complete the deal, the Scottish Office paid at least £6m to construct the short approach roads.[4] After the consortium which won the bridge contract had started building, the government remembered that there should have been a public inquiry to decide whether or not the bridge was necessary. The consortium was told to stop building while the inquiry was taking place, and was paid £2m in compensation. Even so, the islanders claim, construction did not entirely cease. From the offices in which the inquiry was being held, they could, they maintain, see the coffer dams being built in the kyle.

Most of the public inquiry's proposals, such as a separate lane and cheap or free tickets for local people, were ignored, but one recommendation was respected by the Scottish Office. This was a reduction of the height of the bridge by six metres, in order to reduce its visual impact. John Campbell, who is an engineer, calculated that the change must have saved the consortium £2m. But instead of paying the companies less for building a cheaper bridge, the government decided to pay them more, on the grounds that it had caused them inconvenience. Another £2m of taxpayers' money disappeared.

Three million pounds was spent on hiring consultants (who were appointed without competition) and buying land (which was massively overvalued).[5] A further £3m was allocated by the Labour government, to compensate the companies for reducing the islanders' fares. In other words £16m was handed over by the government to fund a project described as 'privately financed'. When the ferries were removed, the Exchequer lost a further £1m a year in profits it could no longer collect.

The islanders were furious, but the investors must have been delighted. The companies which built the bridge spent, according to the Public Accounts Committee, a mere £500,000 of their own money. In eighteen years of tolling, they would collect, the committee determined, £37m.[6] As the Liberal Democrat MP for Skye, Charles Kennedy, later pointed out in Parliament, the Public Accounts Committee had greatly underestimated the potential gains. The contractors were allowed by the government to charge so much interest that by 2005 £1,000 collected at the toll booths would discharge only £573 of the debt they were deemed to be owed.[7]

The arrangement was so lucrative because, as the National Audit Office reported, the consortium had the government over a barrel.[8] It knew that the Scottish Office was desperate to launch the government's first privately financed project. It knew that once it had won the contract it could tear it up and demand whatever it wanted. The contract stated that no more than £6m of government money would be spent. The consortium demanded more. The contract said that the consortium would carry the risk of falling traffic levels. The consortium told the government to carry the risk. The developers should pay for the approach roads, the contract said. The consortium was having none of it. The tolls were not supposed to rise above the rate of inflation. The developers insisted on another 30 per cent. The contract required that the companies arrange their own finance. The consortium said the government must arrange a loan from the European Investment Bank. One after another, the Scottish Office agreed to everything the developers demanded, until the deal the government struck bore no resemblance to the one it had offered.[9]

The Scottish Office then sought advice about the financing of the bridge. It turned to the Bank of America for help. This was a curious decision, for the Bank of America was also a member of the consortium which had been awarded the contract. It was rather like asking a football team to provide the referee. The bank, acting in the capacity of the government's independent adviser, told the department that its financial plans were sound, and that it should go ahead with the deal.[10] Once the Scottish Office was committed, the consortium to which the same bank belonged then told the department that it could not build the bridge without more money. When questioned by the Public Accounts Committee, the civil servants who brokered the deal admitted that the bank's assurances had been unreliable.[11] They had accepted them without taking legal advice.

But perhaps the most surprising and dangerous concession of all concerned the amount of time the consortium would be allowed to run the toll and how much it would be allowed to charge. To this day, the government maintains that the tolls are likely to be removed after fourteen years. But during negotiations with the consortium, the Scottish Office quietly raised the maximum time limit to twenty-seven years.[12] At the same time, it failed to impose a cap on the profits the developers might make. A parliamentary answer shows that the toll company took £3,254,000 from the Skye Bridge in 1997.[13] If that year was typical and the toll period lasts for twenty-seven years, the bridge which cost £25m to build will extract, at today's prices, some £88m from one of the poorest places in the British Isles.

The Public Accounts Committee concluded that the government's methods were 'contrary to good practice, unfair and imprudent'. Its failure to work out in advance whether or not a privately financed bridge was the best option was 'highly unsatisfactory'. One of the committee members commented that the government could have got just as good value had it financed the project with his Visa card. The Skye Bridge was 'a licence to print money'.[14]

*

John lit another cigarette. His fine yellow face glowed for a second in the gloom. A boat horn sounded from the harbour. From another room in the hotel came the faint screech of a fiddle: a band was rehearsing for the evening ceilidh.

'But the Public Accounts Committee,' he said, 'told only half the story. The rest was outside its terms of reference. Either that, or they didn't understand what they were looking at. Read the reports, then come back and see me, and I'll tell you what's really been happening.'

*

The Crofter's Kitchen café, on the Skye side of the bridge, was in uproar. One hundred people had crammed into the restaurant and the foyer, singing, laughing and shouting over the din. It was Saturday 4 July 1998, and the people of Skye had come to celebrate their independence from America.

The concession to run the bridge, they had found, had, by mysterious means, become the property of the Bank of America. Most of the money they paid at the tolls would be transferred to the bank's headquarters in California. Skye had become, according to their press release, part of 'a US banking gulag', a 'colonial penitentiary' in which they had been held to ransom. They would use Independence Day to demand their release from their imperial masters.

At precisely the time advertised, the hilarity that filled the café came to a halt, and the residents quietly filed out into the car park. A big man with a ginger moustache had brought out a clipboard.

'Right, everybody, you're going to stand in alphabetical order at ten-yard intervals. Flags and music at the front. So listen as your state is called out.'

As he announced the names of the American states, a series of strange creatures stepped up and took the placards that had been printed for them. 'Florida' went to a gigantic orange carton, whose ingredients were listed as 'Pure Florida Orange. Diluted with Scottish Office Mandarins'. Illinois was taken by a lean septuagenarian in wide suit, white tie and trilby, holding a violin case. Mississippi went to a ghoul in a white hood and cape. A middle-aged woman in a racoon-tail hat, with two dead teddy bears slung from a pole, came forward when Montana was called. When all fifty had taken their placards, the big man called out, 'Skye.' The remaining protesters took banners reading 'Welcome to Skye, the £5.60 state', 'Bank of America: The bank that likes to say Gimme' and 'Give me your tired, your hungry, your £5.60'.

A man in a red steward's jacket marshalled people along the pavement as they took their places, making sure that they stood ten yards apart. Three men in full tartan, bearing the saltire and an upside-down stars and stripes, took the head of the line. An accordionist struck up 'The Yellow Rose of Texas' and the Fourth of July Independence from America March set off past the permanent sign the protesters had legally installed on the roundabout ('Beware: Bogus Toll Collectors Ahead') and over the bridge to the mainland.

Motorists hooted and waved as they passed. The people marched, polite, disciplined, in time to the music. They stopped at the toll booth. The postmaster, claiming to be Bill Clinton's special representative, made a short speech. He apologized that the President couldn't be with them in person: he had, regrettably 'gotten held up in the bathroom, helping one of his interns to grasp the essentials of the body politic'. But on his behalf, 'I would like to welcome you to the fifty-first state of America, and thank you sincerely for all the contributions you've made to our federal tax-take . . .'

Several people were interviewed by local news crews, then, as orderly as ever, the protesters marched back across the bridge.

*

The protests had begun with a simple campaign of non-payment. The people of Skye would arrive at the toll booths and refuse to pay for the privilege of getting on or off their island. The result was chaos. The Northern Constabulary had to bring in officers from as far away as Sutherland, and within a few months its entire annual overtime budget had been exhausted.

The toll company changed its tactics. It stopped calling the police, and simply refused to let the non-payers pass. So the islanders devised new means of frustrating their captors. On some days they would pay the toll penny by penny, blocking the bridge for hours on end. On others they would bring cardboard cheques so large that they wouldn't fit through the tollbooth window. Soon before I arrived, they had discovered that the collecting company banked its money on Fridays, so thirty people were planning to arrive at intervals on a Saturday morning with £100 notes and no change.

The islanders had discovered that the company empowered by the government to collect the tolls had changed its name, while the deed which appeared to allow it to charge the money remained the same. So Robbie the Pict bought the discarded company name – 'Skye Bridge Tolls Ltd' – and insisted that he, and not the consortium, now had the legal right to collect the money. When the company protested, he offered to sell them the original name for £1m, and demanded that they 'remove our good name from the documents which you are using for the purpose of exacting money from road users'.[15] 'I've got a right,' he told me, 'to collect the tolls. One of these days I'm going to set up in a garden shed and, if the police come, I'll tell them I've got the paperwork: it's them you should be arresting.' The protesters put in a bid to buy the bridge, and another to acquire the ferries that used to run across the kyle. Both were, unsurprisingly, rejected by the Scottish Office.

Once a month since the bridge had opened, the campaigners had organized a demonstration, in order to keep the issue in the public eye. They devised a new theme every month. When the minister responsible for the bridge erroneously assured the islanders that if they didn't want to use it they could take an alternative route, they brought the system to a standstill by driving round and round the roundabout leading to the bridge, looking for the alternative exit.

Unlike many protests further south, these were initiated and run by middle-aged and older people. Among the organizers were a painter and decorator, a Gaelic broadcaster, the postmaster at Portree, a retired miner, a checkout assistant, five teachers, an engineer and three GPs. 'It takes a lot,' one of the protesters told me, 'to make us angry, but when we do get angry, we don't give up.' They were careful always to ensure that the protests remained lighthearted: as a result no campaigner had been arrested for any offence more serious than obstruction. They had maintained a high profile in the Scottish press, and generated a great deal of public sympathy. The local brewery brought out a batch of Extortion Ale in support of the protest, road-haulage companies instructed their drivers not to pay the tolls. Hotels and pubs throughout the Highlands and Islands gave discounts or free drinks to the protesters. The Skye Revolt had spread to the mainland.

*

In a youth hostel in Kyleakin the protesters gathered, soon after they left the bridge, to plan the next phase of their campaign. They were formidably organized. The meeting was chaired by Drew Millar, the postmaster and a member of the Highland Council, who had already been fined fifty times for obstruction. He spoke at tremendous speed, and marshalled the meeting with a scowling, fiery sympathy which seemed to me to be the most useful attribute a chairman could possess. He asked John Campbell to present the latest research, then asked Robbie for a legal report. The Pict told the meeting that he believed the Secretary of State was acting outside the law when he had signed the revised toll order. He had devised several new legal challenges, but needed more criminal cases to peg them to. The meeting agreed to have more people arrested for obstruction. They chose a day on which to drive to the toll booth at thirty-minute intervals, refuse to pay, block the road and wait for the police. Someone volunteered to ring round and find twenty people to do it. There was a brief discussion about the following month's protest. A theme and a tactic were chosen, the tasks were assigned and, within forty minutes, the meeting, passionate, cordial, disciplined, had broken up.

*

A herring gull stood on the locomotive of the early morning train to Dingwall and filled Kyle station with cynical laughter. Nets had been stretched across the far platform to dry. On the road leading down to the station was a fishing boat, parked on a row of sleepers and surrounded by traffic cones. Across the water, Kyleakin hid its face in the skirts of the hills.

The lambs grazing beside the track fled the train. An otter nosed into the bladderwrack on the shore of Loch Carron. Curlews strutted officiously across the mud. At the head of the loch, dead trees, dry and barkless, the picked carcasses of dinosaurs, lay white as bones where the river had dumped them in its winter spate. An arrow slit of sunlight incised the far side of the glen.

*

In the National Hotel in Dingwall, Robbie the Pict, crammed into a three-piece suit, savaged a monstrous breakfast: sausages, scrambled egg, tomatoes and two racks of toast. As he ate, he briefed the small crowd sitting at his table. He advised one man on how Dingwall's royal charter could be used to protect its inhabitants from paying parking fees, another on the means by which contraventions of the Act of Union allowed Scotland to sue for independence. He told a third that yes, the blues band he fronted, playing the mouth organ and mandolin, would be able to do a gig for him.

'Sit down, pal. Have a cup of coffee.'

He talked as relentlessly as he ate.

'The public has been asked to build the mangle, then to put their hands in it. They think we're *gadgies*. But they'll not be writing this in their CVs in a wee while.'

A fifth man arrived. He was worried, he said, that a local businessman had too much influence with the council.

'Oh Christ, aye, I wouldn't worry about him. He's just a Daimler-driving pseudo-Christian.'

'Which Church?'

'Bank of Scotland.'

The last piece of toast disappeared and Robbie pushed back his chair.

'Right, let's go and beat the bastards.'

Outside the court, Robbie the Pict spoke in a low, urgent voice to one of the protesters, his big hands corralling the air. Police and court ushers walked past them, in and out of the doors. None failed to exchange a word with the Pict.

'How, Robbie, how ya doing?'

'Not too bad, Dougie, how are you?'

'You leave that poor sheriff alone now, Robbie.'

'Ach, Tom, he enjoys it. Keeps him young.'

Dr Shona Bird, the defendant, a retired GP and the image of affronted respectability, in bifocals, pearl earrings and a cashmere cardigan, listened carefully and nodded.

Like the seats in a theatre, the benches in court stepped down towards the defendant's box. The young man whose case preceded Dr Bird's must have felt the whole court breathing down his neck. Men in black frock coats or military uniforms glared at him with cold disapproving eyes, their mouths proud and pursed, from dingy paintings high on the walls. Among these haughty guardians of the court's authority were those pillars of legal rectitude Sir James and Sir Alexander Matheson, the men who, in the mid-nineteenth century, forced the Chinese to trade in opium.

It was a grim little case, in which a young man driving

an overloaded car had fallen asleep at the wheel and crashed, killing a little girl sitting in the back. Since the crash, he had started seeing the girl's sister, and now her family was split down the middle. The factions sat several benches apart, behind hard, angry faces.

Sheriff Forbes was a big, florid man in magnifying spectacles. He spoke in a singsong, clerical voice, hitting the terminal consonants so hard that his tongue bounced off them with a sigh. 'Applying an objective test-er ... The Toyota braked-er ...' His theatrical patience was pitched in perfect counterpoint to the theatrical impatience of the Procurator Fiscal. The fiscal, Mr Hingston, whose role is roughly equivalent to that of a crown prosecutor in an English court, was a thin, sallow, good-looking man with a JFK haircut and, curiously, a lurid Winnie-the-Pooh tie. He turned his back on the defendant while questioning him, head thrown back, interrogating the mouldings, responding to the mumbled replies with long, sibilant intakes of breath. Fast, flitting, alert, he feigned an exasperated neuralgia that made everyone shift in their seats.

When the young man was pronounced guilty, he turned with trembling grey lips to where his girlfriend sat. As the court cleared, one of the men from the frontbench faction turned to face a man from the backbench faction.

'I'll see you outside, Neal.'

'Y'fucker.'

The police pushed them apart. From outside came the sound of shouts and scuffles.

*

'All stand!'

The sheriff re-entered the court. Dr Bird stood upright

in the defendant's box, hands crossed in front of her. She gazed steadily at the sheriff's face. He smiled at her.

'Now, Dr Bird-er, are you familiar with the procedure?'

'I'm learning.'

'Can we take it-er that you're over twenty-one?'

Mr Hingston interjected with a fleeting grin. 'That remains to be challenged.'

Dr Bird began outlining her defence against five charges of non-payment. She could not, she argued, be sure who it was who was asking her to pay the toll. He had no uniform, he did not introduce himself, and provided no evidence of lawful authority to collect tolls. Indeed, the issue of who was and who wasn't legally empowered to collect them was in dispute. So, though she had tickets, she didn't offer them to the collector.

'Dr Bird, you were questioned by the police on these occasions. You replied "In my opinion, to levy tolls in any part of the UK is illegal and immoral and should be resisted."'

'Yes.'

Mr Hingston turned to the wall and questioned it with weary incredulity. 'So could you tell me what on earth that's got to do with to whom they should be paid?'

'They're separate matters.'

The prolonged intake of breath. 'Exactly.'

'They *are* the highest tolls in Europe, Mr Hingston.'

The sheriff, benign and owl-like, listened carefully to the arguments, his head cocked slightly to one side, then leant back in his chair. He summed up, then paused.

'There is clearly ample evidence to conclude who was making the demand-er. I have little difficulty in concluding that the finding should be guilty on each charge.' He leant forward, fingers knitted, and I thought I saw the flicker of a smile. 'I propose to deal with them-er by way of admonition.'

A few minutes later, the Pict was standing in the defendant's box, his shoulders stretching his suit, great ringed hands gripping the rails.

'Mr Pict-er, good morning.'

'Your Lordship, good morning. It's only one small matter which, if I may, I'd raise before the court.'

Robbie the Pict, his rumbling voice filling the court, explained that in several of the cases against him, a plea of 'not guilty' had mistakenly been entered, when in fact he had made no plea. The case immediately plunged into the most fantastic complexity, as Robbie, the sheriff and Mr Hingston tried to untangle the technicalities of two and a half years of adjudication. The fiscal trudged through a wilderness of paperwork, and his high, nasal voice creaked on and on. 'Intermediate diet . . . warrant for 28 July . . . bill of application . . . September . . . January . . . October . . . bring it back into process . . . pleas to competency . . . leave to appeal given on certain grounds . . .' I was lost immediately.

Robbie lowered his head like a bull and answered in a growling, respectful voice. He seemed to agree with what the sheriff said, and when the court rose and we stepped into Dingwall's uncertain sunshine, I assumed he had lost his point.

'Ach, no, pal. We've got them gubbed.'

Robbie explained that he had simply been carving a handful of charges away from the others so that they could be heard separately. The fiscal thought he was doing something quite different. 'They've never understood the game we're playing. They thought we were trying anything that came into our heads, one at a time. At first they thought we were playing snap, then brag, then poker. They still haven't tumbled to the fact that it's whist, and we haven't told them what the trumps are.'

He looked at his watch. 'I'm starving. I musta missed my breakfast.'

*

Three hundred and seventy-eight protesters had already passed through the Dingwall Sheriff's Court. On the first day of proceedings, 198 defendants were called. 'To make us feel like common criminals,' John Campbell had told me, 'they would always bring up one or two drunken drivers ahead of us. There were the poor wee sods, still hung over, expecting a nice quiet court. And there we were, kilts, banners, the lot. We filled the court and the witness rooms. In the end it was like being back at school, because all they did was call out the register and we said "Present". They couldn't do anything with us.'

From the beginning, the protesters claimed, it was clear that their cases were as much political as judicial. Even the procurators fiscal seemed perturbed by the Crown's decision to treat the alleged wrong-doing as a criminal rather than a civil matter. When the defendants applied for help, all of them, irrespective of income, received the same reply from the Legal Aid Board. 'The Board is not satisfied,' the letter said, 'that it is in the interests of justice that legal aid be made available to you.' Their appeals against this decision were turned down on the same grounds. They were, as a result, left to tackle a fiendishly complex suite of legal arguments without access to lawyers. Robbie the Pict and

John Campbell spent weeks reading legal textbooks, briefed the first defendants, then encouraged them to coach the next people who came to court.

At first, the Procurator Fiscal's Office did not want to prosecute. It was instructed to do so by the Lord Advocate, who is appointed by the Scottish Office. One judge, Sheriff Cameron, described the prosecution's case as 'the lowest end of frivolity – it shouldn't be in my court'. He was never asked to preside over the cases again. Instead, another Sheriff, Jimmy Fraser, oversaw the majority of the prosecutions. People were convicted on the strength of what seemed to them the flimsiest and most contradictory evidence. In one case, one policeman alleged that the defendant was travelling in a red van from Kyleakin to Kyle. Another said it was a green car travelling from Kyle to Kyleakin. The defendant was pronounced guilty.

The 378 defendants were tried on the evidence of just eight or nine policemen and the manager of the toll booth. These witnesses had to remember the details of up to thirty cases at a time, in some instances nearly two years after the event. The standard of proof, Robbie claimed, fell through the floor. One defendant was told by the court that it did not matter to within three days when the alleged offence had taken place.

Even so, soon after the trials began, the protesters secured a significant victory over the Crown, when Sheriff Fraser threw out the prosecution's case on the basis that the toll order did not specify who should pay. The prosecution went to appeal. In Scotland, the Lord Justice General is supposed to canvass opinion among senior judges as to which is the most suitable to preside over the bench at an appeal. In this instance, he appointed himself, overruled the sheriff and granted appeal to the Crown. The Crown's appeal was heard within ten days. An appeal by the protesters, by contrast, was still pending two years later. Even so, Robbie the Pict succeeded in winning leave to appeal on five separate grounds: an extraordinary achievement for an amateur, and testament both to the islanders' perseverance and the questionable nature of the judicial process.

When the old Lord Advocate was promoted to Lord Justice General, the new Lord Advocate decided to drop most of the charges and concentrate on the prosecution of a few protesters, whom the Crown alleged to be ringleaders. 'We did win,' John Campbell told me. 'We beat them because the system couldn't cope. People with fifteen charges in the system were let off on the grounds that they were not persistent offenders. We broke the back of the courts.'

The authorities, however, had no intention of making life easy for the defendants. There was a sheriff's court in Portree, on the Isle of Skye, but the Crown insisted on trying all the protesters in Dingwall, one hundred and twenty miles away. Because of the caseload, and the etiolated nature of the sheriff's court's procedures, some defendants had to turn up in court as many as fifteen times to defend a single case of the non-payment of £5. On most of these occasions, they would simply be asked whether they were present and then told to go home again, but it meant taking a day off work, travelling two hundred and forty miles and paying the tolls both ways. A man who refused to turn up to one of these 'intermediate diets' received eleven days in prison. 'They are trying to wear us down,' Robbie the Pict told me, 'but they won't succeed. We will raise the petrol money penny by penny to come here.'

Robbie was locked up on his fiftieth birthday. He was

convinced that they chose the date deliberately: the non-appearance warrants had been hanging over him, unenforced, for weeks. Friends turned up from all over Britain to celebrate at his house, and had to do so without him.

Even so, the protesters told me, they wanted the trials. It was, Robbie said, 'the only opportunity we had to object and appeal. All the usual democratic channels were closed. The last chance was to put your head in the conviction noose. It's a sad indictment of colonial rule by Westminster, that the last niggers of the empire have to stand on the trap doors to have their say.'

And the proceedings were not without humour. One man was asked by the sheriff whether he was a lawyer. He replied that he was not. 'In that case,' said the sheriff, 'I can't hear you.' 'I said,' replied the defendant, 'I AM NOT A LAWYER!' John Campbell sent Mr Hingston a Christmas card, entitled 'I have a dream'. The procurator fiscal was shown thinking. In the thought bubble was Robbie the Pict saying, 'Overwhelmed by your brilliance we have no alternative but to plead guilty.' Hingston had it framed. But 378 peaceful, respectable people had been prosecuted and, in most cases, fined for resisting the licence a foreign company had been granted, to charge them an entry fee every time they wished to go home.

*

Robbie the Pict drove me back to Skye in the ancient official Mercedes of the 'Scottish People's Mission'. He drove like a maniac, making 85 m.p.h. on the worst A-road in Britain. When a tourist's car ahead of him hesitated at an S-bend, he overtook it before I realized what was happening, uttering, as he passed the other driver, 'You're a numptie, pal.'

Workmen on the road, a farmer, even a policeman, all waved to him, and the Pict lifted a massive forefinger from the wheel in reply.

At the height of the non-payment campaign, Robbie the Pict's car was stopped twenty times in five weeks. He was investigated for non-registration, using false plates, possession of a stolen vehicle and possession of a stolen engine. He was not prosecuted for any of these alleged offences, but the Pict missed appointments and was held up for precious hours which should have been devoted to preparing briefs. He struck back. One afternoon, he set up his car for immobilization, removing the door locks and the ignition. He drove round the toll booth on the grass verge. He was arrested and the police tried to remove his car. Policemen claim to be able to break into any car within twenty-one seconds, but by seven o'clock the next morning, Robbie's Mercedes was still parked beside the toll booth. The police hired a forklift truck but in removing the car succeeded in putting the fork through the petrol tank. The steady leakage filled the police garage with fumes, and they were forced to allow the Pict to take his car away before the place exploded. The police were furious, but they never stopped Robbie again.

As he drove, the Pict explained the legal challenges he had discovered. Most of them concerned the consortium's authority to collect the tolls. When the toll order was made, Robbie argued, the Secretary of State was supposed to have published a statement giving the consortium permission to demand payment. In its haste to approve the deal, the minister had, he maintained, failed to do so. The Statutory Instruments Act, 1946, Robbie found, made the matter clear: if defendants could prove that an order had not been signed and officially published, they could not be prosecuted for failing to abide by it.

The protesters' argument looked incontestable. But at the trial of a seventy-year-old non-payer, the government produced at the last moment a document which, it claimed, gave the consortium its authority.[16] This document, the Labour Secretary of State for Scotland, Donald Dewar, later told Parliament, 'represents the Secretary of State's written consent to these arrangements'.[17] The protesters examined it and saw that it represented no such thing. All it was, they contended, was a memo to the developers from the Scottish Office, without a date or an ISBN number. It had never been published or even signed by the Secretary of State. Robbie sent the memo to Professor Robert Black QC, widely regarded as Scotland's foremost expert on legal procedure. His response was unequivocal. 'I have absolutely no doubt,' he replied, 'that this document does not constitute any form of consent by the Secretary of State. It simply says that the parties either have or will enter into various agreements.'[18] Even the solicitor who drew up the document on behalf of the contractors described it as 'very minor' and 'peripheral'.[19] The Scottish Office, under duress, admitted that the memo had not been published. It seemed to be, in Professor Black's words, 'a pretty fatal flaw ... the clincher'.[20] When Robbie raised the matter, the sheriff announced that his plea was 'rubbish' and told him to 'shut up'.[21]

Robbie discovered, moreover, that the memo had failed even to mention the company now collecting the tolls, apparently on behalf of the Bank of America. The company named was Skye Bridge Tolls Ltd. The collectors, according to their sworn testimony in court, were employed by Miller Civil Engineering. The contract between the government and the developers had clearly stated that the right to collect the tolls could not be handed from one company to another without the Secretary of State's consent. This had not been given.

Robbie argued that if the document was not lawful, the people taking the money were acting in a criminal capacity. He appealed and applied for a Writ of Interdict against Miller Civil Engineering for the unlawful collection of tolls. In March 1999, Lord Eassie, the Lord Advocate, ruled that Robbie was right: the Scottish Office document did not constitute consent to collect tolls. To the islanders' astonishment, however, he declared that this was 'irrelevant'.[22] Consent, he decided, had instead been confirmed in writing in April 1998, when, in response to the islanders' arguments, the government had testified to the court that Miller was allowed to collect the tolls. But if the government's testimony in court was the first written authority granting the company the right to collect the tolls, then surely, Robbie argued, any cases heard before the government testified were invalid? His appeal was dismissed.

By February 1999, three of the protesters' appeals against conviction had been heard by Lord Rodger, the Lord Justice General – Scotland's chief judge. Lord Rodger, the campaigners believed, may have been involved in a conflict of interest. Because judges are not supposed to review cases on which they have given advice, the Scottish Office insists that 'the Lord Justice General will never involve himself in an appeal which began as a prosecution during his tenure in the office of Lord Advocate'.[23] But one of these three cases started during Lord Rodger's tenure. If, as Lord Advocate, he had instructed the procurator fiscal to prosecute the protesters involved in that case, then by hearing the appeal he would have been reviewing his own decision. There is only one means of determining whether or not Lord Rodger did instruct the procurator fiscal, and that is to examine the contents of a letter he sent on 6 November 1995, in response to the prosecutor's request for guidance. But in August 1999 the campaigners discovered that the Scottish Office had forbidden publication of this letter until 2070.[24] Lord Rodger dismissed all three of the islanders' appeals.

*

We drew up at the toll booth. The ticket collector leant out of the window.

'Ah, Robbie. Now listen. We need a harmonica player for the motorbike trials gig this Saturday. Will you do it for us?'

As we drove away, Robbie shook his head. 'I'm doing the man out of a job, and he wants me to come and play the moothie.'

*

John Campbell stood at the window, watching the rain spatter on the glass. Outside, the mountains were hooded in cloud. He sat down and tapped his pen on a pile of papers.

'The full story of this scandal has never been told, and probably never will be. But we can be sure of several things, which suggest complicity at the highest levels of government.'

The House of Commons Public Accounts Committee had concluded that the taxpayer had received a terrible deal from the bridge, that the contracts had been badly negotiated and the wrong advice had been taken. But this was just the beginning of the story. John Campbell's account, supported by the dossier he had given me, starts in 1990.

Among the leaked documents in the parcel the islanders received were two reports for the Scottish Office by a company called JMP Consultants Ltd. One of them was a dummy 'Invitation to Tender', the other a 'Concession Agreement'. They were dated March 1990. They formed the basis of the contract the government eventually struck with the developers. The 'Invitation to Tender' contains a section called 'Developer's Toll Proposals': it appears to have been written by a potential developer. It lays out precisely how much drivers should be charged.[25] These proposals were almost identical to the real proposals for levying a toll, published two years later by the Scottish Office. In other words, a developer appears to have helped to write the contract which condemned the people of Skye to paying such extortionate fees.

As their investigations advanced, the islanders stumbled across another strange chain of events. According to the Scottish Office, the bridge is owned by a consortium called Skye Bridge Ltd, which is composed of three firms: two construction companies and the Bank of America. But by the time the bridge opened, the *Herald* discovered, the ownership had changed dramatically. One thousand shares had been issued. The Bank of America possessed 997 of them, while the remaining three were in the hands of 'Bank of America nominees'.[26] The bank, in other words, had become the sole controller of the bridge. The other companies involved were employed merely to collect the tolls on its behalf and transfer the money to America. The Scottish Office had twice issued misleading statements about this arrangement.

The contract for the Skye Bridge prohibits the consortium from changing the ownership of the bridge without informing the Secretary of State. In 1998, the Scottish office told the *Herald* that it 'has been aware of these shareholding arrangements since 1991'.[27] But during both the public inquiry, in 1992, and the National Audit Office investigation in 1997, the Scottish Office maintained that the bridge was still controlled by the three original members of the consortium.

There are several reasons why the Scottish Office might have been less than frank about the bridge's change of ownership. The idea that the rights over part of Scotland's infrastructure are wholly owned by an American company, and that most of the money extracted so painfully from the impoverished people of Skye is expatriated, was likely to rub salt into an open wound. The Bank of America, previously known as the Bank of Italy, has a blemished record. In November 1998, it settled with the 250 American government agencies which had sued it, after admitting that it had improperly shifted unclaimed payments into its own accounts, instead of returning them to the public bodies to which they belonged.[28] The bank, moreover, will have wanted to buy the concession from the other companies only if it believed that the crossing would be more profitable than the people of Skye had been told.

The government's problem was compounded when the Bank of America merged with NationsBank, based in North Carolina, in September 1998. An investigation by the *Herald* showed that the Scottish Office, contrary to the requirements of the contract, had not been officially informed about the merger.[29] Again, however, the government failed to act. The islanders were less than ecstatic when they learnt that, following the merger, the outgoing President of the Bank of America received a 'golden goodbye' worth $100m.[30]

John Campbell looked into the financing of the bridge. The Skye Bridge, according to the Miller Group, cost £25m to build.[31] The Scottish Office initially contributed £13m. The European Investment Bank added a further £13m. Private investors paid in £7.5m, the contractors £0.5m, and 'a commercial bank' £6m, making a total of £40m.[32] The bridge, in other words, was 60 per cent over-financed. The only explanation the islanders could suggest is that the investors believed the bridge was going to make a great deal of money, and wanted to buy a stake.

When the consortium complained that it couldn't raise the money it needed on sufficiently favourable terms, the government agreed to ask the European Investment Bank to help. The bank's purpose is to fund projects which boost the livelihoods of people in the less developed parts of Europe. It is legally bound to lend money only when 'funds are not available from other sources on reasonable terms'[33] and to support only those schemes which do not 'distort competition'.[34] Funds for the construction of the Skye Bridge were, as shown above, hardly lacking. The removal of the ferries on the day the bridge opened did not distort competition: it eliminated it. The loan, it appears, was therefore illegally obtained by the government.

The bridge's financial arrangements became even more mysterious when the residents discovered that Miller Civil Engineering is paid £770,000 every year for collecting the tolls.[35] Though the ferries, unlike the toll company, used to collect the money on both sides of the kyle, and pay their collectors the full union rate, they spent just £116,000 per year on the same task.[36] The collection costs of the tolls, at present prices, will add up to £18.75m by the end of a twenty-five-year concession. These costs will be added to the money that needs to be made from the bridge before the developers are deemed to have been paid off. The islanders have no means of discovering whether or not the costs are fairly incurred. Indeed, as Miller Civil Engineering won't tell them, they are unable to discover how much nearer they are to paying off the bridge than they were when it opened. When their MP, Charles Kennedy, asked the company how much it took during the National Mod – the huge Highlands cultural festival which was held on the island in 1998 – 'I received,' he told Parliament, 'a courteous reply saying that the company does not reveal its figures. As the local Member of Parliament I am not allowed to know how much the company made out of that major national event. That is a disgrace.'[37] The islanders have yet to discover how the Scottish Office will decide when enough money has been sent to the Bank of America for the tolls to be removed.

Indeed, the whole process has been clouded in secrecy. Though the Skye Bridge is part of the national infrastructure, and though it is ultimately financed by the taxpayer and the toll payer, almost every aspect of its commissioning and funding has been deemed by the government to be 'commercially confidential'. During one court case, forty pages of text were excised from the contract between the bridge builders and the Scottish Office before the document could be discussed in court. To this day, none of the defendants knows what it contains, but believe that the missing section might have been critical to their defence. At the public inquiry, the Scottish Office misled the inspectors when it claimed that the costs of the ferry service 'are not broken down by individual routes',[38] meaning that it did not know how much each route cost to run. The ferries' costs, it said, were also 'commercially confidential', even though the government ran the service itself.[39] The leaked reports later showed that the Scottish Office had been using the broken-down costs of the ferries as part of its feasibility studies.[40]

*

So the people of Skye must pay a fee to an American bank every time they want to go to or from their island, despite the fact that most of the costs of the bridge have already been met by the taxpayer. The bridge was built with the assistance of a loan illegally obtained by the government. It was 60 per cent over-financed and, thanks to commercial confidentiality, no one knows how profitable it will be. The concession agreement was written with the help of a developer, and the Scottish Office misled both a public inquiry and a government body. Six hundred people have been arrested and 378 prosecuted on the basis of a government order which the foremost expert on Scottish legal procedure has described as fatally flawed.

The government had no need to use the Private Finance Initiative to build the Skye Bridge. Not only has it spent almost as much public money on this private development as it would have done if the project were a public one, but, as Skye lies within a regional development area, it could also have asked the European Union to provide nearly all the money required for a toll-free crossing. The means of financing this bridge have nothing to do with saving public money. Far from Westminster and the offices of the national newspapers, out of sight, out of mind, Skye was the ideal location in which to launch a corrupt and unpopular initiative, in which private companies were granted monopolistic control over public works.

*

The people of Skye had every reason to believe that a Labour government would overturn the tolls. In 1995, Brian Wilson MP, who was to become the Minister for Industry in the Scottish Office and, later, a minister at the Department for Trade and Industry, described the Skye Bridge project as 'a shocking story of ideologues using a remote place for an experiment that they could not have got away with anywhere else'. The toll regime, he announced, was 'immoral, unacceptable and unjust', while the people of Skye were the 'near-monopoly prisoners of ... ruthless commercial interests'.[41] In 1996, he joined the demonstrators, marching over the bridge with a pipe band, and announced that 'the Tartan Toll Tax' was 'an injustice which will not be meekly acquiesced in'.[42] In the same year, Calum MacDonald MP, who is now a minister in the Scottish Office, asked his opposite number: 'Isn't it about time that he listened to the weight of public opinion ... and scrap[ped] this damaging and unpopular toll regime?'[43]

The local Labour candidate for the 1997 General Election, Donnie Munro (formerly the lead singer of Runrig), told voters that 'The Labour Party are committed to work in partnership to abolish the tolls within the shortest practicable timescale'.[44] The Scottish Labour Party published a full-page advertisement to this effect in the *West Highland Free Press* one week before the election.[45]

But a clue to Labour's real intentions lay in its manifestos. Its manifesto for the Highland region promised that it would devise 'a strategy for the elimination of tolls ...

within the shortest practical timescale'.[46] If anyone on Skye had chanced to read it, however, they would have discovered that the separate manifesto for the whole of Scotland, by contrast, was promising only to 'examine the toll structure'.[47]

Soon after the election was won, the ministers whose party had promised to eliminate the tolls announced that this would be impossible. It would, they maintained, cost £30m to buy out the contract: more in other words than the bridge cost to design and build.[48] How they arrived at this remarkable figure no one can tell, not least because they have maintained the official line that the bridge contract and all other relevant documents are 'commercially confidential'.

Brian Wilson told *Scotland on Sunday*, 'It's just a lie to say that either I or the Labour Party promised to abolish the tolls.'[49] When the islanders requested that they be allowed to reopen the ferry service and run it in competition with the bridge, Mr Wilson told them it was a 'silly stunt'. They pointed out that, in opposition, he had supported the idea of maintaining a competing ferry service. When the islanders wrote to Geoffrey Robinson, then the Labour minister responsible for the Private Finance Initiative, and he raised their complaints with Henry McLeish, Minister for Home Affairs at the Scottish Office, Mr McLeish wrote back warning that corresponding about the issues raised by the protesters 'is not, I am sure, the best use of our time and taxpayers' money. . . . I am sure you will understand my reluctance [to commit] scarce Departmental resources to dealing with the views of a small, but vocal, minority'.[50]

It would not be fair to suggest that the new government has done nothing to tackle the problem. After sustained demands by both the islanders and opposition parties, Donald Dewar, the Secretary of State for Scotland, agreed to reduce the tolls for residents, but only if they bought books of twenty tickets in advance. This, the islanders pointed out, would help only those who left the island frequently, leaving the majority of the residents no better off. According to the Public Accounts Committee, however, the new deal was negotiated so badly that the compensation the government paid to the consortium for reducing these tolls was likely to make the bridge even more profitable than before.[51] The government commissioned a survey to discover what the islanders felt about the bridge. Residents were disappointed to discover that the company chosen to conduct the survey was none other than JMP Consultants. They were also concerned that the way the questions were phrased was likely to affect the results: they were asked, for example, how many more crossings they were making now that the bridge had been built, but not how many fewer.

'What hurts us most,' John Campbell told me, 'is the sense of betrayal. These ministers were campaigners before they got into power. Now they're just suits.'

The islanders expected that the positions of some of those involved in the bridge might have been reviewed. They were particularly interested to know what would happen to Professor James Innes. This was the man who, as Deputy Chief Engineer at the Scottish Office Roads Directorate, had incorrectly informed the public inquiry that the government did not have a breakdown of the ferries' costs. This was the man who signed all the major documents pertaining to the bridge. This was the man who admitted to the Public Accounts Committee that his sole source of financial advice for the scheme had been the Bank of America. Before the election, Professor Innes had been promoted to Director of Roads at the Scottish Office. After the election, he was promoted again: he is now the head of the Scottish Office's Transport and Planning Group.

He is not the only Scottish Office official involved in the Private Finance Initiative to have prospered. In January 1998, Charles MacLeod, who worked on the Treasury's Private Finance Panel at the Scottish Office, left the civil service to join Miller Construction, a company belonging to the Miller Group, which built the Skye Bridge. He became the joint head of the company's Private Finance Initiative unit.[52]

In July 1999, Harold Mills, the retired civil servant who had drawn up the Skye Bridge contract between the government and the developers, was appointed, by the Scottish Office, to a new post. He became chairman of the government-run ferry company whose service between Skye and the mainland had been terminated on the day the bridge opened. He would be paid £22,000 for a one and a half day week. His appointment was greeted with outrage, and not only by the Skye Bridge campaigners. Of the four people who appointed him, three were his former colleagues, among them the man who had moved into his old job when he retired. The fourth was a man whose appointment to the board of the housing agency Scottish Homes had been made on the strength of the recommendations of the Scottish Office Environment Department – of which, at the time, Mr Mills was secretary.[53]

The Bank of America has also thrived in Britain. Before the general election, the consortium to which it belonged won the contract to build the privately financed A30 dual carriageway in Devon. Since the election, it has become the lending bank for the £1bn Private Finance Initiative contract to update and operate London Transport's ticketing services.

The court cases grind on – the islanders have now taken their appeals to the European Court of Human Rights and the European Court of Justice. But the demonstrations have diminished. Exhausted and impoverished by their fight, the people of Skye no longer have either the energy or the resources to sustain the pressure they exerted during the first three years of tolling. But they have not given up, and some say they never will.

*

I walked back to Portree through a sour land of broken crofts and abandoned cultivation, the ridges and furrows of pre-Clearance fields fossilized, then rusted with bracken. Cattle cried and paced the shallow water of a loch.

On the bus to Glasgow, I took out the Public Accounts Committee report and read it for the second time. One sentence caught my eye before I fell asleep. 'We note,' it stated, 'the Department's assurance that lessons have been learned from this project, though they have not said what these are.'

CHAPTER TWO

Hospital Cases –
The Corporate Takeover of the
National Health Service

Tom McAllister slid the No Smoking sign off the table, shuffled it out of sight with his feet, then lit a cigarette. A waitress in a checked apron stacked the chairs on the tables and ran a mop across the floor. Outside, the people of Coventry hurried home through the gathering darkness. The shutters in the rest of the arcade slithered down, one after another, and hit the ground with a crash.

He waved his free hand around the restaurant proprietorially.

'I'm directly responsible for twenty-six of these shops. All the wiring, the electrics, just about every sort of handiwork there is. They're a good firm, very sympathetic. I moan, of course – show me one person who's employed who doesn't moan. But I'm a hard worker and I'm happy working for them.'

Tom McAllister had been reared by hard work. His father had owned a small farm in Airdrie, 'but he pissed it up against the wall. He became a plasterer's labourer and a hod carrier, but I tell you, he could talk to you about any subject under the sun. The house was stacked with books of learning. He could recite verses from the *Iliad* and poetry of all kinds.'

Tom's mother gambled, in a small way, incessantly. The twelve children were brought up on little besides lentil soup. 'She bought an electric cooker on the never-never, but she forgot to put any money by for the electricity. After two weeks, she sold the cooker for a tenth of what she bought it for, and after that she cooked on a two-bar heater set on its side. She drew the curtains while she was cooking. If there was a knock on the door, pots and pans would go flying as everything was put back to normal. It was terrible – but we could see the humour in it.'

At the age of eight, Tom was taken to a Barnado's home. Eight years later, he was sent to the Isle of Arran. 'It was hard, but I wouldn't have missed it. Setting out near-on bare-arsed at six on a winter's morning in a lobster boat. Or out crawling on your hands and knees along a row of turnips, with sacks wrapped round your legs to keep the mud out. At the time I thought, no thanks: give me a warm cell in an approved school, any day. But now I'm grateful for it.' He took an apprenticeship at British Steel, qualified as an electrical engineer, and moved to Coventry in 1990. But the instinct for injustice and fair play he had developed in the west of Scotland had never left him. It was he who introduced me to the next, astonishing chapter in the story of Britain's Private Finance Initiative.

I first met Tom McAllister in a car park behind the Skye Bridge, where he and the other protesters had gathered for a demonstration. He and his partner had taken a holiday on Skye soon after the bridge opened. When they found out what had happened to the islanders, they were horrified, and, on the way back home, refused to pay. He was arrested and charged but, thanks to a series of spectacular legal mishaps, had yet to be successfully prosecuted. From then onwards he had returned to Skye almost every month to attend the demonstrations, marched with the saltire at the head of the processions, and failed to pay on fifteen occasions. From a dog-eared folder in the back of his van he drew a ragged cutting from the *Coventry Evening Telegraph*, dated 30 June 1998. Between an article about a six-year-old Coventry boy with the same name as the England goalkeeper and a report about a gas cooker that had burst into flames in a house in Nuneaton, the paper reported the furious dismissal by the local hospital's chief executive of criticism of the hospital's planned Private Finance Initiative project. The claims that the scheme would lead to 'massive staff cuts' and 'fewer beds', he told the paper, were 'absolute rubbish'. On the contrary, it would employ more doctors and nurses and 'secure a full range of services'.[1]

'The moment I saw the words "private finance",' Tom told me, 'was the moment I thought I should look into it. My MP is Geoffrey Robinson, who was the minister responsible for the Private Finance Initiative. So I went to see him, to talk about the Skye Bridge and find out what was happening to the hospital. He was very pleasant, a nice bloke really, no airs and graces about him. He'd buy me a pint, no problem. We talked a bit about the bridge, and he seemed quite sympathetic. But then I raised the matter of the hospital. You know, it's a funny thing, but he wouldn't talk about it at all. He ducked and dived, changed the subject and wouldn't let me bring it up again. It made me suspicious, so I looked into it a bit. And I'll tell you something. What we've seen on Skye is just the beginning, a taster for what's starting to happen all over the country. And what's going on in Coventry is, if anything, even worse than what's happening on Skye.'

Tom's coffee had grown cold, and the waitress was tutting ominously as she mopped around our table. We ducked under the security screen and out into the wet autumn night.

Tom shifted a newspaper, a clipboard, a mobile phone and a Cornish pasty off the passenger seat of his van, while I read the warrant for his arrest stuck proudly on the inside of his windscreen. We drove out along Corporation Street and onto the ring road. From behind the cluttered windscreen I could see only concrete pillars, bright lights and the voids they framed. We pulled up in front of the Walsgrave Hospital and sat in the van with the engine idling.

'Labour,' said Tom, 'has broken a lot of promises since it came to power. But what it's doing to places like this is worse than anything else.'

*

In 1993, the Conservative government informed the National Health Service that it was introducing a new rule. It would release no money for major hospital building works until the NHS had first considered financing the new works privately. The private sector, the government maintained, would run hospitals more efficiently, and therefore more cheaply, than the public sector. Private companies would build new hospitals and let them to the National Health Service. They would also take care of all the 'non-clinical' services, such as catering, cleaning and portering, leaving the NHS to concentrate on looking after patients. By mobilizing private capital, the government would be able to open more hospitals than the Exchequer alone could afford. By cutting the costs of peripheral services, it could plough more money into caring for patients.

Labour poured scorn on the idea. Far from providing more money for healthcare, private companies, the party maintained, would suck funds out of the NHS. 'The future of services will be driven by the short-term priorities' of the companies involved, Harriet Harman, then the shadow Health Secretary, claimed in the summer of 1996. 'NHS employees will be strangers in their own hospital – public servants in a privatized hospital'.[2]

But when Labour came to power, far from abandoning the Private Finance Initiative (PFI), it cleared the remaining obstacles out of the way. As a result, in 2000 it was able to announce that public projects worth some £20bn would be privately funded by 2003.[3]

At first, the Labour government hinted that public bodies like the NHS would be able to choose whether or not to seek their money privately. Before long, however, it revised its position. 'When there is a limited amount of public-sector capital available, as there is,' the Health Minister Alan Milburn announced in July 1997, 'it's PFI or bust.'[4]

*

Twenty years ago, Coventry had five hospitals. One was bought by Warwick University, which plans to demolish it to build a library. One is now a Safeway supermarket, a third is being turned into a £3m 'superpub'. The services they provided have been absorbed by the remaining two: the Coventry and Warwickshire in the centre of town, and the

Walsgrave, just outside the city's ringroad. Though the Walsgrave is only thirty years old, both hospitals are run-down and need refurbishment.

In the early 1990s, the National Health Service planned to renovate the Walsgrave hospital. This would have cost around £30m, which the government was reluctant to provide. In 1997, after the Labour government had indicated that no substantial public funding would be available, the NHS Trust submitted a new plan: for the privately financed demolition of both the Coventry and Warwickshire and the Walsgrave hospitals, and the construction of a new hospital on the Walsgrave site.

The trust's financial plans were kept out of the public domain – indeed, they were considered so sensitive that they were not even placed in the library of the government's own PFI Task Force. But as details began to leak, local people became increasingly concerned. Coventry, comprehensively bombed by the Luftwaffe, had been rebuilt on a radial pattern – the roads connecting the city centre to the ring road are like the spokes of a wheel. Whereas patients and visitors could travel to the city centre hospital by taking a single bus from almost any point in the city, Coventry's urban geography ensures that getting to the out-of-town hospital is very much harder for the 39 per cent of the city's people who don't possess a car. Even someone living just a mile away from the Walsgrave Hospital, for example, has to take one bus to the city centre, and another back out to the ring road.

It was also obvious to residents that the new hospital would be smaller than the current Walsgrave, and considerably smaller than the two old hospitals combined. Though the chief executive of the local NHS Trust assured them that the efficiencies of a modern hospital, operating on a single site, would allow more patients to be processed at less expense, local people could not see how the demolition and rebuilding could fail to be accompanied by cuts in services. They were mystified by the trust's approach. Why did the NHS persist with this plan, which, they felt, was bound to lead to fewer beds and fewer staff? Why were the existing hospitals not renovated, as the health authority had first proposed? This seemed to many to be both the most effective and by far the cheapest option; it would also allow both hospitals to stay open. A long-running petition to save the city centre hospital gathered 120,000 signatures.

In July 1997, the government published plans to build fourteen new hospitals under the Private Finance Initiative. Many of Coventry's residents were relieved to discover that the Walsgrave was not among them. They were also, however, painfully aware that this meant there were no viable plans for the renovation or renewal their hospitals required. The NHS drew up a new business case and, in April 1998, Alan Milburn, the Health Minister, announced that a single hospital worth £174m would be built on the Walsgrave site under the Private Finance Initiative. The project, he announced, would 'allow for a sound foundation for the further development of excellent health services in Coventry well into the next millennium'.[5]

At first, the Labour-dominated City Council supported the NHS plan, but at the end of October 1998, just as I arrived in Coventry, it suddenly changed its mind. The new hospital, it realized, not only would be less convenient for residents, but also threatened its plans to regenerate the city centre. It begged the National Health Service to build the new hospital on the city centre site instead. When the health trust refused, the council made an astonishing offer. It would lend the trust £20m and hand nine acres of its own property to the NHS, if only it would change its mind. The trust, again, refused.

All this seemed most peculiar, and the residents of Coventry began to suspect that there was more to the NHS decision than met the eye. They were right. Coventry's new hospital plans were being driven not by the needs of its people, but by the needs of the private companies hoping to profit from them.

*

I had heard about the health authority report on the Walsgrave Hospital from several sources, but no one would agree to send it to me. It was, I was told, strictly confidential and extremely sensitive. I had no right and no good reason to see it. I had given up trying when a brown envelope arrived in the post. It contained no letter and no acknowledgement slip, just a dull-looking document with a plastic binding, marked 'Confidential' and titled 'The Walsgrave Hospitals PFI Development'.[6] It wasn't hard to work out why I was not supposed to see it.

The report was written by two eminent public health scientists and a distinguished economist. It contained a compact economic analysis loaded with acronyms and tables. Though the paper was just twenty-four pages long, it took me several hours to understand everything it contained. It is, in its quiet, technical, mathematical way, one of the most explosive documents I have ever read. It demonstrates unequivocally that the government's plans for the NHS spell the end of accessible, affordable, universal healthcare in Britain.

*

Private companies would be interested in demolishing the old hospitals and building a new one on the out-of-town Walsgrave site only if the scheme promised them a healthy profit throughout the hospital's twenty-five- or thirty-year contract. The new hospital, the report revealed, would have to make a surplus four times as big as Coventry's hospitals made in 1998 if it were to be profitable. The NHS Trust would have to pay the consortium which won the contract £36m a year at current prices. There was only one way of finding this money: by slashing the numbers of both beds and staff.[7]

All NHS trusts want to treat patients more swiftly and send them home earlier, reducing the need for large numbers of beds. But it is widely understood that this can be achieved only if they employ more staff, as a higher turnover of patients places a greater medical and administrative burden on doctors and nurses. It is widely acknowledged, too, that doctors and nurses tend to be overworked rather than underworked, which is bad for them and bad for patients, as they are more likely to make mistakes when they get tired and stressed. Because of both the number of people needing treatment and the pressures on existing staff, Coventry Health Authority had already been warned by its consultants that there was 'little scope for significant reduction in bed numbers'.[8] Yet, the confidential report revealed, the contract being offered to the private companies bidding to build the hospital would be affordable only if Coventry were to lose

25 per cent of its all-purpose beds, and 560 – or 20 per cent – of its staff.

The health trust had assumed, the report's authors found, that the number of admissions to Coventry's hospitals would decline rapidly over the next decade, and that doctors' surgeries and clinics would take on more of the patients the hospitals had cared for. But there was no evidence to support either assumption, and no extra money for the surgeries and clinics. There would, in other words, be nowhere for Coventry's patients to go.

Perhaps most astonishingly, the report revealed, no one in authority had sought to answer the most obvious question of all: was a new hospital necessary? No one had tried to find out whether or not Coventry's needs could be met by renovating its existing hospitals, even though this option was far cheaper than building a new one. It seemed unlikely that the Walsgrave, whose construction had commenced in 1966, needed complete demolition and rebuilding. As half the hospital beds in Britain are in accommodation that was built before 1914, knocking down the Walsgrave was, it seemed, hardly the National Health Service's most pressing need.

While a publicly funded renovation of the existing buildings would have required, according to the health authority's earlier assessment, a one-off payment of around £30m, the full-scale demolition of both hospitals and the rebuilding of a smaller hospital with fewer beds and fewer staff, out of town, would cost the taxpayer £36m a year, for decades to come. And because the £174m for the new hospital excludes the costs of equipment, the health authority would be forced to provide an equipment grant to the new hospital worth £25m – almost as much as the entire publicly funded renovation scheme would have cost, had it been allowed to proceed.[9] Renovating the existing hospitals might have made economic sense and might have been better for Coventry's patients, but the contract for renovation would have been too small to make it attractive to a private consortium. This option, in other words, had to be rejected not because it was too expensive, but because it was too cheap.

The option of building the new hospital in the city centre also had to be discarded. 'A City Centre hospital', the Coventry Health Authority conceded, 'would improve access to care, improve public health and contribute to the City Council's strategy for regenerating the heart of Coventry.'[10] It would create jobs in the part of town where unemployment is highest, and cause less environmental destruction, by building on land that had already been developed, rather than on green fields. But the city centre site was smaller than the Walsgrave site. This meant that there was no surplus land which private companies could sell for other developments in order to boost their profits.

It might seem incredible that the health trust and the health authorities, whose sole purpose is to administer healthcare in Coventry and Warwickshire, could make such fundamental mistakes. But, the report suggested, the 'mistakes' had been made for a good reason. Just as the people of Skye were told that if the bridge were not built through the Private Finance Initiative, it would not be built at all, the Coventry and Warwickshire Health Authorities had been left in no doubt that if they did not apply for a PFI scheme, they needn't apply at all. They swiftly came to see that either they had to devise a scheme which was attractive to private investors, or they would have to make do with their existing facilities, unrenovated and ill-equipped for the demands of the twenty-first century. They had, in other words, to invent a project which would make money for private companies, rather than proposing one which would best meet the needs of Coventry's people. The scheme, the confidential report found, had been 'progressively tailored to fit the needs of private investors'.[11]

*

In December 1998, Coventry Health Authority launched a 'consultation', to allow the public 'to express a view' about the location of the new hospital.[12] This was all they were allowed to do. Both a publicly funded hospital and the refurbishment of the existing buildings were ruled out in advance. Once those choices had been eliminated, it soon became clear that the decision over where the new hospital should go was similarly constrained. Though the health authority agreed that a city centre site would be 'preferable for reasons of access and city centre regeneration', and that it would 'provide clinically acceptable new hospital facilities', it had 'reluctantly concluded that the hospital should be built on the Walsgrave site'.[13]

There was only one major reason for this assessment, but it was an insuperable one: the private sector would reject a city centre development, as it would take too long (because all the facilities on that crowded site would have to be moved out before building could start) and release no spare land. A delay in building the hospital would mean that the consortium chosen to construct it would demand an extra £20m from the NHS.[14] There was also 'the possibility of liquidated damages being required for each week of delay to the project'.[15] As a result of these pressures, the health authority concluded, 'the Walsgrave Hospital option is the only viable one open to us at present'.[16] Residents must have wondered what on earth the consultation was for.

Not only had the decisions been made in advance, but residents were required to comment on them without the benefit of the most important information of all: the data contained in the devastating confidential report. While three other studies were cited in the consultation document, neither there nor in the minutes of the public meetings held by the health authority was the report even mentioned. It was as if it had never existed. Even so, the people of Coventry voted decisively to reject the health authority's choice. Eighty-two per cent of those responding to the consultation chose the Coventry and Warwickshire site in the city centre, while just 11 per cent opted for the Walsgrave.[17]

In January 1999, an extraordinary thing happened. Geoffrey Robinson, the minister in charge of the Private Finance Initiative, who, four weeks earlier, had been forced to resign over his undeclared loan to the Trade and Industry Secretary Peter Mandelson, rebelled. Now that he was no longer constrained by his governmental duties, and could act solely as a constituency MP, he started lobbying against the very development he had championed while in office. But the health authorities and the NHS Trust were unswayed by the local MP, by the council, and by the results of the consultation. They knew that a privately financed hospital on the out-of-town site was the only option they had: it was, as the Health Minister insisted, 'PFI or bust'. The state had set out to hand control of its functions to private companies, whatever the cost might be.

*

71

It would be comforting to believe that Coventry's plans were exceptional, that a dreadful mistake had been made in this city which might, before it was too late, be recognized and cleared up, above all that it would not be repeated elsewhere. But the disaster awaiting healthcare in Coventry is one which looms over almost every new hospital building plan in Britain.

Projections commissioned by the British Medical Association show that the health trusts running the first fourteen hospitals to be built under the Private Finance Initiative will lose a total of 3,700 beds.[18] On average, 26 per cent of the beds belonging to the English health trusts experimenting with the initiative will disappear,[19] while the health trusts in Scotland will lose 30 per cent.[20] The nursing budget will decline by between 10 and 20 per cent as a result of the scheme. According to a study by a consultancy company which works for NHS trusts and the Department of Health, every £200m spent on privately financed hospitals will result in the loss of 1,000 doctors and nurses.[21]

A later report on the affordability of the Private Finance Initiative published by the *British Medical Journal* found that bed numbers will decline by an average of 31 per cent in privately financed hospitals.[22] The South Manchester and Worcester trusts would lose around 40 per cent of their places. Fifty per cent of the beds, a further study shows, will disappear from Durham's Dryburn Hospital.[23] Only Carlisle is projected to lose less than 10 per cent of its beds, and this, according to doctors in the town, is because the new facility will be 'more like a doss-house' than a hospital.[24] The contractors planned to squeeze eighty-eight beds into wards originally designed for seventy-six. To fit them in, they would have to cut the number of toilets to one for every thirty-eight beds, and reduce the width of the corridors until they were so narrow that a hospital trolley could not be turned around in them.[25] According to Carlisle's consultants' committee, the plans are 'clinically unworkable'.[26]

In June 1998, in response to public pressure and in order to try to meet his promise to cut the NHS waiting lists, Frank Dobson, the Secretary of State for Health, pledged that an extra 2,000 beds would be provided by British hospitals, and a further 1,100 saved from closure, at a cost to the Exchequer of £500m. In February 2000 his successor, Alan Milburn, indicated that he would raise the target to around 4,000.[27] The first wave of privately financed hospital building alone will eliminate almost all the extra beds they have promised to fund.

*

The Private Finance Initiative will reduce not only the number of Britain's hospital beds but also the number of Britain's hospitals. Most of the PFI plans involve the closure of all but one of a given trust's hospitals. In simple geographical terms, healthcare will become less accessible, especially for the 32 per cent of British households with no use of a car. Many of the new schemes, like the planned hospitals in Swindon, Edinburgh and Durham, will be built on greenfield sites beyond the peripheries of the towns they serve. The hospitals scheduled for closure, in order to find the money with which to build the new ones, are, in every case, at the heart of the towns or cities they serve.

To provide enough money to pay the fees and leases required by private companies, NHS trusts must sell everything they can lay their hands on. They will have to question the need for every service they provide, and if they can find a means of justifying its removal, the service and the building which houses it will have to be dismantled, so that the land on which it sits can be sold. In Durham, the health authority decided that the only way in which it could find the money the private contractors required was to sell part of the site on which the new hospital would be built to Tesco. Nigel Martin, who stood for the Liberal Democrats in Durham in the 1997 election, revealed that 'the prospect of putting a large supermarket in an area that is already congested fills me with horror. But unless we get the Tesco, there is grave doubt that we will get the hospital'.[28]

In May 1999, the Private Finance Initiative became one of the principal issues dividing the parties contesting the Scottish elections. Four months earlier, the Scottish *Sunday Mail* had uncovered 'a secret property deal' between the companies building a new Royal Infirmary on the outskirts of Edinburgh and the NHS. Four of Edinburgh's hospitals were to be closed down, and their services transferred to the new site. The land they occupied was being sold for a song to the companies. This 'sweetener' was worth, according to Scottish property experts, some £200m. The Scottish Office had refused to disclose details of the deal to the public on the grounds that it was 'commercially confidential'.[29]

Even before the land deal came to light, Scottish taxpayers had learnt that the consortium of four companies was due to reap £990m from a project which, had it been publicly financed, would have cost the public purse £180m.[30] The result of this staggering public expenditure was that Edinburgh would find itself with 200 fewer beds and 890 fewer staff. The city could ill afford to lose them. In January 1999, Keith Little, the head of the Royal Infirmary's Accident and Emergency Department, resigned on the grounds that a shortage of beds had made his job impossible. Patients were being left on trolleys for up to ten hours before beds could be found for them.[31]

*

The health trusts and boards negotiating these deals argue that fewer hospitals and fewer beds do not mean fewer treatments. New technology means that patients can be discharged more quickly. New techniques allow GPs and social services to care for people who would otherwise have to stay in hospital. This is true, up to a point. But day surgery, which allows patients to be discharged before they are given a bed, stopped expanding in Britain some years ago. GPs and social services are already short of money. Most importantly, a faster turnover of patients, making use of fewer beds, requires an increase in the number of doctors and nurses, but every trust making use of the Private Finance Initiative will lose clinical staff. There is no slack in the system: Britain, according to the economist Dr Jean Shaoul, already has the cheapest public hospital system in the industrial world.

The result of the decline in both beds and staff that the Private Finance Initiative will inevitably precipitate is that hospitals will have to cut corners. They will have to reduce the number of prolonged and expensive treatments they offer, and concentrate instead on patients who are broadly healthy, rather than chronically sick. Their capacity for expensive treatments, such as maternity and accidents and emergencies, will have to be reduced. Those who can afford it will buy insurance and be treated privately. Those who cannot will wait and wait for services which might never materialize.

*

Just as the problems surrounding the plans for a new hospital on the Walsgrave site in Coventry result not from a terrible mistake but from the inevitable unfolding of the Private Finance Initiative, so the impending reduction of beds and staff nationwide is an unavoidable consequence of taking private money. Like the Walsgrave scheme, the price of all the new projects has been massively inflated in order to make them what the NHS calls 'PFI-able': attractive, in other words, to private investors. Between the first proposal for a hospital replacement or refurbishment and the conclusion of a final deal with private consortia, the British Medical Association has found, the cost of the schemes has risen by an average of 72 per cent.[32] The cost of renewing the Princess Margaret Hospital in Swindon, which was built in the 1970s and is still structurally sound, rose 229 per cent: from a £45m renovation to the £148m construction of a new, smaller hospital, several miles from the town centre.[33]

Health workers also question the assumption that private operators, being supposedly more efficient than public operators, will run a cheaper service. Roger Tanner, the Consultancy Director at NHS Estates, suggests that private companies could save the taxpayer money only through 'omissions, a smaller area, or lower specification':[34] which means either fewer services or worse services. Companies can reduce the wages of hospital porters, cleaners and caterers, but these people are already among the worst-paid in Britain, and any money the taxpayer saves by paying them still less has to be refunded by the taxpayer through income support.

The NHS will pay the consortia a fixed fee every year. In theory, this will come from the so-called 'surplus' or 'capital charge' it currently returns to the Treasury. But there are two problems with this arrangement. The first is that the NHS's current 'surplus' is not a surplus at all, but simply an accounting convention. The money is sent straight back to the health service after it has been paid to the Treasury. Under the Private Finance Initiative, this money will be handed, instead, to the companies operating the new hospitals: it leaks out of the NHS, in other words. The second is that the 'surplus' amounts to just 6 per cent of the NHS trusts' budgets. Private companies will not invest in building and running hospitals unless they can guarantee their shareholders a return of at least 12 or 14 per cent. So where will the rest of the money come from?

Running the cleaning, portering and catering contracts yields a maximum of 3–4 per cent annual profits for private operators. If beds and staff have already been cut and the remaining facilities are desperately overstretched, there will be no room for further 'efficiencies'. The only way in which the private companies can make the money they need is for the National Health Service to give them subsidies.

The first way in which the NHS does this is by allowing the consortia to sell off surplus land. The second way is by diverting the money that was to have been spent on looking after patients into paying the private operators' fees. The first ten privately financed hospitals to be completed, the British Medical Association calculates, will need a subsidy of £220m.[35] Swindon's new hospital alone will require an NHS subsidy of £43m – almost as much as the £45m with which the health service would have completed the entire renovation of its Swindon hospitals, had it been allowed to run the project itself.[36] The scheme which, government ministers tell us, will bring money from the private sector into the health service will instead drain money from the health service into the private sector.

*

But the issue which worries doctors, nurses and NHS managers most is that the transfer of money from the public to the private sectors is accompanied by a transfer of control. Soon after it came to office, the government commissioned a review of the Private Finance Initiative. One of its recommendations was that the government's commitments to private companies should get priority, and the money promised to them would never be cut.[37] The recommendation was adopted as government policy in September 1997.

From that point on, the needs of private contractors were given legal and constitutional priority over the needs of public services. Any future cuts to the NHS budget will have to come from the money allocated to employing doctors and nurses and treating patients, rather than the money allocated to paying leases and service charges to private companies.

This becomes particularly alarming in view of the length of the contracts struck between the NHS trusts and the private consortia. Most run for between twenty-five and thirty-five years, some for as long as sixty. It is surely inconceivable that the needs of the hospitals run by these consortia will remain unchanged throughout the contract. As some of the tasks the private companies carried out for the National Health Service become redundant, the NHS will want to stop requesting and paying for them, and use the money, instead, to pay for essential services. But the contracts it has been forced by Treasury rules to strike with private companies expressly forbid this: it will have to continue buying the services they offer throughout the length of the contracts, whether it needs them or not. 'The NHS,' the British Medical Association complained, 'could find itself with a facility which is obsolete in ten or twenty years' time, but for which it will still have to pay for thirty years or more'.[38]

Gradually, as hospital schemes are tailored to meet the needs of companies, as clinical services are cut to pay for the contracts with private operators, as hospitals are scaled down, beds, doctors and nurses shed, and as the only secure and unassailable part of the NHS budget will be that part pledged to private operators, the consortia will come to control the National Health Service. Companies whose shares are traded on the Stock Exchange are legally obliged to maximize their value. Whether they want to behave like philanthropic organizations or not, they are unable to do so. As they gradually take over the NHS, they will run it not according to the needs of the patients, but according to the needs of their shareholders.

None of these considerations, however, has deterred the government. By April 2000 it had commissioned thirty-four privately financed hospital developments at a cost of £3.5bn. The six publicly funded developments it authorized in the same period will cost just £217m. The corporate takeover of Britain's National Health Service has begun.

*

At first sight, the government's enthusiasm for a programme which carries so many costs and hazards looks mysterious. Why should a Labour government which has pledged to cut hospital waiting lists and increase bed numbers, to expose the work of the state to scrutiny and to keep a tight rein on public spending, both now and in the future, back an initiative which seems destined to achieve precisely the opposite?

Government ministers offer three explanations. First, because it mobilizes private capital, the Private Finance Initiative allows the government to start more schemes than it would otherwise be able to commission. The construction and renovation of hospitals, prisons, schools, the London Underground, courts, benefit offices and police stations, condemned by a tight public budget to years of delay, can be commenced immediately if private companies agree to pay for it.

Secondly, while the government concedes that the Private Finance Initiative has proved to be more expensive in at least some of the schemes started or completed so far, overall it is likely to save the taxpayer money. Ministers point to a study conducted by the consultants Arthur Andersen in 2000, which suggested that an average of 17 per cent will be saved by the twenty-nine PFI schemes they surveyed.[39] Thirdly, because private companies, rather than the government, provide the capital, the money spent on new projects does not contribute to the government's 'public sector borrowing requirement'. This, in theory, helps the government to maintain a tight grip on inflation. A low borrowing requirement also allows it to qualify for European Monetary Union. These are worthy aims, but there are serious problems inherent in all three official justifications.

There is no question that, if it did not have a budget surplus, the government could start more projects under the Private Finance Initiative than it could if it was constrained only to use public money. But spending under the PFI today will mean less money for new government projects in the future. As the Private Finance Initiative expands, future payments to private companies are likely to number among the government's major expenses.

The Labour Party has long been aware of this problem. Before the 1997 General Election, Alastair Darling, then shadow Chief Secretary to the Treasury, pointed out that 'apparent savings now could be countered by the formidable commitment on revenue expenditure in years to come'.[40] After the election he became partly responsible for implementing the policy which, he knew, would reduce the amount of money available for future spending.

More importantly, many of the Private Finance Initiative's savings are likely to be illusory. While a straightforward comparison between the cost of building a new hospital with private finance and the cost of building it publicly might favour the private option, if a new hospital is being built only because the private sector is not interested in renovating existing properties, the comparison is meaningless. If the savings are achieved, moreover, by cutting staff and reducing wages, then costs are simply transferred to other people and other parts of the state. The Arthur Andersen study the government favours also assumes that much of the risk of running privately financed projects is carried by the companies, rather than the government, and it has costed this risk accordingly. The report was an honest attempt to answer the questions the Treasury posed, but hospital contracts suggest that in practice the companies are adept at passing their risks back to the public sector. A study which took all these factors into account would be likely to show that the Private Finance Initiative is an exorbitant means of building and running Britain's infrastructure.

Indeed, when fully costed, many privately financed schemes prove to be considerably more expensive than comparable publicly funded projects. The government's Highways Agency initially maintained that privately financed roads were 15 per cent cheaper than state-built roads.[41] The National Audit Office discovered, however, that the agency had used the wrong discount rate. Of the first four private roads completed in Britain, two were more expensive than they would have been if publicly funded.[42] The campaigning organization Transport 2000 extended the analysis with the help of a number of parliamentary answers, and found that when various hidden costs were taken into account the private roads turned out to be two and a half times more expensive than public roads.[43] When Transport 2000 asked the Highways Agency where its optimistic figure had come from, the agency responded that its figures were 'commercially confidential'.[44]

The Channel Tunnel rail link would have cost £1bn, had it been publicly funded as originally envisaged in 1989.[45] Instead, a private consortium was asked to build the link, and was given £5.7bn worth of land and public money to cover its costs. In 1998, it asked the government for another £1.2bn. The government refused, but later agreed to underwrite a £3.7bn loan to the consortium as part of a £5.8bn 're-financing' deal.[46]

Some privately financed schemes do seem to be cheaper than similar publicly funded projects. The government calculates, for example, that private prisons cost between 8 and

15 per cent less to build.[47] However, according to Richard Tilt, the Director-General of the Prison Service in England and Wales, 'the great majority of the cost reduction comes from the payment of much lower wages and poorer conditions of service for staff working in the private sector'.[48]

It is not obvious how these and other savings in the prison service could be regarded as efficiencies. Parc Prison, near Bridgend in Wales, which is run by Securicor, will save, according to the government, £53m over the life of the company's contract.[49] But even before it was officially opened in November 1997, the prison suffered eight minor riots and two suicides.[50] The Prisons Minister, Joyce Quinn, admitted that the prison lacked adequate work and training, drugs testing and visitor facilities.[51] According to the Prison Reform Trust, by April 1998, just five months after it had been opened, the prison had thirty fewer warders than it needed, due to 'an unexpectedly high turnover of staff'.[52] Disruptive prisoners were being transferred from Parc to the publicly-run HMP Cardiff, as Parc's staff could not cope.[53] Within a year of the prison's opening, Securicor had been fined £105,000 for, among other offences, failing to honour its contract.[54]

In February 1999, the government cancelled its contract with an American company called Wackenhut Correction Corporation, which was running workshops at Coldingley Prison in Surrey. A leaked audit by the Home Office alleged that the prison's managers had shown 'a total disregard for fundamental tenets of government accounting and Prison Service financial policy',[55] after their accounts revealed what the auditors believed was 'a deliberate attempt to circumvent control systems'.[56] Wackenhut is one of the most controversial private prison operators in the United States. Within eighteen months of opening, its two prisons in New Mexico suffered several riots, nine stabbings and five murders: the consequences, critics maintain, of impossible conditions caused by cost-cutting.[57] But in August 1999 the Home Office announced that Premier Prisons, the consortium Wackenhut controls, would build and run a new prison at Marchington in Staffordshire. In October 1999 the government awarded a new, ten-year contract to Premier to run Doncaster Prison. Premier also controls prisons in Kilmarnock and Nottingham, and the immigration detention centre at Gatwick.

Cost-cutting by a private company also appears to have been responsible for the disasters which beset the Passport Agency in the summer of 1999. When Siemens Business Services won the £120m contract to install and run the Passport Agency's new computer system, it claimed that it would reduce costs by sacking some of the agency's staff, while cutting the time taken to process passport applications. As *Computer Weekly* magazine pointed out, these aims were incompatible: 'reducing staff in anticipation of a new system's introduction', it noted, 'is madness'.[58] But the madness was driven by a Private Finance Initiative contract which ensured that Siemens was paid according to the savings it delivered. The predictable result was that the average waiting time for passports at the Liverpool office of the Passport Agency did not fall, but rose from eleven days in May 1998 to forty-one days in May 1999. This threw the entire passport system into chaos, and disrupted the holiday and business plans of thousands of people. Siemens, however, continued to draw its fees for this increased efficiency, and the government – anxious perhaps not to draw attention to the cause of the crisis – refused to penalize the company. The costs of the new service, in other words, were not transferred to the company enjoying the benefits.

We should not, perhaps, be surprised that private projects are likely to be more expensive than comparable publicly funded ones. Borrowing money costs companies more than it costs the government, as companies are less credit-worthy than nation states. Companies, unlike the state, also expect to make a robust profit. According to the accountancy firm and PFI advisers Chantrey Vellacott, health consortia hope to make between 15 and 25 per cent a year from privately financed hospitals.[59]

As a result, the Private Finance Initiative will, in the long term, add substantially to the public sector borrowing requirement. At the end of 1997, an unlikely row broke out between two of the most staid of Britain's financial institutions, the Treasury and the Accounting Standards Board. The board was concerned to ensure 'that Parliament is not misled over the extent of the payments it is committed to make in the future'. Some projects, it claimed, should really be counted against the borrowing requirement. Otherwise the Private Finance Initiative, the board maintained, could be viewed as what accountants call 'an off-balance sheet fiddle': a debt hidden from public view but which the government would eventually have to pick up.[60]

*

The Private Finance Initiative might be damaging to the taxpayer, but it's a blessing for private companies. 'The PFI,' according to the Department of the Environment, 'offers real benefits to the private sector in the form of increased business profit'.[61] According to Adair Turner, then the Director-General of the Confederation of British Industry, the government had to be 'open-minded and realistic'. 'If the government cannot accept occasional excess returns in publicly sensitive areas,' he warned, 'it shouldn't seek to transfer the risk in the first place.'[62] Companies can make these 'excess returns' in places they had scarcely dreamt of exploring before. The PFI, according to Sir Alastair Morton, a member of the government's Private Finance Panel and co-chairman of Eurotunnel, is 'the Heineken of privatization – taking the private sector to the parts of the government machine not reached by previous privatizations'.[63]

It shouldn't, in view of the Private Finance Initiative's potential profitability, be too surprising to discover that big business has lobbied hard, both to see the scheme expanded, and to take control of as many elements of the initiative as it can. It has been, so far, almost wholly successful. As soon as it took office, the Labour government commissioned a review of the PFI, which reported on 23 June 1997.[64] It gave the Confederation of British Industry nearly everything it asked for.

The CBI wanted the Treasury's Private Finance Panel (which, it felt, was too heavily dominated by civil servants) scrapped and replaced with a Task Force composed of industry representatives.[65] It got it. By 1 July 1997 the old Private Finance Panel had been discarded, and a Treasury Taskforce was put in its place. The head of the taskforce, Adrian Montague, was a merchant banker who has worked on the Channel Tunnel, the privatization of British Rail and the Skye Bridge. All eight of his deputies were drawn from large private companies.[66]

The CBI told the government that it wanted the Private Finance Initiative to reflect the needs of business. 'The new Taskforce', the government's report recommended, 'must maintain frequent and active liaison with the private sector.'[67] The government should 'allow businessmen to help to run the Private Finance Initiative', the CBI insisted, and grant the CBI 'Formal recognition . . . as active partners'.[68] The government did as it asked. The departments' private finance units, its review concluded, 'must be strengthened by the addition of deal-making and project management expertise to be acquired initially from the private sector'. It would look into 'CBI involvement' in the training of civil servants.[69]

Even before the new government took office, the Department of Health had already acquired its 'project management expertise' from the private sector. It hired Robert Osborne, the head of Special Projects at Tarmac, which is one of the major builders of privately financed hospitals, to run its private finance unit. The appointment was welcomed by the industry as 'marvellous news for construction. What everyone has been crying out for has been more understanding, and less suspicion, of contractors from the Department of Health.'[70] Labour was furious, however. Chris Smith, then the shadow Health Secretary, claimed the appointment raised 'serious questions' about a potential conflict of interest.[71] In January 1998, Robert Osborne moved straight back into Tarmac, where he became the head of its Private Finance Initiative division.[72] Though Mr Osborne was doubtless able to bring back to Tarmac the inside knowledge he had acquired at the Department of Health, and though this was precisely what Labour, in opposition, had feared, the government's front bench raised not a squeak of protest. In 2000, the government handed still more control to the corporations, by privatizing the PFI Taskforce.

*

The Private Finance Initiative, in other words, has been redesigned until it does precisely what business wants. But in becoming accountable to the private sector, the initiative appears to have sacrificed accountability to the public. Whereas the public financing of public infrastructure can, in principle, be scrutinized by the electorate, the details of privately financed deals are guarded almost as fiercely as military secrets.

The Conservative government claimed that 'commercial confidentiality' prevented it from revealing details of the contracts and the costs of the Private Finance Initiative. The sensitivities of the private companies with which it dealt were so delicate that it insisted that even the National Audit Office should be denied an automatic right to inspect the books of the companies providing government services. Alastair Darling, then Shadow Chief Secretary to the Treasury, complained that using commercial confidentiality 'to hide the truth about the extent of the taxpayer's commitment from the public is inexcusable'.[73] So objectors to some of Britain's most controversial privately financed projects have been mystified when the doctrine of 'commercial confidentiality' has been used by Mr Darling's administration precisely to 'hide the truth about the extent of the taxpayer's commitment from the public'.

The Birmingham Northern Relief Road, for example, will cut through twenty-seven miles of the West Midlands greenbelt. It is destined to obliterate two Sites of Special

Scientific Interest, destroy scores of homes and pass within a few yards of three schools. The project is, as a result, deeply unpopular with the communities it bisects. The Conservative government, which commissioned the road, failed to complete a cost–benefit analysis. So the World Wide Fund for Nature asked Keith Buchan, a consultant who has worked for the government's transport department, to conduct an analysis on its behalf. He discovered that the new road would cause more congestion than it solved.[74] His assessment seems to be supported by the traffic models presented to the road's public inquiry by the last government, which showed that the Birmingham Northern Relief Road (BNRR) would cause traffic jams on all the major roads it was linked to, and would increase traffic on the northbound M6 by 40 per cent.[75] But the new motorway, which, like the Skye Bridge, will be a privately financed toll road, stood to make a tremendous amount of money for its backers. In opposition, Labour promised never to allow it to be built. Frank Dobson, at the time opposition environment spokesman, told local residents: 'Labour is opposed to the building of the BNRR. This road would cause a great deal of environmental damage, with both noise and air pollution harming the health and amenities of local people ... Labour would not build the BNRR.'[76] Residents claim that when John Prescott, who later became Secretary of State for Environment, Transport and the Regions, was campaigning for the General Election, he told them that the road would be built 'over my dead body'.[77]

So local people were astonished when the Labour government announced that the Birmingham Northern Relief Road would go ahead. They were even more astonished when the party which had committed itself unequivocally to transparency in the Private Finance Initiative revealed that it had changed its policy for reasons which were 'commercially confidential'. Local people assumed this meant that the contract with the consortium building the road contained huge 'cancellation charges': money the government would have to pay to the private companies if it dropped the project. They took the government to court, arguing that the public had a right to see the contract. At first the judge ruled that parts of the contract should be made public. Then he reversed his ruling, leaving residents to pick up a £50,000 legal bill. To this day, no one knows precisely why an administration which had identified the road as a roaring white elephant has been forced to let it go ahead.

For all its protestations of openness, the government continues to insist on secrecy. According to the Treasury's Private Finance Taskforce, 'Preliminary discussions, on a confidential basis, might be held with ... construction companies and developers; manufacturers; ... bankers/financiers/insurers'.[78] Private companies will be able to discuss the future of the country's infrastructure with the government before the electorate has been consulted or informed.

*

Secrecy is not the only way in which private interests and public interests clash. In 1996, Jack Straw, then the Shadow Home Secretary, argued that it is 'morally unacceptable for the private sector to undertake the incarceration of those whom the state has decided need to be imprisoned ... almost all people believe that this is one area where a free market does not exist'.[79] 'We shall', he announced, 'certainly make no new [contracts] and, within the existing budget, shall take back into the public service privatized prisons as soon as contractually possible.'[80]

Within a week of taking office, he had decided to 'sign those contracts' for privately financed jails which were 'in the pipeline'.[81] A month later, he renewed one private prison contract and signed contracts for two new ones. A year after Labour came to power, he told the Prison Officers' Association that all new prisons in England and Wales would be privately built and run, and that his promise that private prisons would be transferred to the public sector no longer stood.[82] By April 2000, a total of five privately run prisons had opened, two were being built, and contracts for another two were being advertised.

Jack Straw had good reason to be suspicious, in opposition, of privately built and run prisons. In the United States, prison-building companies lobby and bully state and federal authorities to introduce tougher penal policies and increase the incarceration rate, with striking success. As the power of government declines and the power of corporations increases, it is not hard to envisage a situation in which law and order policies are driven by financial vested interests. This is a prospect which appeared to thrill Adrian Montague when he was head of the government's PFI Taskforce. 'The prison sector', he boasted, 'is becoming a commodity product. It is almost on a production line.'[83]

*

Among the many costs of the Private Finance Initiative is the transfer of control and ownership of the nation's critical infrastructure to private business, whose interests are often wholly distinct from those of the electorate. Complicated and confidential, it has been able to penetrate areas of public life whose overt privatization would be politically impossible. It has enabled companies to harness the great untapped resources they coveted, sustaining their share prices by turning public capital into private cash. The purpose of the Private Finance Initiative is to deliver the assets of the state to the corporations.

CHAPTER THREE

Breaking Point –
The Smashing of Southampton

Ida Hayter's tiny bony hands slipped and shuffled over the pile of ancient papers: shop bills as frail as tissue paper, photographs, brown and brittle press cuttings, letters whose ink had faded to the palest lilac.

'Ah, 'ere it is. That's the one I was on about.'

She held up a photograph of a girl in a white dress sitting on a high-backed wooden bench beside a young chimpanzee, which was about the same size as she was. In neat white ink in the corner of the print was written: 'Miss I. Hayter. The youngest monkey trainer in Great Britain'.

'I'm the one on the right.' She wheezed with laughter, then wiped her mouth with her fingers. 'They don't flatter you any down here. They look at the photo and say, "Beauty and the Beast," and I say, "That's nice." Then they point to the monkey and say, "That's the Beauty." No, they don't flatter you any.'

The bell on the door rang and a man came in. 'Morning, Ida.' 'Morning, dear.' The shop assistant busied around with change and carrier bags while Ida kept talking.

'They got me to train the chimps and the capuchins,

since I was five. We used to sell 'em to London Zoo. They were pretty dear, mind you. We 'ad them dog-faced baboons as well. I didn't like them.' She spread out the pile of papers on her lap. 'This was all before the war. First war, I mean.'

Another customer came in and bought some wild bird seed.

'They used to march down 'ere to take the boats over to France. And that's when we had to send our cats with them. They took 'em to kill the rats in the trenches.'

She put the photos aside. 'A load of old history.'

Ida Hayter's grandfather had taken over the pet shop in St Mary Street, Southampton, in 1888. For seventy years she had run it herself: only after her first stroke had she stopped weighing and bagging up the pet food and keeping the accounts. She was still renowned as the city's foremost expert on animal keeping, and people came from all over Southampton to ask her advice.

'I'm the last of the Mohicans. I 'ad a couple of shop assistants. But I've seen them off. They're all passing off and leaving me behind. I'm an old relic. I should have retired years ago. But where is there to go, love? This is a dear old place. I'd like to spend the rest of my days here before I pop off. I can get me pension across the road. Doctor there, chemist there. I've got me papers and fags next door, and the wash'ouse across the road, come back washed and ironed. Me fruit and veg from the market. I mean, how can I move?'

She looked around the shop, at the cracked yellow paint on the wooden walls, the little gas heater, the bags and boxes of dog biscuits, chocolate bones, hamster food, canary mix, millet and sunflower seeds, and shook her head. 'Now I'm getting chucked out like an old boot.'

*

Ida Hayter's shop was not scheduled for immediate demolition, though it was, she believed, due to be torn down during the second phase of St Mary's 'regeneration'. But the covered market and many of the other shops and businesses which drew customers to St Mary Street were about to be removed and this, Ida feared, would precipitate the collapse of much of her trade. The oldest part of Southampton, whose streetplan still reflects the pattern of the settlement which some historians describe as 'the first English town', was, she believed, about to lose its heart.

No one disputes that the St Mary's area is in desperate need of renovation. It suffers, according to Southampton City Council, from 'some of the worst deprivation in the whole of the United Kingdom'.[1] Twenty-seven per cent of its residents are unemployed, and its ethnic minorities, who comprise around a third of the population, are particularly deprived. Cut off from the rest of Southampton by a dual carriageway, and overwhelmed by new shopping developments on the other side of the city centre, St Mary Street, once the hub of Southampton's retail trade, has shrivelled. Some of its premises are boarded up, some have been turned into sex shops. The number of stalls in its covered market has fallen, in twenty years, from sixty to twenty.

So the residents of the district were delighted when they discovered, in 1995, that the council was applying to the government for a massive injection of money in order to 'bring life and vitality back' to the area 'so that people want to shop, meet and do business there'.[2] The City Council asked the government for £26m, and promised to find a further £52m from other public bodies and private companies. This would be, the council boasted, a 'regeneration programme which is the largest in the South East of England, outside London'.[3] The money, it promised, would transform the economy of St Mary's, create jobs for thousands of people and turn the area into a clean, healthy, well-integrated urban village.

But as the council's plans unfolded the people of St Mary's were horrified to discover that, far from regenerating their district, boosting its businesses and drawing in new trade, the council was intending to demolish it. Many of the shops and older buildings and most of the market were to be torn down and replaced by private housing and a smart piazza. Scores of small businesses would disappear, and the ancient and intimate character of the district, which both residents and council advisers had described as its greatest potential asset, would evaporate.

At first the council's plans seemed incomprehensible. But as the residents investigated, they slowly began to make sense. The council, they discovered, had become enmeshed in a series of glutinous conflicts of interest. Its regeneration programme, as a result, had been subtly redeployed until it ceased to serve the interests of the community, and matched, instead, the needs of two private companies.

As I have travelled around Britain, talking to local people and reading about the plans for their regions, I have come to see that this is a problem which attends development schemes throughout the nation. Scores of local authorities, whose task is to represent the public interest, appear to have been swayed instead by private imperatives. In some cases the problem has become so grave that planning permission could reasonably be described as being offered for sale to the highest bidder.

The councils' power to decide which places can be developed and what should be built there is the single most important agent of our quality of life. It determines whether or not a city or district has sufficient employment, and whose needs that employment meets. If people are under-housed, or if local housing serves only the wealthiest people, it is because the planning system has failed. The quality of an area – whether it provides enough green spaces, attractive views, a vibrant community, safe streets, in other words all the factors which determine whether a place is pleasant and habitable or grim and bleak – depends overwhelmingly on the planning decisions made by the local authority.

There are two ways of making fantastic quantities of money very quickly in Britain. The first is to be the director of a privatized utility. The second is to be a property developer who knows how to make the planning system sing to his tune. Britain's property market is, for the best of reasons, rigged. Only 12 per cent of the nation's surface is available for development, as the remainder has been desig-nated for farming, forestry or nature conservation. Within the 'development zones', certain areas are allocated to certain uses: you can, for example, build a superstore or an office block in one part of town but not in another.

This zoning helps to protect both the countryside and the quality and character of towns and cities. But it also means that development land, and in particular land for certain kinds of development, is artificially scarce. The result is that the price of this land is much higher than the price of land outside the relevant development zones. Farmland in lowland Britain, for example, generally costs between £1,500 and £2,500 an acre. Land right beside it, but within the development zone, can fetch £500,000 an acre or more. In the City of London, where planning permission for vast, luxurious office blocks can be expected, land changes hands for as much as £15m an acre.

This means that a single council decision, determining whether or not a piece of land falls within a particular zone, can turn a person of average means into a multi-millionaire. Crooked councillors can, if they are careful, make millions for friends and colleagues, and property development is the source of nearly all the sleaze stories involving local authorities. But individual, criminal corruption is not my theme. There are a host of legal and institutional means by which developers can get what they want, whether or not their needs correspond to the public interest.

Councils, as everyone knows, are always short of money. Increasingly they must rely on sources other than the council tax and government grants if they are to meet local people's needs. Individual councillors with political ambitions also discover quickly that the more wealthy and powerful allies they can enlist, the better they are likely to do. While local authorities can help make property developers a great deal of money, the developers, in turn, can render favours of various kinds, financial and political, to local authorities.

Sometimes the help they provide is crude – simple cash payments, for example – and sometimes it is far subtler, but the net result is the same: council decisions which should have been taken with the widest possible public interest in mind come instead to serve the narrowest private interests. The land which lies under our feet, our homes, our economy and our lives is deployed, in many places, to work for speculators and against the rest of us.

The widespread co-option of local authorities is matched by the corruption now contaminating the planning functions of central government. The government's Department of the Environment, Transport and the Regions is responsible for national planning policy, and is the ultimate arbiter of certain individual development decisions. Chapter 4 details my investigations into the conflicts of interest within this department. As far as I can discover, these have never been exposed before. They are, I believe, as grave and alarming as any of the allegations of institutional corruption that this government has faced so far, and appear to explain some of the otherwise inexplicable decisions the department has made.

But I am getting ahead of myself. First I must tell the story of St Mary's in Southampton, for it illustrates some of the local diseases which have come to infect the development of the places we inhabit. It is a stupendous scandal, which has never been investigated before. Like many planning issues, it is complicated, and needs a little explanation.

*

The Single Regeneration Budget is the money provided by the government to fund new development and improvement schemes, to reduce deprivation and social exclusion in the inner cities. The money is supposed to boost jobs, to support and promote local economies and businesses, and to enhance the quality of both the environment and the infrastructure. The budget is not intended to fund the regeneration schemes it supports in their entirety, rather it will only be handed out if the people applying for it can find matching money from businesses and other public bodies. It must be administered by a partnership composed of public and private bodies and local people.

It is, in theory, an excellent idea, bridging the gap between local people's aspirations and their affordability. In some places the Single Regeneration Budget has restored confidence to places previously sunk in dereliction and despair. But the government's demand for matching funding, which is not an unreasonable one, entertains both opportunities and one substantial problem: what the providers of private money want is often at odds with what local people require. In theory, the Single Regeneration Partnerships, which oversee the disbursement of the money, should balance these competing interests, tempering the corporate requirement for profit with the needs of the community. In practice, as the *Local Government Chronicle* points out, the partnership 'has effectively come to mean a collaboration between public and private sector. The vacant space between is filled by a community sector ill-informed and ill-advised, struggling to understand and always involved too late to actually participate – feeling that they are only seen when they are dragged out to show a visiting group of government office dignitaries around their homes'.[4] This is the experience of many of the people of St Mary's. The scheme designed to serve the public interest has instead been subtly redeployed to assist strictly private concerns.

*

Ian Loveridge stood under the market awning on a windy day in October 1998, watching the first few drops of rain spotting the tarmac then fading away. One or two shoppers

– an Asian woman in a bright green sari, a large unhealthy-looking white man in spectacles, two students in bomber jackets and torn jeans – passed along St Mary Street. A gust of wind picked up a crisp packet, swirled it around, skidded it across the pavement and over the street, then pinned it against the far kerb.

'I've fought so long for this place,' he told me. 'But now I'm giving up. I just can't carry on any more.'

Ian Loveridge, a builder who had lived in St Mary's for most of his life, had for years been attempting his own, small-scale regeneration of the district. He and other members of the community had drawn up a business strategy for St Mary's and started implementing it. They had opened an art gallery, refurbished some shops and helped them to start trading again. But they had swiftly run out of money. The gallery had closed and the shops were struggling.

So when the Labour-controlled City Council revealed that it was seeking to raise £80m from the government and other sources, much of which was destined for St Mary's, it seemed as if Ian Loveridge's dreams for the area were about to come true. The community he loved, whose slow decay and fragmentation he and the other people of the area had been unable to prevent, was at last to get the help it desperately required.

'Or that,' he told me, 'is what we thought. Instead the whole lot's going to be swept away.'

The first phase of St Mary's redevelopment, which would start in late 2000, would close the market and the market car park, pull down 70 per cent of the buildings on the west side of St Mary Street, shutting fifteen small businesses, and turn the land into a housing estate, a surgery and a square, in which an occasional street market trading from a handful of stalls would be allowed to run. After that, many of the buildings in the rest of the street, including Ida Hayter's shop, would, it seemed, be demolished to make way for similar developments. Ian took me around the market, then up the street. Everyone we met was furious.

Matthew Holmes, Meat and Fish, pulled out a sheet of cardboard, on which was stuck a map of the area, circled and hatched in different-coloured felt pens.

'That's the plans. That's all you're going to get. This is going to be a three-storey doctor's surgery here. They're going to wipe us out.' He scanned the market, then pointed to an older man talking to the proprietor of a fruit and veg stall. 'That's me dad over there. I'm the third generation. There's a few of us on site like that. You add it all up – there's got to be four or five hundred years of trading here. It's heritage, isn't it? So you can see why we're so eaten about it.'

They had, in the last few months, become even more eaten about the plans than before, as the market had been enjoying something of a resurgence. Though it was still cut off from the city centre by the dual carriageway, though the market structure looked increasingly shabby and run down, the number of stalls had grown from twenty to as many as forty on some days.

'This place is crammed in the mornings now. And you get more proper market traders down here on a Thursday, Friday, Saturday, like. But they're going to put us all out, aren't they?'

There was, he told me, no future for the traders if the plans went ahead. There would be no parking for either the stallholders or the customers, and the number of barrows allowed would not be sufficient to pull people in, especially in the winter, as the new, reduced trading area would be unroofed. The traders had been keen to form a cooperative to run the site (which was currently managed by the council) themselves. 'But we'd have to be idiots to take it over at the smaller size.' Instead, he told me, they were preparing to take direct action.

If the market were to close, the stallholders insisted, St Mary's would lose 150 jobs. 'Everything else will follow,' the secretary of the market traders said. 'The sixty businesses in St Mary Street will all go. The market attracts the trade which serves the local shops. It's our biggest draw.'

The market provides St Mary's with more than just jobs. 'This,' said Ian Loveridge, 'is where we meet. It's the community focus. It keeps people together. It's a rather unusual place in today's world. Yes, it's rundown, but they want to take away everything we've got, rather than build on what there is. And it's the one source of cheap food round here. We'll have to go to the supermarket to get a few manky carrots which cost a fortune. It's cheaper to get some Wagon Wheels to fill the kids up. And you can walk to the market. Otherwise you'd have to drive, and a lot of people in St Mary's don't have cars.'

The shops on St Mary Street had also been enjoying a minor renaissance. Though the district was blighted by the development plans, as the banks were unwilling to lend to businesses which might close down soon, several shopkeepers had been renovating their properties and a few new businesses had opened. Some places remained boarded up, but sixty-five of the eighty-five shops on the street were now trading. The regeneration plans foresaw just a handful of shops surviving, scattered around the new piazza.

The first phase of St Mary's redevelopment would

demolish not only the market but also a pub, two cafés, a small supermarket, a hairdresser's, a hardware shop, a fishmonger's, a music shop, a solicitor's office, a sex shop, a candle maker's, a Chinese restaurant, an amusement arcade and a newsagent's. I stopped at Reno's Café, the centre of Southampton's Maltese community, an odd-looking place with green walls, a tapestry of John Wayne in a frame, ships, glass floats, strings of garlic, and Meatloaf playing on the radio. In the window was a green plaster figure wearing a bearded horror mask, which seemed to be a hideous caricature of the proprietor. Men with paint-splattered trousers were drinking tea and savaging enormous plates of tagliatelle and spaghetti. The food was good and very cheap.

Reno sat down beside me.

'I been here eight years. My lease runs for twenty-four years. I thought it would be a job for life, which was good, because I am a single parent, and my daughter is too, and we can bring up my granddaughter while I'm working here. But now, I don't know what we gonna do.'

The council, he told us, was offering just a fraction of the amount of money he needed to relocate his business, and there was nowhere else in Southampton where he could take on a lease at such low rents. 'Today it is all big business. There is no place for the little guy.'

A few yards away from Reno's was a steel door to what appeared to be a boarded-up shop. But when Ian rang the bell the door opened, and we stepped into a dark room full of strange glass bubbles laid out on black velvet. They were, the proprietor explained, 'oil candles': a kind of fancy lamp made of blown glass in which oils of different colours could be burnt. They were sold to restaurants and gift and furnishings shops and, in five years, orders from all over Britain and Europe had allowed a tiny backroom workshop to grow into a vigorous little business with six full-time staff. The phones on the desk rang incessantly. Two people pored over spreadsheets and order forms. In the workshop behind the reception room kilns hummed and boxes built up beside the people who were packing a new order.

Tim Fitzgerald, the proprietor, spread his hands towards the packed shelves of his studio.

'If it all goes ahead it would finish us. There's no way we can move. They don't understand how business works and how much it costs to move a company. Where else will we find a storage space like this, and a workshop with natural light, without spending a fortune? We're having to fight this every step of the way. Yet we desperately need to get on with the business. We don't know what we're going to do. If they close us down, the homes of two directors are on the line.'

He rubbed his fingers across his forehead.

'All this is going to kill St Mary's. This pasteurized piazza they're planning will make it the same as everywhere else. It won't draw the punters in.'

While Tim Fitzgerald feared for his business, it seemed to Ida Hayter that she was losing her life.

'I hope they run out of money before they gets 'ere,' she told me. 'If they pull it down I loses me home, you see. I don't know where they'd put me. I don't fancy going in a 'ome.'

So it wasn't hard, Ian Loveridge explained, to see why he was feeling 'pretty depressed about all this'. But he, like most of the people of St Mary's, had also been feeling pretty puzzled. For one of the most curious aspects of the council's plans to demolish and rebuild St Mary Street was that they were utterly unnecessary.

According to the council, 60 per cent of the properties in St Mary Street 'have reached the end of their useful lives'.[5] Ian, a builder, had looked over a few of them, and found it hard to see how the council could have come to this conclusion. A study conducted by consultants ten years before had recommended 'rehabilitation' rather than demolition. But perhaps there were structural defects that had emerged since then, which he hadn't noticed? He knew the senior partner in a large and well-known engineering firm and asked him to come and take a look at the main block of shops and homes the council was intending to tear down. The engineer examined the buildings one by one then stepped out into the street.

'Yes,' he told Ian, 'it all looks a bit tatty. There's a few things here and there which are going to need doing. But no, they certainly don't need pulling down.'

'Then,' Ian told me, 'he took a long look up and down the street, and turned to me and said, "Isn't it interesting: you've still got all the original Victorian lines here." He looked into it further and told me, "You know, there's real potential here. It'd be madness to demolish this lot."'

Both the early study of St Mary Street, conducted in 1985,[6] and a leaked report from the council's own consultants, dated 1998,[7] pointed out that the market was suffering not from a lack of demand but from its physical isolation. It needed to be reintegrated into the rest of the city centre, by establishing better physical links across the dual carriageway and by promoting it and St Mary's shops throughout Southampton. It needed more parking spaces, rather than fewer.

'There is,' the first study noted, 'an urgent need to attract more trade, keep existing businesses going, and to encourage new ones to open.' St Mary Street should be promoted 'not as a local shopping facility only, but also as a specialist centre serving Southampton as a whole'.[8] 'St Mary Street', the leaked report contended, 'should continue to hold the main market for Southampton. Its retention and improvement as a specialist shopping facility is vital to the image and future of the area.' The regeneration programme should 'encourage the economic re-use of buildings' and 'protect existing shop frontages which add character and quality to the area . . . all properties on St Mary Street . . . should be eligible for grant assistance'. The council should promote 'St Mary's broadly throughout the city to both visitors and businesses'.[9] The council's regeneration plans, which were diagonally opposed to all these recommendations, began, to the people of St Mary's, to look a little mysterious.

*

When the city council's bid for government money was first published, in 1995, local people were so pleased that their repeated requests for help finally appeared to have been heard that at first they scarcely noticed the peculiarities of the council's approach. Southampton City Council's bid for government money had been prepared with the help of two housebuilding companies, British Gas, the Hampshire Constabulary, the Hampshire Probation Committee, the Southampton Chamber of Commerce and several other organizations, but, regrettably, there had been no time to discuss the project with anyone who lived in St Mary's. 'Residents' groups', the bidding document conceded, 'have not actively participated in the preparation of the bid. This involvement has not been omitted but has been delayed due to the bid's complex, diverse and somewhat radical approach to solving some of the problems.'[10]

Failure to consult the residents before submitting a regeneration bid was certainly a radical approach to solving the community's problems. It was not the only sign of innovative thinking in the document. The bid repeatedly emphasized the needs of the people of St Mary's and the council's desire to involve them at every stage of the area's development (except, of course, the first and most crucial one). But buried in a long list of coded figures was the budget for this grand partnership. Of the £80m the council intended to raise, a total of £60,000 would be allocated, across the eight years of the regeneration scheme, to supporting community initiatives, residents' groups and voluntary organizations.

When these curious procedures came to their attention, the residents questioned both the plans the council had submitted and its failure to consult them. But they were assured that nothing in the council's bid was set in stone. If the council got the money it was seeking, it would organize massive community consultation exercises, at which the residents would be able to say what they thought of the plans. If they didn't like them, they would be scrapped and replaced by what the people did want. Nothing would be finally determined until it had been endorsed by the community.

In December 1995, the council's bid was accepted by the government. Southampton was awarded £26m on the strength of a council promise to find twice that amount from other sources, mostly the private sector, and the biggest regeneration programme in the south-east was launched.

*

Just as the council promised, in the autumn of 1996 it launched what it described as 'the biggest consultation exercise in British history'.[11] The consultation, a 'Planning for Real' weekend, in which local people would be able to draw up draft plans for their neighbourhood as if they were council officials, would give everyone in St Mary's and the other areas scheduled for regeneration the chance to comment on the council's strategy and spell out their aspirations. Ian Loveridge was so enthusiastic about this approach that he volunteered to sit on the steering group for the event, believing that this would help him to ensure that the community's opinions were comprehensively heard. But even before the consultation was launched, it had begun to look rather less promising than the residents had imagined.

A document arrived in a brown envelope. No one knew where it came from. It was a leaked copy of a letter from Britain's leading organizer of 'community planning events', the Neighbourhood Initiatives Foundation, to one of the bodies which had helped the council draft its regeneration bid. The foundation had clearly been asked to run the event for the council, but it wasn't remotely pleased about it.

'I am writing to confirm,' it read, 'that the Neighbourhood Initiatives Foundation will not be quoting for the above event and to explain the reasons behind that decision ... Planning for Real enables each community to recognize issues within their own neighbourhood and to decide on their own priorities for the future. To have outside influences deciding on that future does not fit in with that concept.'[12]

As Ian Loveridge and the other residents had not seen the contract that the Neighbourhood Initiatives Foundation had been asked to quote for, they couldn't be sure exactly what this letter meant, or who the 'outside influences' it referred to might be. They found out pretty swiftly.

In November 1996, 'the biggest consultation exercise in British history', organized now by a firm of London architects, opened at the British Gas offices in St Mary Street. Hundreds of people turned up, and the event split into workshops to discuss the different components of the district's regeneration. A powerful consensus began to develop for the expansion of the market and the promotion of St Mary's as a specialist shopping area, which could draw people in from the rest of Southampton. At the workshop on shopping, the residents appeared to be united in their requests for help to turn St Mary's back into one of the commercial hubs of Southampton.

'Then,' Ian Loveridge told me, 'this guy at the back of the meeting says "Yes, but there's boarded-up shops, we've got to be realistic about this, there's not the demand for all these shops." Everyone said, "Who is this bloke?" Eventually the guy running the event asks him who he was. He said it didn't matter who he was. "No," the chairman says, "who are you?" It turns out he was a planning officer on the council.'

The same thing happened at the workshop about 'the quality of the built environment'. The meeting appeared to be reaching a consensus when someone at the back of the room called for 'realism' and suggested that the people's plans might be unworkable. Again the other people in the workshop asked who he was, and they discovered that he worked for a housing association, based in Bournemouth, which the council had invited to participate in the scheme. A similar thing took place at the workshop concentrating on

St Mary Street. A common position had emerged among the residents when someone they had never seen before came forward, took the pen out of the hands of the architect running the workshop and started drawing on the map. His plans bore an uncanny resemblance to those the council had put forward in its bid. Again, the residents asked who he was: he revealed that he was an urban regeneration specialist from outside the city, brought in by the council for the planning event.

'All this,' Ian Loveridge told me, 'was being documented as bullet points, as if this was what the community was saying. At the same time, architects from the Single Regeneration Partnership, who were also in the workshops, were scribbling on yellow Post-it notes which, like everyone else's, were handed up to the front anonymously.'

Despite his misgivings about the activities of the outsiders at the 'community' planning events, Ian Loveridge was confident that the residents' views had been expressed unequivocally. They wanted a doctor's surgery, but not on the site of the market. They wanted new houses, but there was no need to demolish the market and remove the market car park to build them: there was a huge site not far away, where the houses had been bombed flat during World War Two and never rebuilt. It was owned by the council and used as a temporary lorry park. The residents argued that four times as many homes could be built here. The market car park, they reasoned, was unsuitable for housing, as, pressed up against the dual carriageway, it had been identified as one of the most polluted inner city sites in England. Already, the residents said, 40 per cent of the children in St Mary's had asthma, which they linked to the traffic fumes.

They wanted the dual carriageway reduced to a single

carriageway, with a pedestrian crossing to the market. They wanted the traffic within St Mary's calmed and a full bus service – which had been shut down a few years before – restored.

They wanted a secondary school, so that St Mary's children didn't have to be bussed out every morning. They wanted better public transport and better connections to the rest of the city centre. The market should be regenerated and expanded, and promoted all around the city. They wanted cleaner streets and a more pleasant outdoor environment. All this, they reasoned, given that the council had £80m to spend, was not too much to ask.

'After the planning meeting,' Ian Loveridge told me, 'I said to the council, "It's clear what people wanted," and they said, "Oh yes, but there were conflicting views given." I said, "The only conflicting views were between what the community said and what the planning officers said." "Nonsense," they said.'

The people of St Mary's scraped together £7,000 and organized their own planning event. This one was run by the Neighbourhood Initiatives Foundation and, unlike the event the council organized, this investigation of local needs involved only local people. Four hundred people came, and the results were indisputable: the houses should be built on the lorry park, the shops should be promoted and helped and the market should be expanded to 130 stalls. On some days it should be allowed to spill out into the street. St Mary's, they argued, could become a new Covent Garden. An architect drew up their plans for St Mary's revitalization, and costed them at £2.5m, a fraction of the regeneration budget.

So the residents were astonished when, eight months

after the official community planning event, the council published its new plan for St Mary's and the surrounding areas. In all important particulars, it followed the plans outlined in the bid the council had presented to the government nearly two years before. Though the community had shown that it was fiercely opposed to the original plans, nothing of substance had changed.

'The Community Planning Event,' the council wrote, 'was an opportunity for people to "dream their dreams". If a start is to be made on realising any of these dreams, the approach needs to be tempered by practicality.'[13] 'The City Council does not believe there is a long term future for Kingsland Market . . . If no financially sound proposals come forward alternative uses must be found. The community may benefit more from the land being used for a new health centre and other local facilities. A more appropriate market facility would be encouraged within a new community square.'[14]

The council made no secret of the fact that it intended, as before, to demolish many of the buildings and close many of the shops on St Mary Street. 'It has become clear over the last decade', the plan stated, 'that the mixed shopping role and strung out nature of shopping in St Mary Street cannot be sustained. Its future will best be secured by concentrating shops into a more limited frontage . . . The current public car park, the frontage to St Mary Street and perhaps the site of Kingsland Market provide an opportunity for comprehensive redevelopment.'[15] The council's Head of Planning concluded that 'St Mary's can sustain only a local shopping role – aspirations for a return to a long quasi High Street . . . are unrealistic.'[16]

The leader of the city council warned the residents that

they had better accept the plans. 'This,' he told them, 'is the one opportunity to improve St Mary's. Otherwise it will go on crumbling ... If it does not work this time, there will never be any more government money.'[17]

'It was,' said Ian Loveridge, 'as if there'd never been a consultation. We were simply ignored.'

*

At first, the council's position was unintelligible. What was the point of conducting 'the biggest consultation exercise in British history', only to jettison its findings? Why was the council continuing to pursue plans which had been comprehensively rejected, and which remained deeply unpopular with the people of St Mary's? By the time local people found out, planning permission had been granted, and the businesses on St Mary Street had been given notice of closure. Their properties would be compulsorily purchased.

From the moment Southampton City Council launched a scheme to raise £80m and transform the face of the inner city, its credibility rested on making the project work. Were its bid to have been rejected by the government on the basis that its commercial partners had made insufficient commitments, or were it later to collapse because the private companies had pulled out as the deal wasn't profitable enough, the council, which had announced the scheme so publicly, would have ended up looking very foolish indeed. The political careers of the project's advocates would, effectively, have been brought to an end.

The private developers working in partnership with the council wanted, understandably enough, a scheme which would enable them to make their money as quickly and easily as possible. A piecemeal development, which protected most of the existing buildings, filled in a few small gaps and concentrated on upgrading and repairing rather than on demolition and redevelopment, offered few opportunities for swift and profitable construction. A single cleared site, however, on which the urban fabric could be rebuilt from scratch, was a far more attractive proposition.

To keep the developers and their money on board, the council had to offer them what they wanted. Whether or not the development that served the construction companies also served the community was a secondary consideration: the community had no money, and therefore counted for little. Indeed, the community had specifically to be excluded from the decision-making process at the crucial moment – the beginning – to prevent its demands jeopardizing the developers' interest.

The council, in other words, had to find land – preferably a single large piece of land – with which to whet the developers' appetite. There were two places which could, with comparative ease, be handed over, as both belonged to the council: the bomb site being used as a lorry park and the market and market car park. The lorry park, the council maintains, is unavailable, though it has yet to explain to the satisfaction of local people why this is. The market site, on the other hand, is well located.

By handing over the market and its car park, and compulsorily purchasing and demolishing the shops and houses along St Mary Street, the council would be able to assemble a largely empty two-hectare 'development opportunity' for its commercial partner, Bellway Homes. Bellway would use the site to build ninety new homes, a piazza and a handful of shops to replace the far greater number either demolished or scheduled for demolition. Some of the houses, partly subsidized by public bodies, would be sold below the normal price to council tenants, but most would be released onto the open market. Residents suspected that the subsidized housing would be pushed up against the dual carriageway, while the homes sold on the open market were likely to take the place of the demolished shops and houses on the more salubrious and attractive St Mary Street. The shops had to go to make the new development profitable.

Once that decision had been taken, the others followed automatically. The community planning event was seeded with council representatives and nominees. When, despite the council's best efforts, it still produced a clear mandate for expanding the market and shops rather than destroying them, it was ignored. A 'business survey' and 'property ownership study' of St Mary Street were conducted for the council's benefit. Both were funded by Bellway.[18] The community planning event was part-funded by the same company.[19]

When the council published its plans, eight months after the planning event, it organized a series of public meetings at which its planners explained their proposals. But on these occasions, as before, the meetings were rigged. When the officers had presented their plans, the conference would split into discussion groups, each of which was chaired by a council representative. The full meeting would then reconvene, and the council officers would tell the audience what had been said by their groups. The accounts they gave, the residents claimed, were biased and unrepresentative. But the audience was entitled only to seek 'clarification': the chairs of the meetings tried to prevent people from expressing opposition to the plans. By this time, however, the residents were becoming aware of the council's machinations. Several people ignored the chair and spoke out against the proposals, to resounding cheers. It was, one of the people in St Mary's Street told me, 'a promotional exercise, to allow the council and the regeneration board to claim that they had consulted the residents and found no opposition to their plans.'

The council was prepared to go further still to ensure that the developments it (and the developers) wanted could proceed. In October 1997, it commissioned a large and respected chartered surveying company called Gerald Eve to draw up an Action Plan for the St Mary's developments. The firm looked at the council's plans and the results of the planning event, and suggested to the council that it was in danger of making a serious mistake. Its plans would not be good for St Mary's: it would be better to expand the market and turn the district into a specialist shopping area which could draw people in from all over Southampton and even beyond. The market should be promoted all over the city, and grants should be made available for renovating the buildings on St Mary Street. The district should be reconnected with the city centre: it could become a diverse and economically viable urban village, which provided a home for creative and entrepreneurial businesses; the surveyors suggested that it could be turned into Southampton's Soho. The company endorsed the residents' suggestion that the lorry park, rather than the market and its car park, be used for building new homes.[20]

Instead of taking its consultants' advice, the council tried to freeze them out. It refused to provide the company with the information it needed and told it, without providing any corroborating evidence, that the residents were 'criminals' who had 'bamboozled Gerald Eve' for their own nefarious purposes.[21] The council instructed the company not to consult them any more. Soon afterwards, the council terminated the company's contract. The report drawn up by Gerald Eve was withheld by the council from the planning inquiry into the developments. Local people did not even know of its existence until a copy was leaked to them.

In April 1999 I spoke to Simon Milner, the consultant at Gerald Eve who had compiled the company's report. Over a year after the report was, in his words, 'effectively binned', he said he still found the episode 'very depressing'. 'We found out,' he told me, 'that, without informing us, the council had done a deal with the developers. We knew nothing about it, so we were made to look extremely stupid. Our recommendations for St Mary's would have taken three to five years to implement. But it was vital to the system to engage the private sector, as that was where the money was coming from. Only on that basis will government money be handed out. And the private sector wasn't going to wait three to five years for a plan to be worked out that helped St Mary's rather than hurting it . . . It was outrageous that the council won the bid. There was no basis for handing out that government money.'[22]

The council duly granted Bellway Homes planning permission to knock down the market and most of the buildings on the west side of St Mary Street, and turn them into new houses and a piazza. Towards the end of 2000, the demolition was due to begin. To please a private developer, and thus to secure the money it needed with which to sustain its credibility, Southampton City Council would destroy for ever the part of the city which has best retained its historical character, and that district's chances of engaging in an economy wider than its own. But that was not quite the end of the story.

*

The city council's primary justification for the closure of the market in St Mary's and the downgrading of the district's economy from one which served the whole of Southampton to one which served only its own needs was that both the market and the shops had suffered a severe decline in trade. They had sunk, according to the council's funding bid, into 'commercial obsolescence'.[23]

The market traders and small shopkeepers agreed that their trade had declined overall during the last few years, but argued that its contraction had been neither inevitable nor irreversible. The dual carriageway which formed the western boundary of the district had unquestionably contributed to St Mary's isolation from the rest of the city centre, though, the traders contended, a sensitive crossing, rather than the scary subway, would have helped to re-establish the link. But its fate had been sealed by the city council's flat refusal to promote St Mary's to the rest of the city. There are no signposts leading to the market, it is absent from the tourist brochures publicizing the city and St Mary's is even missing, bizarrely, from the 'City Centre' maps erected by the council in Southampton's other shopping zones, even though it is closer to the city's geographical centre than some of the districts that are marked. As one market trader pointed out, 'A visitor to Southampton simply wouldn't know the market existed.'

The council's promotional activities have, instead, been focused on the new developments on the other side of the city centre. A vast ex–industrial site, fifty-three acres in extent, beside Southampton's West Quay, has been swiftly transformed into 'the largest inner city development in Europe'.[24] The new development contains a huge John Lewis store and a monumental Marks and Spencer's, a 'retail village' featuring McDonald's, Halfords, Allied Carpets, ShoeCity and other national or multinational outlets, and a twelve-acre Rank LeisureWorld 'multi-entertainment complex', containing thirteen screens, clubs, bars, live music venues and several fast-food outlets. A new dual carriageway links West Quay directly to the M27, and there's enough parking for 4,000 cars.

It is, in other words, a huge and spectacular development. It is also the antithesis of what most town planners, urban design specialists and the government's Urban Task Force advocate as progressive city development. Car-dependent and characterless, it threatens the smaller businesses all over Southampton and the surrounding towns, and is likely, as a result, to lead to a massive net loss of employment. *Property Week*, a magazine not commonly associated with radical environmentalism, noted that 'it looks set to rip the guts out of formerly prime shopping areas in the centre ... Provided you can get the licences, the northern parts of Above Bar [hitherto the main shopping street] will be just pubs, pubs, pubs.... While this will no doubt delight the city's huge student population, it is unlikely to do much for the retail mix'. 'West Quay', it continued, 'is an in-town scheme but with all the feel of an out-of-town centre ... Access by dual carriageway will take shoppers out onto either the M3 or M27 without having to go into the centre ... people will not go elsewhere from the scheme.'[25]

In a brochure promoting the West Quay shopping complex, Southampton City Council announced that the development would become 'a new heart' for the city centre, 'the key to reshaping our city'. 'Our ... overall plan for Southampton,' the council's leader announced, 'is now well and truly falling into place.'[26]

The brochure went on to describe the city council's twofold conflict of interest. 'Southampton City Council', it boasted, 'is spearheading the West Quay development . . . It is also the planning authority and has provided part of the land on which the development is taking place . . . West Quay is being developed in partnership with Southampton City Council.'[27] Cases in which a council is both the vendor of a piece of land and the planning authority attracted the attention of Lord Nolan's Committee on Standards in Public Life; they are particularly alarming when the council is also the promoter of the development. It is worth noting that the council was faced with the same potential conflict of interest in St Mary's: the city council was selling the land for which it had granted planning permission, for a scheme it had chosen to promote above the district's other options for regeneration.

The developer of the shopping complex, a property company called Imry (now owned by Barclays Bank), would, the brochure announced, provide 'a £6 million package of benefits for the community in the city centre' as part of the West Quay deal.[28] These included the new dual carriageway, a 'town arena' on the West Quay site, training and a crèche, also on the West Quay site. But there was one 'benefit' the brochure did not mention.

The money Southampton City Council had acquired for transforming St Mary's was not the first disbursement from the government's Single Regeneration Budget to reach the city. Some years before, it had acquired a smaller grant for training, 'business support' and promotional activities. It had established a regeneration partnership which included the property company Imry. Imry's contribution was to provide 52 per cent of the money the council would use for marketing the city centre's shops.[29]

The City Council's promotional budget for the city centre, an area which incorporates West Quay, Above Bar Street, the High Street and St Mary's, was, in other words, being largely provided by the developer of West Quay. When the stallholders and shopkeepers of St Mary's were passed the leaked details of the first Single Regeneration Budget accounts, they believed they had found the explanation for the enduring mystery of why the council had failed, despite their repeated requests, to inform Southampton's people and visitors that St Mary's existed.

*

I took the complaints of the St Mary's residents to John Arnold, the leader of the City Council, and Paul Jenks, the Chair of the Southampton Regeneration Board, who was also Chair of Housing and Regeneration for the council. John Arnold was slim, formally dressed, quite ponderous in his manner and speech. Paul Jenks was younger, rotund, quick, and dressed, incongruously in the smart council offices, in shorts and a T-shirt.

The people spearheading the opposition to the area's redevelopment, Paul Jenks insisted, belonged to a criminal fraternity 'who are manipulating the genuinely held views of others' in order to run illegal activities out of St Mary's. 'I can't substantiate what I'm saying with evidence', he conceded, but there was, he believed, 'a bullying thug who was intimidating people into signing the petition ... against closing the market'.[30]

I asked them about the community planning event. Surely the point of consultations like this was that they canvassed the views of the community, rather than those of the council's planning officers? Paul Jenks answered.

'Not necessarily. Someone has forgotten that planning officers live in communities as do police officers and others. Quite a few of the officers involved actually live in this area. But of course I do recognize what you are saying, that they are holding a professional view. The idea was that their voice is in that discussion as well – not to dominate it or to steer it but to be part of the information input into the whole event.' I suggested that this approach was an unusual one, so unusual that the Neighbourhood Initiatives Foundation refused to bid for the event.

Mr Jenks spoke again. 'That's not my recollection. We asked three consultants to put a bid forward and we ended up with John— I forget his name now.'

I showed him the leaked letter.

'I remember what you're saying now. They have a different approach. Our feeling, with community representatives involved in setting up this event, was: no, we can't have a discussion in isolation from a planning engineer or a planning officer or a police officer without detailed information about how things work.'

What about the similarities between the original bid and the council's final plans for St Mary's? Did this not suggest that the council had made up its mind in advance? Mr Jenks raised his voice.

'No, this is the conspiracy theory, that's bollocks. I am extremely annoyed with it. There absolutely was not a plan. We'll show you the document, you can ask the consultants as to whether they were told there is a master plan they must end up with whether they liked it or not – there wasn't.'

(I did just this, and, as detailed above, they told me that, in effect, there was.) So why, I asked, did the market have to be closed?

'It is,' John Arnold told me, 'a strategic question of changes in shopping habits and for that reason we have to work on the assumption that within the period of the SRB [Single Regeneration Budget] programme the market will no longer be there for whatever reason and therefore in a planning document we have to put in provision for alternative use of the site.'

Since the West Quay development had been started, he told me, St Mary's could no longer be considered part of the city centre. He pointed to the map on his wall. 'That's West Quay and that's where the regional covered shopping centre is being developed. So this is the retail heart of the city . . . St Mary's is off centre and for that reason cannot have a future as part of central retail.'

I asked about Imry's sponsorship of the city centre's promotion. Mr Jenks and Mr Arnold flatly denied that the company had provided money for this purpose. I brought out the leaked Single Regeneration Budget accounts. John Arnold opened his mouth, but Mr Jenks cut in first. 'Fair enough, looks like they have!'

'That,' explained John Arnold, 'is marketing the city centre in the sense of getting people into the city centre.'

'It's not going to tell them to come to St Mary's, is it?' I asked.

'No, no.'

'It's going to tell them to go to West Quay where Imry are the new developers.'

'Yes, that's right.'

'St Mary's,' Paul Jenks explained, 'is a shopping centre but it's not the city centre.'

'You've seen St Mary's,' said Mr Arnold. 'We are not going to tell people in Winchester that they ought to go to

St Mary's to shop, are we? ... Let's get this straight. Imry are paying, if I've got it right, Imry are paying for a city centre manager because we didn't have a city centre manager so that person has been in the post for the past couple of years and part of their job is to bring people into the city centre. The city centre is going to be strengthened by the Imry development and ahead of the process of the Imry development we are trying to encourage more business into the city centre. But it's true that St Mary's isn't part of our city centre and as I say, we don't regard St Mary's as part of the city centre, we don't regard it as part of our potential package ... the whole reason for why St Mary's existed in the forties and fifties has gone and is not going to come back.'

*

Ian Loveridge was close to breaking point. He and other residents had fought the council's plans for two years. They had poured their money, their time and all their energy into trying to save the distinctiveness and vitality of St Mary's, and now had nothing left with which to campaign. He had been hit particularly badly by an arson attack on his mother's antique clothes shop. In July 1997, while he was running the campaign against the council's plans, he, his girlfriend and his girlfriend's children woke up to find black smoke pouring into their flat above the shop. They were extremely lucky to have escaped alive, but the collection of period costumes his mother had spent thirty years amassing was incinerated. The police said the fire had been started in three places, but they were unable to discover who was responsible. It had helped to shatter Ian's confidence.

'I always thought of myself as really strong,' he told me.

'But the strain of it all was so bad I ended up on sleeping tablets.'

It seemed to him that he had been wasting his time. 'The council has used the community's plight to get its money, but it simply wasn't prepared to listen to us. It wasn't interested. I can't stay here and watch everything I love being destroyed. It'd kill me. I'll just leave Southampton when the bulldozers come in.'

The bulldozers, however, are coming in all over the country. They are destroying not only the fabric of our cities and our countryside, but also the democratic procedures designed to protect it.

CHAPTER FOUR

How to Buy Planning Permission – The Department of the Environment's Conflicts of Interest

Even the most prosperous parts of London have surprisingly deep pockets of poverty, and the Royal Borough of Kensington and Chelsea, perhaps the richest place in Britain, is no exception. The ward in which Linda Wade lives is surrounded by fabulous wealth, but 38 per cent of its inhabitants live in 'social housing': homes subsidized for people who are too poor to buy on the open market.

As head of her residents' association, Linda Wade discovered that one of the major concerns of the people she represented was, like that of impoverished people throughout Britain, traffic. While many of the residents are too poor to buy a car, they carry much of the cost of other people's car use. The wealthy tend to move away from busy roads, leaving the poor with the noise, the danger and the pollution. This is one of the reasons why children in social class five – the bottom of the official economic register – are five times more likely to be hit by a car than children in social class one.[1]

In July 1997, the government decided to remove some of the obstacles impeding drivers passing through the borough. It insisted that Kensington and Chelsea turn three of its roads into 'red routes': narrow urban motorways designed to speed up the traffic. The people living beside these roads believed that this would make their surroundings less habitable, as the volume of traffic would increase. Members of her residents' association would be affected by all three of the red routes, so Linda Wade began exploring the possibilities for challenging the government's decision.

They were, she found, limited. The residents' objections would be heard only if she could force the borough council to confront the government and hold a public inquiry into the impact of the red routes. This meant that she had to seek judicial review in the High Court. Linda Wade knew that the chances of success were poor and that the costs of failure could be high. Legal aid for judicial review is hard to obtain: if any members of a community group opposing a development have more than a certain amount of savings, then the group has to carry its own costs and often – if it loses – those of the council. Such cases are also hard to win: the residents had to demonstrate that a council's decision not to hold an inquiry was 'unlawful, perverse or procedurally improper'.

But the residents were desperate: the traffic was already bad enough, and it was hard to imagine what life would be like if it became still worse. So, on behalf of thirty-seven residents' associations, Linda Wade and three others, none of whom are particularly wealthy, went to court. They lost. In February 2000 they were handed the bill. The council had costed the work of its legal department at £120 an hour, and added a 36 per cent 'handling charge'.[2] The residents had also been forced to hire lawyers, who, among other tasks, had to dissect the 700-page document the council had submitted to support its case. Linda and her three colleagues were handed bills amounting to £150,000. The council warned them that, if necessary, it would send in the bailiffs to recover its money.[3]

'If we had stood to make money out of the outcome of this case, I could understand why we should have to carry the council's costs,' she told me. 'But all we were trying to do was to prevent people's lives from deteriorating, which is surely what the council should have been doing in the first place. They are outpricing dissent.'

Going to court might appear foolhardy, but it was the only means the residents possessed of influencing a decision which would have a major impact on their lives. The planning system in Great Britain, which at first sight looks orderly, well balanced and fair, is thoroughly rigged. While the plan the residents of Kensington and Chelsea were confronting was initiated by the government, the imbalances in the system are used by corporations to devastating effect. Distortions in the planning process are among the most potent means by which they ensure that their needs are met, even when they conflict directly with those of most of the public.

*

In every other country in the European Union, local people who disagree with a council's decision to approve a development can use the planning system to object to it. In Britain, by contrast, only developers can appeal against a council's decision. It's a gross imbalance, which is never more evident than in cases where the council ignores its own local plan, approved after months of public consultation, and grants planning permission for a development which no one had envisaged. In these cases, all local people are entitled to do, short of taking the drastic and often ruinous route of legal action, is to ask the Secretary of State for the Environment to override the local authority and 'call in' the decision. Unfortunately, secretaries of state will do anything for a quiet life. Aware that every case they handle carries an enormous burden of paperwork, they tend to call in as few applications as possible.

The Labour Party is well aware of this problem. In 1994 it pledged that when it took office objectors would have an 'automatic right of appeal . . . in cases where there has been a departure from the local plan'.[4] But soon after the 1997 General Election, the Junior Planning Minister, Nick Raynsford, announced that this promise would not, after all, be kept.[5] Indeed, in August 1999 he compounded the injustice, insisting that the number of cases the Secretary of State is asked to call in should be further reduced.[6]

While local people are forbidden to appeal against a council's decision, property developers make full use of the special privilege they enjoy. When they launch an appeal, big development corporations purchase the best barristers and planning consultants money can buy. Local people, by contrast, have to fight the appeal with their own resources. There is no financial support for objectors, and there are no official sources of free advice. Preparing a case that will stand up to critical and legal scrutiny at an inquiry can take months and cost a fortune in legal fees, consultation and research. As most inquiries are held during the working day, people have to take time off work to attend. Objectors may be humiliated by developers' barristers: I have come across cases in which ordinary men and women with no legal qualifications have been reduced to tears. And the sole positive outcome of all this expense, time and stress, as far as the objectors are concerned, is to keep things as they are.

The local authority will, of course, be among those who argue against the development, and it can be expected to hire a barrister to make its case. But fighting an inquiry can be inordinately expensive, especially as the entire costs of the exercise, including the developer's legal fees, can be awarded against the council if it loses. On several occasions, councillors have been warned that they could be personally liable for costs if they reject a development. As councils run out of money, they are becoming ever more reluctant to risk the expense of a confrontation. Developers find that the threat of going to appeal is often enough to persuade a local authority to cave in and grant them planning permission.

Even if the development company loses the appeal, it needs only to wait for two years before submitting an identical application. Developers, adept at playing the long game, apply again and again for the same scheme until the resources and resistance of local people have been exhausted. In the absence of sustained objections, the local authority is likely, finally, to grant permission.

The only remaining means of challenging planning decisions are judicial review or an appeal to the Local Government Ombudsman. The ombudsman's powers are limited. He can make decisions based only on the narrowest technical criteria, and objectors have to demonstrate not only that the local authority is guilty of maladministration but also that the development would have been rejected if the case had been handled properly. Curiously, the ombudsman has no power to enforce his recommendations.

*

So the planning system, even when it works precisely as it is designed to, tends to discriminate against local people and in favour of development corporations. But it does not work precisely as it is designed to. For the councils charged with making nearly all the country's development decisions are often deeply compromised by their involvement with developers.

Situations like Southampton's, in which local authorities find themselves in the dangerous position of promoting a scheme for which they must later grant or refuse planning permission, are common. Councils often grant planning permission for land in which they have an interest, and in some cases appear to sell consent to the highest bidder. In Oxford, for example, a leaked memo from the city council's Director of Property and Leisure Services announced that permission for a huge and controversial leisure complex to be built on land owned by the council had been granted by the planning committee 'on 26 June 1996'. The memo was circulated on 25 June 1996 – the day *before* the committee was due to meet to discuss the case. The decision, in other words, appears to have been made before the development had been officially considered.[7] The developer was prepared to pay £3m for the council's land: more than the council believed it could obtain from other buyers.

But this is not the only means by which the property developer's path appears to be smoothed by money. Companies can, quite legitimately, give money or benefits in kind to a local authority as a condition of receiving planning permission. In theory there's nothing wrong with this: it seems fair that developers should be expected to pay for the new road junctions or bus services their schemes demand.

But the principle is easily abused. In the early 1990s, as local authority budgets collapsed, developers began offering inducements in return for planning permission which had nothing whatever to do with the schemes they were proposing. They would offer, for example, to build a swimming pool on the other side of town in return for planning permission for a new housing estate, or they would simply give the council a cheque, with which it could do whatever it wanted. While most people regard these inducements as bribery, local authorities describe them as 'offsite planning gain'.

The superstores were particularly keen to stretch the principle. In 1995, Safeway (which trades as Presto north of the border) wrote to the Western Isles Council in Stornoway on the Isle of Lewis, after the Co-op had applied for planning permission to build a rival store. 'Should your council decide to turn the Co-op's application down,' Safeway's Regional Development Director offered, 'then Presto would be willing to develop an all weather playing surface on the park suitable for sports such as football, hockey, etc. We have priced the provision of such a facility at £375,000, inclusive of fees, and would be willing to make this available to the Council for this purpose should the Co-op's application be refused.'[8]

The council was astonished. 'The suggestion in your letter indicates a new dimension to the concept of planning gain,' its Chief Executive replied, 'and I am frankly aghast and very seriously perturbed by your improper approach which seeks to interfere in the Council's proper consideration of a planning application submitted by one of your trading competitors.' He would, he warned, take 'legal advice as to whether your request constitutes professional impropriety on the part of your company.'⁹ When he did so, he discovered to his amazement that Safeway's offer was perfectly lawful.

Today, following a good deal of public scrutiny and complaint, offsite planning gain deals appear to be rather less common. But developers have found new ways of using their money as a means of persuasion.

*

In 1997, West Berkshire Council had a problem. It had been told by the Government that it must find room for thousands of new homes: the final figure, approved in 1999, was 9,000. It had few ex-industrial sites on which to build them, and one of the most beautiful rural landscapes in southern England to defend. The council knew that any major housing proposal was likely to be controversial.

But in deciding to support a scheme to build 1,700 new homes on 350 acres of Sandleford Park – a strange and striking landscape to the south of Newbury, believed to have been designed by Capability Brown – the local authority seemed to be walking straight into the guns. The site occupied rising ground overlooking a wide lowland plain. The new town's visual impact would be exacerbated by the unapologetically tall houses at its centre: it would, the developers bragged, 'fit prominently into the skyline'. The development, with its own centre, its shops, school and surgery, would alter Newbury's shape and orientation, destroying, local protesters insisted, 'the essence of our market town'. Its opponents calculated that the scheme would generate an extra 4,000 car journeys a day in a town which, despite its new bypass, continues to suffer from congestion and traffic pollution. Though the most pressing need in South-East England is for low-cost homes, most of the new housing in the Sandleford scheme would be expensive. Though housing land in West Berkshire is in desperately short supply, the development would be widely dispersed, with houses built at just a fraction of the density government advisers recommend.

Local people found it hard to see why the council was, in the words of one officer, 'putting most of our eggs in the Sandleford Park scheme', particularly in view of the fact that an old army depot at Thatcham, on the east side of Newbury, had recently become available for new building. The old depot could accommodate a major housing scheme at a small cost to the environment, as it had already lost its ecological and landscape value, was surrounded by buildings and was close to the railway station. The council was also beginning to discover that Newbury itself, with its old bus station, car parks, vacant plots, large gardens and derelict offices, offered opportunities for new housing. They also questioned the council's failure to take a strategic approach to the development of the district: while Newbury has no unemployment and too few homes, in 1999 the council granted permission to Vodafone, now the biggest publicly traded company in Europe, to site its world headquarters outside the town, massively increasing the pressure for new housing. Why, objectors wanted to know, was the council planning to destroy one of the district's most stunning landscapes in order to build a whole new town, without either devising a plan for reducing housing pressure or assessing the chances of fitting many of the new homes onto other sites? The answers evaded them until they found out about the deal that the council had negotiated with the Sandleford Park developer.

District councils are supposed to produce a 'Local Plan' about once every ten years, to determine which places should be set aside for development, and what sort of development can be pursued there. Some areas might, for example, be allocated for housing, others for industry or shopping, while the majority of any rural district will be devoted to farming and other green spaces. Developers then know where they can expect to receive planning permission for the schemes they might propose, and where it is likely to be refused.

The council's draft Local Plan is subjected to an inquiry. Developers who have bought or acquired an interest in a piece of land will argue fiercely that it be demarcated as a building zone. If they succeed, they can make a prodigious amount of money. People who believe that developments will damage their quality of life, or fail to meet their needs, will argue against them. The council is supposed to represent the public interest, seeking to strike a balance between the overall needs of the district and the immediate wishes of developers and local people. It will appoint lawyers and expert witnesses to argue its case, providing impartial advice on behalf of the whole community. Their task is to help the government inspector presiding over the inquiry to decide whether or not the council's draft plan is good for the district. This is how Local Plan inquiries are supposed to work. In Newbury in February 1998 the inquiry took a rather different course.

There were, as might be expected, several housing developers backing rival schemes for inclusion in the West Berkshire Local Plan. As the inquiry progressed, some of them began to display a certain amount of puzzlement at the enthusiasm with which the Liberal Democrat-controlled council and its expert witnesses and barrister appeared to support the Sandleford development. The lawyer acting for one of the competing construction companies began to suspect that something was seriously wrong. No one knows whether his question was prompted by a shrewd calculation or an inspired guess, but he asked the council a question which would ordinarily have been considered ridiculous: who was paying for the council's barrister and expert witnesses? The answer which everyone expected was 'Us, of course', for the local authority, as the representative of the public interest, is expected to pay for its own impartial advice. But in this case the council's representative replied that the backers of the Sandleford scheme, a large but little-known company called Trencherwood Homes Ltd, had contributed to its legal fees and paid for the council's landscape consultant.[10]

This was news not only to the residents of Newbury, but also to most of the district councillors. They discovered that for the past two months their officers had been negotiating with Trencherwood, in order 'to save public money'.[11] The officers insisted that there was no conflict of interest. Stella Manzie, the council's Chief Executive, told the *Newbury Weekly News* that 'the deal was limited to Sandleford Park, where Trencherwood and the council shared the same objective'. It was, she insisted, 'less than likely' that the council would broker a similar deal elsewhere.[12] 'Trencherwood's contribution,' she added, correctly, 'is perfectly legal.'[13] The arrangement, the head of the Environment Committee told opposition councillors, 'would have come to light . . . in the fullness of time'.[14]

Local people were furious. They demanded to know whether these were the only payments that Trencherwood had made to the council. At first, officers were evasive. But in early March they admitted that Trencherwood had, in fact, also paid the fees of the council's agricultural consultant.[15] They were pressed again by the *Newbury Weekly News*. Three weeks after Ms Manzie had insisted that 'the deal was limited to Sandleford Park', the council admitted that three other property developers had helped to meet its expenses at the Local Plan inquiry. McAlpine, Trafalgar House and a company called Queensgate Homes had all paid for the council's expert advisers. Developers contributed a total of some £100,000 to the council's costs.[16] The council's purportedly independent advice, in other words, on which the inspector's decisions about the future of the district would be made, had been systematically financed by the developers hoping to benefit from its plans.

West Berkshire Council argues that it would have supported the developments in question, whether or not the developers had paid its fees. This may or may not be the case. But hard-nosed development companies are not in the habit of giving money to local authorities when nothing can be expected in return. It is hard to see how the council could have failed to find itself obliged to its generous sponsors, and locked into a particular view of the developments. Janet Griffin, the Newbury woman who led the resistance to the scheme, told me: 'It's legal, but it's bribery. We trusted the council and they let us down. It makes you wonder what else is being cooked up by them.'

West Berkshire Council certainly gave local people plenty of reasons to remain suspicious. In July 1998, they discovered that the council had asked Trencherwood to apply for planning permission for the new town at Sandleford Park by January 1999 – thirteen months before the inspector was due to present his report on the local plan – so that the council could grant permission to Trencherwood the moment the inspector allowed the development to proceed.[17] The council failed to demand that Trencherwood conduct either an environmental impact assessment or an historic landscape assessment of Sandleford Park.

Local people suggested that the company had called in its debts. 'The council is trying to push this through as quickly as possible,' Janet Griffin told me. 'It seems to me that they think this will get them less trouble from people like us. They're wrong. We're going to fight them in every way we can.'

The uproar the revelations caused forced the council to conduct an internal inquiry into the Local Plan deal. Its report revealed, by contrast to the Chief Executive's assurances, that Trencherwood had also paid for both the council's draft planning brief for Sandleford Park and its presentation to the public. Alfred McAlpine Homes, Trafalgar House and Queensgate Homes, the report confirmed, had paid for experts who would otherwise have been hired by the council. The council would not reveal how much each of their contributions was worth, however, 'for reasons of commercial confidentiality'.[18]

The report appeared to endorse the officers' decision to accept this help, as it had saved the council both time and money. It argued that deals of this nature are now being accepted by other councils, while 'local authorities increasingly play an "enabling" role' for developers. 'Finance is now increasingly supplied by the private sector, not least through the Private Finance Initiative', it argued.[19] Councils, in other words, should no longer seek to be financially independent of the developers applying to them for planning permission. Alarmingly, as the report suggests, this perspective appears to be taking root among local authorities all over the country.

To the disgust of the council and the delight of many local people, in February 2000 the government's planning inspector rejected the Sandleford Park scheme. Ominously, however, he turned it down not on the basis that the decision-making process was compromised, but because the council had not examined alternative sites for the new housing. No one in authority appears to believe that there is anything wrong with the idea of councils taking money from the corporations hoping to profit by their decisions.

*

You might imagine that the development companies' power over local authorities – exercised by means of money, political influence or the democratic deficits in the planning system – is sufficient to ensure that they get what they want, while the people seeking to restrain their excesses are silenced or ignored. But the problems and abuses I have documented so far are the least of the distortions corrupting development policy in Britain.

The final arbiter of planning matters in England is the Secretary of State for Environment, Transport and the Regions, who, at the time of writing, is also the Deputy Prime Minister, John Prescott. He and the ministers and officials in his department are responsible both for establishing the planning policies which guide the decisions councils make, and for granting or withholding planning permission in difficult and important cases. Mr Prescott and his department, in other words, are the regulators of development in England. It is, therefore, critical that their judgement remains unclouded by any considerations other than the merits or demerits of a particular planning application, or (when setting national policy) the development needs of the nation as a whole. They exercise, or so we are led to believe, their judgement on behalf of us all.

But Mr Prescott and his department preside over the British government's starkest conflict of interest. The sector they are supposed to regulate is also, bizarrely, the sector they are charged with promoting.

The previous, Conservative government prided itself on its adherence to free-market principles: business, it maintained, should keep itself afloat, without government support. There was, of course, a certain discontinuity between rhetoric and reality. While small firms were left to sink or swim in the stormy waters of unmediated competition, large companies enjoyed the benefits of an endless supply of life rafts from the government. But most of these came from the Department of Trade and Industry, which still has a mandate for supporting business. The last Conservative Secretary of State for the Environment, John Gummer, made much not only of his free-market principles, but also of his environmental credentials: he was, he liked to claim, the greenest Secretary of State there had ever been. So it comes as something of a surprise to discover that, under his guidance, the Department of the Environment expanded and enhanced the special favours it rendered to construction companies – identified by many as among the foremost threats to the environment in Britain – to the extent that Mr Gummer became the champion of the very industry he was supposed to be restraining.

In 1993, John Gummer installed a new division within the Department of the Environment called the Construction Sponsorship Directorate. The CSD, according to the department's annual report, 'aims to help all sectors of the UK construction industry, including the building products and materials sectors, succeed in their domestic, European and international markets. It is the advocate within Government and the European Union for these industries ... It also acts as the focal point within Government for the property industry.'[20] Its 1996 budget was £26m: more, in other words, than the department provided for maintaining the National Parks of Great Britain or addressing the massive task of detoxifying its contaminated land.

It was not hard to discover what the Department of the Environment meant by being the construction industry's 'advocate within government'. 'Our aim', the Construction Sponsorship Directorate's mission statement boasted, 'is to promote improvements to the policy and legislative framework in which the industry works.'[21] It was committed to 'the review of legislation to remove unnecessary regulatory burdens'.[22] What makes this objective particularly interesting is that all the key elements of the 'legislative framework in which the industry works' – planning, health and safety, building regulations and environmental protection – are overseen by the Department of the Environment. What Mr Gummer was doing, in other words, was creating a lobby within government for the removal of the very legislation he was supposed to be defending and enforcing.

The lobby was well briefed. Its annual report explained, 'The department assists and promotes the construction industry through: consultation at ministerial and official level with representatives of the industry and Ministerial and official attendance at construction industry events ... Regular briefings are held with Ministers to give industry representatives the opportunity to raise issues of concern.'[23] The

Department of the Environment press office assured me that 'The industry itself tells us precisely what it is they want and where they want it focused'.[24]

This was not hard to arrange. Thanks to what the department described as 'a continuing programme of staff interchange with industry',[25] industry representatives came to occupy some of the key positions within the Construction Sponsorship Directorate. Sir Ian Dixon, of the construction company Willmott Dixon, was knighted for his services to the directorate. Both his son and Rick Willmott, another scion of the firm, were seconded into the CSD. Sir Ian later wrote, 'We were instrumental in the wholesale improvement of the industry's sponsorship by government which included a meeting with the Prime Minister in April 1994, several meetings with cabinet Ministers, a regular fortnightly briefing with the Construction Minister and a revamped Construction Sponsorship Directorate within the DoE.'[26]

Every year John Gummer, the greenest-ever Secretary of State, and his junior ministers set out on trade missions with the directors of UK construction companies. In 1995 and 1996, Gummer helped sell their wares in Israel and the occupied territories, India, the Philippines, Syria, Brazil, Argentina, Chile and Peru: countries not exactly renowned for matching development to the needs of people and the environment.

But John Gummer did not just lobby within government against the legislation he was in charge of enforcing: he also helped to organize the industry lobby that applied pressure to his own department. In 1995, he established a quango called the Construction Industry Board, whose purpose was 'to provide strategic leadership and guidance for the development and active promotion of the UK construction industry'.[27] The board was composed of the Department of the Environment, which provided 50 per cent of its funds, and the five major construction lobby groups, brought together for the first time, by the department, to form a single and far more powerful organization. Its Chairman was Sir Ian Dixon and its President was John Gummer.

The Construction Industry Board aimed both to promote the industry nationwide and to lobby for better treatment by the government. One of its early complaints was that 'planning constraints are inhibiting a faster growth in the housebuilding sector'.[28] The board's five industry lobby groups launched a campaign, with the CIB's help, called 'Britain Needs Building'. Its target audience was the Department of the Environment.

While John Gummer worked tirelessly to promote the industry he was supposed to be regulating, his deputy, the minister Tony Baldry, whose departmental duties included, intriguingly, both planning and construction, was even more helpful. Writing about his ministerial experiences, he recalled his eagerness to assist the people he was supposed to restrain. 'Industry representatives spoke of the need to have more access to government and I readily offered the facility of a fortnightly briefing with myself as construction minister. I recall that the senior civil servants present were uneasy about my offer, but the first "Baldry Briefing" was held on 25 November 1992. More than sixty of these briefings were held during the next three years and they became a key element of a new and vibrant arrangement for the Government's sponsorship of this essential industry. Representatives of the CIC [the Construction Industry Council – one of the biggest industrial lobby groups] were ever-present at the briefings, many of which were led and organised by the Council's officers and staff.'[29]

The conflicts of interest in which Messrs Gummer and Baldry revelled might help to explain some of the hitherto unfathomable decisions their department made. Environmentalists were repeatedly astonished when the greenest-ever Secretary of State oversaw some of the most environmentally destructive decisions any British government has made.

He agreed, for example, to the construction of Manchester Airport's second runway, even though it was deeply unpopular with local people, destroyed one of the most stunning landscapes in the north-west of England and had been dismissed as unnecessary by transport consultants, on the basis that the expansion of air travel to and from the region could be accommodated by using derelict land around Liverpool Airport. His department rejected a House of Lords proposal for a register of contaminated land, which was urgently needed to protect householders and organize proper detoxification efforts, but which was stoutly resisted by the construction industry. The Department of the Environment suggested, to the fury of many Tory MPs, the relaxation of greenbelt guidelines. Mr Gummer offered special dispensation for new 'stately homes' to be built in the countryside. For three years he mysteriously failed to introduce a moratorium on the construction of out-of-town superstores, despite repeatedly claiming that he was about to deliver one.

None of these decisions make sense if we see John Gummer as a diligent defender of the nation's fabric, addressing seriously his responsibility for planning control and environmental protection. They become comprehensible only when we remember that, as well as regulating development in Britain, he was also promoting it.

But while this conflict of interest budded during the Conservatives' term of office, under Labour it has blossomed.

*

It is clear that John Prescott did not, at first, understand what was expected of him. From the beginning he knew that he was the development industry's regulator, but he did not seem to appreciate that he was also supposed to be its promoter. When, soon after the 1997 General Election, the contract for the cladding of the Millennium Dome was awarded to a German company, Mr Prescott lamented Britain's failure to supply the material. It was, he said, 'a sad reflection on the competency of the industry'.[30]

The response was swift and furious. 'I can't understand,' growled Graham Watts, the Chief Executive of the Construction Industry Council, 'what his problem is. It is supposed to be his job to act as advocate for it [the construction industry] in government. He needs to sit down and think about his role rather than to just knock the industry.'[31]

'We have a lot of work to do,' the chief executive of one of Britain's biggest construction companies commented, 'to educate Old Labour people like Prescott.'[32]

Mr Prescott got the message. Seven weeks after he bemoaned the loss of the Dome contract, he had clearly come to understand his curious duties perfectly. 'I want to be a champion for your industry,' he told a construction industry conference. 'I am proud of what you can do, your hard work in all weathers, your export achievements and the ingenuity of your engineering. I want to work actively in partnership with the industry to solve problems and to improve performance. I want to offer you fresh ideas.'[33] The visits, the special briefings, the official attendance at construction industry events started all over again.

But while John Prescott, suitably educated and chastened, girded his loins to champion the industry he thought he was supposed to be restraining, it was his junior minister, Nick Raynsford, who was sent into battle most often on the development lobby's behalf. Mr Raynsford's enthusiasm for his interesting task outstrips even that of his predecessors.

Soon after taking office, Nick Raynsford told *Building* magazine: 'I see my job as a combination of creating a climate in which the industry can do well – like unblocking the Private Finance Initiative – and helping the industry itself rise to the challenge, equipping itself to be leaner, more effective and more successful . . . There is no question of construction being downgraded [in the department's priorities]. Quite the opposite . . . Anyone who thinks there is no commitment from the government is utterly misguided.'[34] All this was perfectly clear and uncomplicated – except for the fact that Mr Raynsford was also one of the Department of the Environment's three planning ministers.

Nick Raynsford left little room for doubt about where his loyalties lay. The Department of the Environment, Transport and the Regions' 1998 annual report informed its readers that, as well as helping the construction industry to become more efficient and innovative, Mr Raynsford would be working 'to improve the effectiveness of trade associations and other industry groups',[35] by which, it seems, it meant the lobby groups which were seeking to influence his own department.

The Construction Industry Board, still 50 per cent funded by the DETR, had announced that it would 'lead the implementation of a strategy to improve the industry's image'.[36] To this end it launched two public relations projects. The first is called the Considerate Constructors Scheme. At first sight, it looks like a fine idea: builders are encouraged by the scheme not to be lewd or rude, to dress properly and to be considerate towards residents and local businesses. But it seemed unlikely to achieve much as, in the Construction Industry Board's words, 'The level of regulation involved in joining the scheme should be minimal.'[37] Instead of enforcing codes of behaviour, the scheme should concentrate on producing 'well-designed literature and eye-catching posters displayed on prominent sites'. The board insisted that there should be no independent monitoring of the project. 'Any local-authority involvement would be of an advisory rather than policing nature.'[38]

The point of the scheme, the Construction Industry Board pointed out, 'is that the industry would be seen to be self-regulating'.[39] 'The alternative', according to *Building* magazine, 'is far worse: a Construction Industry Consumer Protection Bill.'[40] The Department of the Environment, in other words, is paying for an unpoliced, unmonitored promotional scheme whose purpose is to avoid the consumer protection regulation the department would otherwise introduce. 'We want', said Nick Raynsford, 'to see the industry take pride in its reputation, not to have to apologize for it.'[41]

With help from both Mr Prescott and Mr Raynsford, the Construction Industry Board also organizes an event called National Construction Week. The first week, much to the amusement of the victims of late builders, lasted eleven days. The second one, in April 1999, was delayed by six months.

One of the week's main purposes is 'to highlight how environmentally conscious Britain's builders are'.[42] 'Many youngsters', the CIB notes, 'may think the industry is a despoiler of the environment. We need to correct this misconception.'[43] On hand to help were those staunch defenders of the environment and sponsors of the week, Blue Circle Cement, Hanson plc (which owns the Amey Roadstone Corporation), Tarmac and McAlpine. Both government-aided weeks also incorporated 'an event to influence MPs'.[44]

The meetings which the Conservative minister Tony Baldry organized appear to have been enhanced and extended by Nick Raynsford. The government refuses to reveal whom Mr Raynsford meets or how often he meets them, but it's possible to piece together at least part of the picture. The lobby group the Construction Industry Council was pleased to report that 'A series of "new-look" Ministerial discussions with Ministers from our Sponsoring Department (DETR) began in October 1997'.[45] *Building* magazine was told that 'twenty movers and shakers with construction expertise regularly meet to advise construction spokesman Nick Raynsford on policy'.[46] The House Builders Federation records that during the 1997 Labour Party Conference 'we had a very worthwhile meeting with Nick Raynsford, minister for construction, who kindly gave us a long and valuable slot in a very full diary'.[47] The Construction Confederation hosted a meeting at the conference, at which Nick Raynsford sat with the confederation's chairman and president, by whom he was lavishly praised.[48]

The British Constructional Steel Association is pleased to note that 'Good relations have been established with the new Government', especially with Mr Raynsford.[49] This happy circumstance could account for the otherwise incomprehensible fact that the government has teamed up with both the British Constructional Steel Association and the British Cement Association to launch a 'government sponsored campaign to increase the commercial and industrial new-build market'.[50] The campaign conflicts directly with another Department of the Environment objective: to encourage the renovation and re-use of existing buildings in the name of sustainability.

In March 1998, some of Britain's biggest housebuilding companies started lobbying Nick Raynsford to ask him not to apply new regulations – which insist that new houses are more accessible to disabled people – to 'starter homes'.[51] The regulations had been brought about largely through the work of the Access Committee for England (ACE), a forum for disabled people's charities which was mainly funded by the Department of Health. ACE was to play a major role in ensuring that the regulations were enforced. Four weeks after the builders' lobby began, the Department of Health, following 'consultation with the Department of the Environment, Transport and the Regions',[52] cut ACE's entire core funding, forcing the group to fold.[53]

Most construction companies appear to agree with the view expressed by a trade body called the Construction Clients' Forum that 'there is no real need to employ lobbying organisations. These points can be made in periodic meetings with ministers and civil servants.'[54] But others prefer to hedge their bets. The Construction Confederation, the British Quarry Products Association and the National Council of Building Materials Producers were all paying a lobbying company called Lowe Bell Political a monthly retainer for providing access to members of the Labour government after the 1997 General Election. The trade bodies' contact at Lowe Bell, according to *Contract Journal*, was Ben Lucas.[55] Mr Lucas was previously head of Tony Blair's briefing unit during the General Election campaign. He was central to the 1998 'cash for access' scandal, which exposed the fact that lobbyists with close links to Labour were being paid by corporations to secure meetings with ministers and policy advisers. Mr Lucas's 'work for the Construction Confederation included arranging meetings for the body with the No. 10 Policy Unit and with Labour MP Stephen Byers [now Secretary of State for Trade and Industry] ... giving the Construction Confederation the opportunity to make amendments to Labour's draft Business Manifesto.'[56]

Another company which featured prominently in the cash for access scandal was GJW Government Relations. One of GJW's directors, Derek Draper, boasted to a journalist that, in May 1998, he had obtained for the chief executive of the House Builders Federation a meeting with a Downing Street policy adviser, to talk about greenbelt policy.[57] I have found that GJW's government connections were even better developed than the newspapers have discovered.

A year before the General Election, GJW launched a joint venture with the public relations company Mistral, whose purpose was to help companies 'ease the path for planning applications'. The package the two companies offered included 'Lobbying of MPs, councillors and those who influence them', as well as 'media work', 'community relations', and 'crisis management'. GJW's spokesman explained, 'The reason for coming together is that for many years we have done a lot of work on controversial planning consents, such as MCA's theme park proposals for Rainham Marshes.'[58] Rainham Marshes is the biggest Site of Special

Scientific Interest in Greater London, and the theme park, had it obtained permission, would have destroyed it. The joint venture was launched with the help of Keith Vaz MP, who at the time was the Labour front bench spokesman for planning and regeneration[59] (he is now Minister for Europe). In other words, Mr Vaz, like Mr Raynsford, Mr Gummer and Mr Baldry, was helping the lobbyists who would be lobbying him.

The department argues that its support for the construction industry will secure public benefits, including an improvement in health and safety standards and environmental sustainability. Its 'Rethinking Construction' initiative identified a number of demonstration projects, which would show how construction can create 'a better and more sustainable environment'.[60] They included a drive-through McDonald's, five giant superstores, a Rugby Cement Works, a new motorway and part of a nuclear power plant.[61]

*

Mr Raynsford, as Planning and Construction Minister, worked as hard as Mr Gummer to sell the construction industry's wares abroad. Since May 1997, he has led trade missions to the Philippines, Poland (twice), the Czech Republic, Jordan, Egypt (twice), Turkey and Brazil. Mr Prescott, the Secretary of State for the Environment, has promoted the construction industry in China and India. Between them, they have sought to help British companies win foreign contracts for roads, airports, dams, pipelines and power stations.

In some cases, the trade missions have been disguised as humanitarian aid operations. A Department of the Environment press release, issued in September 1999, revealed that 'A delegation from the UK construction industry led by . . .

Nick Raynsford has returned from a harrowing visit to Turkey with a determination to help with the reconstruction of the earthquake-torn country . . . "We were deeply moved by what we saw"', Mr Raynsford reported. Britain, he decided, would provide some 'much needed technical assistance in planning for redevelopment'.[62]

The assistance took the form of a £1.5m 'assessment', jointly funded by the Department of the Environment and the construction companies. It wasn't quite as disinterested as Mr Raynsford suggested. Lawrence Hoskins of the construction firm Balfour Beatty, who was chairman of the consortium conducting the assessment, gave the game away. 'We will put the effort in and hope it will lead to business. We are all companies that exist to provide work for our employees and benefit for our shareholders. If the results of our efforts were turned into work for other European companies, it would be a real disappointment.'[63] As the bill for rectifying the earthquake damage amounted to some £4bn, of which £2bn had already been promised by international organizations, the rewards for construction companies which had got their foot in the door were likely to be significant.

Mr Hoskins's company, Balfour Beatty, has already been involved in humanitarian issues in Turkey. It has been negotiating to help construct the Ilisu Dam in Anatolia. Critics of the Turkish government allege that the dam has been designed to assist its ethnic cleansing programme: it will drown the ancient town of Hasankeyf, the Kurds' cultural heartland, flooding 25,000 people out of their homes and forcing them into government-controlled model villages. The dam will also enable Turkey to hold Syria and Iraq to ransom by controlling the flow of the River Tigris.

Two organizations have been particularly prominent on Mr Raynsford's trade missions. Representatives of the construction company Kvaerner accompanied the minister to Jordan, Egypt, Poland and Brazil. In Egypt, the project to which Mr Raynsford devoted most of his time was the 'Media City' development run by Kvaerner in Alexandria.

The other organization is a trade association called the British Consultants Bureau. The minister's visit to Brazil was, according to the Department of the Environment, Transport and the Regions, timed to 'tie in with a visit being organized by the British Consultants Bureau'.[64] In Egypt, the department reveals, 'members of the British Consultants Bureau gave a half-day seminar in Cairo to promote their capabilities'.[65] When commercial officers from twenty British embassies were being briefed by the department about the construction industry, they were given a presentation by the British Consultants Bureau.[66] When Mr Raynsford visited Poland and the Czech Republic, he led 'a DETR – British Consultants Bureau trade mission'. The DETR trade mission to Kazakhstan in June 2000 was prepared and organized, again, by the British Consultants Bureau.

The government's promotion of Kvaerner is unusual, for Kvaerner is not a British company but a Norwegian one: Kvaerner plc is a wholly owned subsidiary of Kvaerner ASA, registered in Norway. But the company enjoys the distinction of having more of its employees seconded into the Department of the Environment, Transport and the Regions than any other organization.[67] This could, perhaps, account for its curious pre-eminence on Mr Raynsford's trade missions.

The prominence of the British Consultants Bureau is just as intriguing. All the trade missions in which the BCB was involved were assisted by a sub-section of the Construction Directorate called the Construction Export Promotion and Materials Sponsorship Division. The head of this division is called Richard Wood. By coincidence, Richard Wood, I have discovered, also sits on the Advisory Council of the British Consultants Bureau.[68]

This is not the only peculiarity overseen by Mr Wood's division. The official policy of the Department of the Environment is to reduce greatly the amount of stone quarried in Britain for hardcore or aggregate: the material with which roads are built and certain foundations laid. In the government's words, this is because of 'impacts . . . in terms of noise, dust, heavy traffic movements, and damage to landscapes and valuable habitats'.[69] The massive quarries carved out of some of the most stunning landscapes in Britain are extremely controversial. They are also, for the most part, wholly unnecessary. Eighty-two per cent of the aggregate Denmark uses is recycled – it comes from demolished buildings and torn-up roads. In Britain, only 10 per cent is recycled, and most demolition waste is dumped in landfill sites. The government's policy looks plain: 'ways of minimising future demand will need to be considered'.[70] According to Mr Raynsford, 'The Government is committed to a more sustainable construction industry and we encourage the use of recycled materials which have clear and positive environmental advantages.'[71]

The unofficial policy of the department is to encourage companies to dig as much aggregate out of the ground as possible and sell it abroad. Far from 'minimizing future demand', it has been helping British companies to maximize it. Mr Raynsford has taken Tarmac and the Amey Roadstone Corporation (ARC), two of the country's biggest aggregate quarrying companies, abroad to sell the fabric of Britain to as many customers as possible.[72]

In 1996, Mr Wood's division set up an Export Action Group for building materials, whose purpose is 'to stimulate enhanced export activity within the industry'.[73] Like the other bodies established by the Department of the Environment to 'advise on improving Government assistance to the industry',[74] it consists of the department itself and the department's major lobbyists. In June 1997, Mr Raynsford boosted its work by launching an Export Action Centre for sending British building materials overseas.

A few months later, the Department of the Environment organized a new public relations offensive for the quarrying industry called 'Minerals 98'. The DETR and the Department of Trade and Industry spent £72,000 on the initiative, which they ran with the help of companies and trade bodies like ARC, Pioneer Aggregates, the British Cement Association and the Quarry Products Association. The companies used the occasion to lobby against the tax on aggregate that the Department of the Environment was proposing as a means of encouraging recycling. Yet again, the Department was paying the industry to lobby against its own policies.

At the 1998 Labour Party Conference, Labour's 'Green Business Evening', hosted by the Environment Minister, Michael Meacher, was sponsored by Aggregate Industries, a big quarrying company which, soon afterwards, was taken over by Tarmac. The result of all this lobbying was to help delay by nearly three years the promised tax on aggregate. When it did materialize, in the March 2000 budget, it was lower than the government's own researchers (who had been employed to cost the damage caused by quarrying) had advocated: the public would continue to subsidize the destruction, noise and pollution caused by the industry.

*

The conflicts of interest which govern the Department of the Environment, Transport and the Regions have resulted in planning policies which are, if possible, even more hostile to the environment and ordinary people's quality of life than John Gummer's were. John Prescott, who came into government with what appeared to be genuinely green intentions, is turning into one of Britain's principal environmental hazards. He has made several extraordinary decisions. His compromised ministers have made many more.

While insisting that he wants underused housing to be brought back into circulation in order to reduce the pressure on greenfield sites, Mr Prescott has repeatedly refused to remove a financial incentive which helps encourage the rich to buy two homes while the poor have none. The owners of houses which are not permanently occupied need pay only half the amount of council tax they pay on homes they inhabit throughout the year. This contributes to a major problem: large numbers of the houses built ostensibly to solve Britain's urgent housing crisis have instead been sold abroad as speculative investments. In 1997, a remarkable 50 per cent of all the new homes built in Central and Inner London were purchased in the Far East. Domestic demand is also strong. There are 224,000 second homes in Britain, which is, coincidentally, roughly equivalent to the official number of homeless families and single people. In some rural areas, villages have been almost entirely bought up by second-home owners, and prices, as a result, have risen so fast that local people cannot afford to buy. Council tax is, of course, only a small part of the cost of owning a second home, but the rebate helps to make it affordable, and make this trade in eviction profitable. It also helps ensure that more houses need be built by the construction industry.

In 1998, John Prescott overturned a planning inspector's recommendation, to approve a greenfield industrial development on a 150-acre site near Sutton Coldfield, even though an ex–industrial site nearby could have accommodated it. The 'brownfield' land would have been more expensive for the developers to build on. In 1999, he refused to call in the decision to allow Vodafone to build its headquarters on a greenfield site outside Newbury, even though the scheme offends every planning principle Mr Prescott claims to uphold.

His ministers have been even keener to embrace the needs of industry while ignoring the needs of the environment. Nick Raynsford has, like the House Builders Federation, repeatedly pressed for low urban densities and more greenfield development, even though Mr Prescott's own advisers have shown conclusively that the urban regeneration the government seeks will only materialize if cities remain compact.[75] Planners, Mr Raynsford says, should be 'more flexible and positive in their approach to development'.[76] He has promised the British Council of Shopping Centres that he will fight to prevent protracted delays to major new retail schemes.[77] He appears to have been partly responsible for the government's U-turn on proposals to tax out-of-town parking places, arguing against his department's own official recommendations and in support of the superstores' objections to them at Labour's 1998 local government conference.[78] In 1999, Mr Raynsford was promoted, becoming the senior Planning and Housing Minister. But he retained his responsibility for promoting the construction industry.

Richard Caborn, who was until 1999 Mr Raynsford's boss, presided over one of the government's more spectacular broken promises. Before the 1997 General Election, the Labour Party promised to protect the Forest of Dean in Gloucestershire from proposals to quarry it for aggregate. The current MP for the Forest of Dean, Diana Organ, was elected on the party's promise, which featured prominently in her election leaflets. She was furious when Richard Caborn announced that he had no intention of honouring the pledge. He also refused to call in a proposal to quarry a million tonnes of limestone a year from the heart of the Peak District National Park. Faced with a conflict between the Department of the Environment's pledges to reduce the amount of quarrying in Britain, and its offer to help the mining industry sell its products abroad, Mr Caborn discovered that he could not keep both promises.

Most importantly, the Labour government has removed some of the few remaining safeguards designed to ensure that development responds to public need, rather than just corporate greed. In November 1999 John Prescott announced that 'for the first time the planning system will be required to promote competition'.[79]

The government, the Department of the Environment has announced, will 'speed up' the planning process in response to 'business need'. Its consultation paper *Modernising Planning* proposed still more radical means of assisting developers. It suggested that special 'orders' could be issued, authorizing the construction of major developments such as airports and nuclear waste repositories. 'National policy statements' outlining 'the need for and benefits of major projects' would 'avoid unnecessary speculation and debate at subsequent planning inquiries ... [so that] time is not wasted at inquiry going over issues which have been settled'. When issues are 'settled', of course, local people have no means of affecting their outcome. The paper suggested that only 'major landowners' and 'local groups with membership of 50 people or more' should be allowed to speak at public inquiries. Dissenters would have to form a membership organization and encourage people to join it before the inquiry could hear their objections.[80] All of these measures, in other words, further tilt the balance of decision-making towards developers and away from local people.

A report published by the department in January 1999 warned that business was being hampered by 'an increasing anti-development mood'. It suggested that 'clear proactive policies' were needed to assist 'business development'.[81] In April 1999 Richard Caborn gave some indication of what these might entail. Preparation of Britain's regional planning guidance, he suggested, should be 'business led'. 'We propose to produce a guide for business on how to become more closely involved in the planning process', he revealed.[82]

Development in Britain is already our greatest source of inequality. While hundreds of thousands are homeless, and some 30,000 elderly people die of the cold each winter because their homes are unfit for human habitation, every city bristles with new office blocks and superstores. Land desperately needed for affordable housing is used instead to build exclusive developments of luxury homes. While parks and community centres deteriorate, new leisure facilities for those who can afford to pay handsomely are springing up all over Britain. These are symptoms of our loss of control over the planning process.

When we are unable to ensure that construction meets our needs, the key decisions about how we live are taken by people who hope to profit from our exclusion. When planning is in the hands of the developers, development will always work against us.

CHAPTER FIVE

Economic Cleansing –
How the Superstores Conquered Britain

For some of the ewes in the market pens, the journey to the abattoir would be a mission of mercy. Half bald, hips sticking out of their fleeces, speckled with dags and scabs, they coughed and groaned as the buyers leant over the bars to squeeze their backs.

'It's the old stagers today,' someone told me. 'This lot are only skin and grief.'

They were scarcely worth the slaughter fees. Since the rouble had collapsed and the Far Eastern market had shrunk, the price of sheepskins, most of which are sold to Russia and Asia, had fallen from £8 to 20p. A few of the better animals would be sold as mutton to halal butchers, the rest would be turned into pet food and 'manufacturing meat': for pies, kebabs and ready meals. The farmers had left them in the stalls and gone: one man told me he couldn't bear to see how much his work was worth.

The auctioneer stepped up onto the gangway above the sheep pens, briefly registered the small crowd of burly men in padded waistcoats and tweed hats and cleared his throat.

'Right, off we go then. Five Cheviot ewes, one Texel tup,

all good ones. Twenty pound I'm asking, twenty pound I've got. Twenty pound and you're out. Half, half, one, one half, two, two and a half – '

'He's got no meat on him,' one of the buyers muttered.

'I've seen worse,' his neighbour said.

' – three! Three half, you're out now, Mike, four, four, I've got four – '

'I'd rather put my money on the horses.'

'A three-legged one would give you better odds than this lot.'

' – four, four half, five, five, I've got five. At twenty-fives, Clive!' The auctioneer hit his clipboard with his biro and immediately moved to the next pen.

'Here we are, gentlemen, just what the housewife wants, no fat.' The buyers laughed.

'Any warranty on them, Percy?'

'Yes, lifetime guarantees on every one.'

The old 'cull ewes' sold for as little as £2 apiece. With slaughter fees of £8 or £9 each, the buyers maintained that they could find around 50p in profit on each animal.

Those men, on that chilly morning in Brecon market, in mid-Wales, in March 1999, were furious. The world, they felt, had turned against them.

'They're brainwashed in the bloody schools. A lot of these teachers think it's a wonderful thing to be vegetarian, see.'

'I lost a friend three weeks ago. Just went out to the barn and hanged himself. He saw no bloody future, raising animals to be bastard burnt. And we're still importing meat from bloody Ireland, where they've openly got BSE.'

But most of the buyers' anger was reserved for Britain's supermarkets. The big stores, they believed, were killing

British farming, forcing livestock breeders to sell their animals for less than they were worth, then charging higher prices for their meat than the independent butchers levied.

'I have bloody swore black and blue about this,' one man told me. 'We won't have a meat trade left in eighteen months' time. There's a lot of blokes talking about jacking it in at the moment. It's a dismal old story, it bloody is.'

The buyers and farmers in Brecon felt they were being trampled twice by the superstores. For years they had been undercut by what they maintained were anti-competitive practices. Now the livestock market in the town centre was to be closed and the site used to build a new Safeway supermarket. The money Safeway paid for the land had enabled the county council to move the market out of town. The auctioneer thought this was a good idea: there would be less traffic congestion, bigger pens and a new canteen for the drovers and buyers. The others were unconvinced.

'Bloody nonsense, boy,' one of the farmers told him. 'Now listen, now. This town developed around livestock and the markets. People come here to do their shopping as well – it's much better for the market to have it here. A lot of the new markets out of town haven't been as good. Look at what happened in Leominster. They moved it out of town and it's closed now.'

Brecon is a remote, windy market town cursed with appalling weather and blessed with exquisite architecture. On the edge of the Brecon Beacons National Park, it is surrounded by formidable views. The people of the hundreds of farmsteads, hamlets and villages in and around the park travel there to buy and sell, meet their friends and organize their affairs. Tourists come from all over the world, drawn both by the climbing and walking nearby and by the peculiarities of Brecon itself. The town differs from others not only as a result of the presence of many remarkable buildings, but also because of the absence of some of the less engaging forms of development. When I travelled there in 1999, I found a strikingly compact settlement, with little of the peripheral commercial construction or new housing estates which have distorted the shape of so many market towns. It was unusual in possessing no major supermarket. Brecon had a small Kwik-Save and a smallish Co-op, but most of its grocery trade passed through the hands of scores of independent shopkeepers and market stallholders. This was about to change, and many of the people of Brecon were convinced that the new store would destroy their town.

*

The big supermarket chains claim that they have achieved their pre-eminence in this country simply by providing people with what they want. They are, they insist, able to offer their customers better value, more choice and more convenience than British people have ever been able to enjoy before. Supremely competitive, they have beaten their rivals by fair means in a free market.

It is true that the superstores are adept at attracting custom, and many British people do enjoy shopping in them. But the key to much of their success lies not within the market but outside it. They enjoy more political influence than almost any other corporate sector in Britain. Their huge financial muscle helps them to bend both local and national government to their will. This political power appears to have enabled them to trade on terms which would surely not be tolerated in any other area of British commercial life. They offer convenience and choice in their stores only by destroying convenience and choice everywhere else.

*

A small man with a jolly red face bounded into Brian Keylock's shop and slammed a can of beer onto the counter.

'Put it in the fridge, Brian, and drink it when Wales win tonight.' He bounded out again. Brian Keylock laughed, put the can away, then carried on scrubbing and hosing down his chopping block.

A tall gangling couple came in, both of whom towered over the butcher.

'Mrs Clarke!'

'What about me?' the man asked. 'Ignore me, will you?

'And Mr Clarke. I couldn't see you, you're too small.'

'Is it going to be worth watching, like?'

'Yes, because we'll win. Now what about a raffle ticket for Cancer Relief? You'll get a French rugby shirt if you win.'

'What would we want one of them for?'

'Well, Mrs J— bought two strips of tickets, and when I asked her why she said, "Just think of all the big men who might have been inside it!" And she's seventy-seven.'

'Oh, all right, then.'

Brian sold them some chops and told them to pray for Wales. He turned to me with a sigh.

'You don't get this sort of thing in the supermarket, you see, George. It's like a family here. Safeway say they're bringing choice to Brecon. But there are nine butchers in town already. You've got nine choices. If we all disappear, you'll have no choice. The fishmonger has already closed down. Clothes shops have closed down. It's bad enough without the Safeways, and you don't need a crystal ball to see what's going to happen when it comes. Look at Monmouth. They call it "the town for sale". It's got seventeen vacant premises. Go to Leominster. Since that thing arrived there, the town is dead. They'll do the same to us. This isn't for the good of Brecon, it's for the good of Safeway.'

He started packing up his shop.

'I'm not moaning about losing my job, George. I'm moaning about losing my life. And it's not just me. Who's going to fill these slots when we've gone? More charity shops, more building societies? The country's run by idiots.'

Everywhere I went in Brecon, I heard the same story. The people I stopped on the street told me that the superstore would ruin the place. People came to the town, they said, because of its peculiarities: the ancient buildings, its small scale, the quirky and engaging shops. The new supermarket would make Brecon more like everywhere else.

They also mourned what they sensed would be the loss of the social cohesion the small shops consolidated. 'These places,' one woman told me, 'are what stick us all together, see. They make us talk to each other. You can't avoid it.'

But above all the people I spoke to felt that they had been misled.

*

Brecon does not have a conventional district council, but is governed by the Brecon Beacons National Park Authority. This body is not directly elected: sixteen of its members are drawn from the county councils within the park's boundaries; the remaining eight are appointed by the Secretary of State for Wales. The authority makes the planning decisions on which the town's development depends. In 1998 it approved Safeway's application to build on Brecon's cattle market. It supported the supermarket at the subsequent public inquiry.

Like Safeway, the authority argued that the supermarket, far from harming the other traders in town, would help them. One of the reasons why many of Brecon's residents travelled to other towns to do their shopping, the authority claimed, was that Brecon had too narrow a range of shops. 'The quality and choice of food retailing', according to the assessment produced by the superstore's consultants and used by the National Park Authority, 'will be significantly enhanced through the introduction of one of the country's premier retailers . . . Shoppers will be attracted back into the town centre.' The only noticeable losses of trade would be felt by the two small supermarkets already in the town. 'No store closures are predicted.'[1]

This assessment, according to the local people opposing the store, was bogus. It was true, they conceded, that many people in Brecon went elsewhere for some of their shopping. According to a study commissioned by the Development Board for Rural Wales, only 39 per cent of the clothes shopping by Brecon residents took place in their home town, while 86 per cent of the townspeople travelled elsewhere to buy large items of furniture. But, as in all towns in mid-Wales, local people were remarkably loyal when purchasing their groceries: 90 per cent of those bought by Brecon's inhabitants are bought in Brecon.[2]

The consultants' assessment, in other words, failed to distinguish between the different kinds of shopping. Brecon's 'leakage' had little to do with groceries, yet the solution to the problem, according to the National Park Authority, was to introduce a bigger grocery store. There was no shortage of evidence to suggest that, far from boosting the trade enjoyed by the town's smaller shops, as the council claimed, the new Safeway would greatly reduce it.

During the 1990s, according to the consultancy Verdict, the number of specialist shops like Brian Keylock's fell by 22 per cent in Britain.[3] The smallest ones were hit hardest: between 1990 and 1996, shops with annual sales of less than £100,000 declined by 36 per cent.[4] Between 1986 and 1997, by contrast, superstore numbers rose from 457 to 1,102.[5] While most towns have suffered substantial losses, the impact has been even greater in the countryside: at the end of 1997 the Rural Development Commission revealed that 42 per cent of rural parishes no longer possessed a shop.

This is plainly not due to an overall reduction in trade: between 1992 and 1997 retail food sales in Britain increased by £18.6bn, or 30 per cent.[6] But while small shops lost 8.5 per cent of their trade between 1990 and 1996, large retailers gained 18 per cent.[7] The two trends – of the decline in small independent shops and the expansion of the superstore chains – appear to be linked.

In 1998, the government published the most comprehensive assessment of the impact of superstores ever undertaken. Its findings were unequivocal. Food shops in market towns lost between 13 and 50 per cent of their trade when a supermarket opened at the edge of the town centre or out of town. The result is 'the closure of some town centre food retailers; increases in vacancy levels; and a general decline in the quality of the environment of the centre ... Even where town centre food retailers suffer an impact, but do not subsequently close, there may still be a concern that this will lead to a general decline in activity elsewhere in the centre, and adversely affect the vitality and viability of the centre.'[8]

It is interesting to note that Safeway's consultants had

made precisely the opposite claim, using the same words: the supermarket, they maintained, 'will enhance and promote the vitality and viability of Brecon'.[9]

Nor was it correct to suggest, as Safeway and the park authority had done, that only the other supermarkets might suffer from the opening of their store. 'Contrary to the widely held perception,' the government's report noted, 'our research indicates that impact is not confined solely to other supermarkets.'[10] Interestingly, one of the places singled out by the report was a neighbour of Brecon's, a market town of roughly the same size, with a similar assortment of shops and stalls: Leominster. When Safeway opened a supermarket there, the report revealed, many of the town's small shops promptly lost 30 per cent of their trade.[11]

Altogether, it is not easy to see how Safeway's consultants and the Brecon Beacons National Park Authority could have assumed that the new supermarket would help the town's existing traders. I asked Jonathon Guscott, one of the park authority's planning officers, how he had arrived at this conclusion. He was familiar with the government's report, he told me, but it was irrelevant, because it dealt largely with 'edge-of-town' stores, and the new Safeway would be built in the town centre.[12]

This claim served only to increase my perplexity. The government's report states repeatedly that it concerns 'edge-of-centre' superstores. The assessment by Safeway's consultants, on which the park authority relies, describes the new store as 'edge of centre'.[13] In the same conversation, Mr Guscott told me that a new road being driven through Brecon, beside which the store would be built, was designed to 'move traffic out of the town centre'. If the road was out of the centre, surely the supermarket served by that road was also out of the centre?[14]

But perhaps the most astonishing of Safeway's assertions, echoed repeatedly by the National Park Authority, is that the new supermarket would generate employment in Brecon. 'Approximately 150 new employment opportunities will be created,' Safeway's consultants claim. 'It will assist in reducing the local unemployment rate.'[15]

Proclamations like this accompany the public presentation of nearly every new supermarket in Britain. In 1997, Safeway announced that it would create 8,000 new jobs over the following two years. In 1998, Tesco boasted that it would boost British employment by 10,000. In 2000 it claimed it would create a further 4,000 jobs by opening grocery stores in Esso filling stations and another 7,000 through online sales. In 1999, Sainsbury's maintained that the hundreds of new 'Sainsbury's Local' stores it planned to open would generate 10,000 jobs. In 2000 Asda promised it would create 27,000 jobs within five years. But these claims are wrong.

Their refutation comes from the most embarrassing source: one of the superstores' own research organizations, the National Retail Planning Forum. It is financed, among others, by Sainsbury, Tesco, Marks and Spencer, Boots and John Lewis (which owns Waitrose). Its report undermines every claim the forum's own funders have made.[16]

The forum studied the changes that had taken place in the areas surrounding ninety-three new superstores. Its analysis, published in 1998, found that there is 'strong evidence that new out-of-centre superstores have a negative net impact on retail employment up to 15 km away'. Total employment in food selling within that radius, it found, decreased by 5.2 per cent. As 'retail employment actually increased by 0.1% in GB outside the 15 km catchment areas', then 'this decline could only be due to the new superstores in the sample'. 'In other words,' the report continued, 'if the superstores had not opened, employment would have risen. All of the reduction in employment that occurred in the catchment areas is attributable to superstore openings.' The ninety-three stores the researchers studied were responsible for the net loss of 25,685 employees: every time a large supermarket opened, in other words, 276 people lost their jobs.[17]

This shouldn't be surprising. The superstores routinely boast about their 'efficiency': economies of scale and clever stock control and delivery systems allow them to shift a great deal of merchandise with very few staff. The New Economics Foundation has calculated that every £50,000 spent in small local shops creates one job, whereas £250,000 needs be spent in superstores for the same result.[18] The supermarkets' expansion relies not only upon increasing the total volume of trade but also upon seizing trade from the economically less efficient – and socially more efficient – employers in the independent sector.

The superstores' impact on jobs, moreover, is unlikely to be confined to retailing. Small shops tend to employ small local businesses for building work, fitting and maintenance. Unlike the superstores, small shops tend to buy their stock through independent wholesalers. They are more likely to buy local produce than the big chains, which often purchase their supplies directly from producers on the other side of the world. The money made by the small shops tends to stay, like their proprietors, in the town in which it was spent.

The money the superstores make is immediately removed. In Brecon, the impact of the new store could be even more damaging than elsewhere, as tourism is central to the town's economy and heavily dependent on its tranquillity and distinctiveness.

*

The big chains insist that their trouncing of Britain's smaller shops is the result of their competitiveness. They are expanding while independent shops are declining, they claim, because they offer choice, cheapness and convenience. Consumer choice, exercised in a free market, favours the big shops over the small. But the market is far from free.

Britain's superstores have mastered the art of offloading their costs. Expenses they and their customers incur are not represented in their prices, but are, instead, carried by everyone in Britain, whether or not they shop in the big chains. This becomes most obvious when one considers the companies' impact on transport costs.

Brecon's shops serve not only its townspeople, but also the inhabitants of the surrounding villages and hamlets. Public transport in mid-Wales, as in most parts of rural Britain, is sparse and irregular, so most of these people come shopping by car. Many of them parked beside the livestock market, or in council-owned car parks elsewhere in the town, in which they had to pay.

Safeway's building covers both part of the livestock market and many of the car parking spaces attached to it. The store has undertaken to replace them with car parking on the other side of the old market, the side furthest from the town centre. This, like the store itself, is served by a new road partly financed by Safeway, which bypasses the High Street, its shops and the grocery market. The store's parking is free.

In theory, people visiting Brecon's small shops could park in Safeway's car park, pay nothing, and walk into town. But while the remaining spaces in the old car park are not far from Brecon's High Street, the new parking is a long way from most of the town's other shops. The new road leads visitors straight to Safeway and its new car park. Shoppers will be faced with a choice between convenient free parking beside Safeway, with a long walk to the other shops, or inconvenient and expensive parking close to the rest of the town. The store will, in other words, reap a massive competitive advantage from the new arrangements. The small shopkeepers complain that Safeway, with the help of the National Park Authority, has turned Brecon round to face the other way.

The free parking the superstores offer their customers is subsidized by everyone in Britain. National Traffic Surveys show that the distance travelled to go shopping increased by 14 per cent between 1989/91 and 1994/96, as the retail chains brought down the cost of driving by offering free, convenient parking.[19] This impact is not confined to out-of-town superstores: a survey of shopping journeys in inner London shows that just 8 per cent of people visiting high street shops arrived by car, compared to 60 per cent of those shopping at a Sainsbury superstore in a similar area.[20] The result is more congestion, pollution and danger on the roads, which is, as Chapter 4 mentioned, often felt disproportionately by the people who cannot afford cars themselves.

The government recognizes that all of us are paying for the superstores' free parking, and in 1997 the Department of the Environment, Transport and the Regions quietly resolved to do something about this. John Prescott planned to include a tax on out-of-town parking in his White Paper on integrated transport. Lawson Lucas Mendelsohn, a lobbying company whose directors all worked for the Labour Party in opposition, warned Tesco that the tax was being considered, more than a year before the White Paper was published.[21] Tesco began lobbying. In February 1998, it also made a £12m donation to the Millennium Dome. While Tesco denies that this was part of a deal with the government, the gift must have done its relationship with Labour no harm. In May 1998, Tesco representatives met John Prescott.[22] His White Paper, which was due to appear imminently, was delayed. By the time it was published, in July of that year, the parking tax proposal had been dropped. Instead the paper called for 'a closer partnership' between local authorities and major retailers to 'identify appropriate measures funded by the private sector to reduce car dependency for access to these developments'.[23] Central government, in other words, would take no action, while contributions by the superstores would remain voluntary.

Supermarkets are similarly adept at making society pay their costs of distribution. The big chains are reluctant to hold much stock, as storage is expensive. Instead they encourage the farms and food manufacturers which supply them to store the produce on their behalf, and operate a 'just-in-time' delivery system. 'This', John Breach, head of the British Independent Fruit Growers' Association, observes, 'frequently leads to very environmentally unfriendly, refrigerated juggernauts visiting farms daily, often collecting just a few pallets of produce'.[24]

The superstores' buying power, their demands for

standardized, easily gradeable produce and their centralized distribution systems have resulted in a profligate use of transport. Out-of-season Coxes are imported 14,000 miles from New Zealand during our own apple season, while our produce lies rotting on the ground. In France, 90 per cent of the apples sold in supermarkets are produced domestically. In the UK, the figure is just 25 per cent.[25] A study by the environmental organization The Safe Alliance found that some of the vegetables being sold in two superstores on the outskirts of Evesham in Worcestershire had been grown just one mile from the town, but before they reached the shelves they had been trucked first to Hereford, then to Dyfed, then to a distribution depot in Manchester, from which they were delivered back to Evesham. The same report noted that all Safeway's dairy produce passes through a single depot in Warwickshire, before being trucked all over the country.

Sainsbury, Safeway, Tesco Distribution, Asda and Marks and Spencer all are or have recently been members of the Freight Transport Association, the lobby group representing the interests of road hauliers. It campaigns against restrictions on lorries travelling through residential areas at night, against constraints on the size of lorries and for increases in the speed limit for large lorries on small country roads.[26]

*

All the large stores deploy what retailers call 'loss leaders'. These are staple products sold at less than the cost of production to create the impression that a store is cheaper than its rivals. Bread and milk are sometimes offered for just a fraction of the market price. In 1999, the big supermarkets sought to persuade their customers that they offered extraordinary value by marking white bread down so far that they were almost giving it away. A senior Safeway executive, whose company was selling loaves for 8p each, admitted that this was a 'crazy price':[27] which seems to mean that it bore no relationship to free market values. Milk rounds and independent bakers, which possess no capacity to cross-subsidize their products, have been eliminated by this device in places all over Britain. Recent legislation in France, Spain and Ireland forbids the sale of goods below cost price, in recognition of the massive economic and social damage wrought by this unfairness. But the British competition authorities have repeatedly refused to intervene.

While they destroy smaller traders by uncompetitive means, the superstores' relations with each other are not quite as red in tooth and claw as their advertising suggests. In 1996, Tesco, Sainsbury, Asda, Safeway, Waitrose and Marks and Spencer as well as twelve of Britain's biggest food manufacturers came together to draw up a pact. They would cooperate on promotions, product launches and distribution.[28] This is not the first time that Britain's biggest retailers have worked together at the expense of their rivals. In 1993, Costco, an American 'discount club' offering goods to its members at prices considerably lower than the superstores charge, sought to open a number of giant stores in Britain. Sainsbury, Tesco and Safeway jointly hired a public relations agency and a planning consultancy in the hope of generating political pressure to prevent the stores from being built. They also took Costco to court, arguing that planning restrictions should be tightened in order to prevent its warehouses from receiving permission. They warned that planning permission for the discount stores would blight the landscape with 'unattractive trading sheds and huge car parks', while 'high streets would suffer'.[29] The chains which had lobbied for years to make planning permission for out-of-town outlets easier to obtain had united to prevent it from being granted, on the grounds that it would cause precisely the kinds of damage for which they themselves are most responsible.

Companies operating in Britain are not legally classified as monopolies until they control 25 per cent of the market in which they trade. Whether or not the superstores qualify depends on how the market is defined. If one assesses all the major sectors in which the superstores trade, then Tesco, the largest, emerges with 17 per cent of the national retail market (twice as high a proportion as ten years before), and Sainsbury has 13 per cent. If, on the other hand, one considers only sales of 'groceries' – fresh and packaged foods and the other consumer staples traditionally sold by smaller stores – then Tesco emerges with 25 per cent of the market, and Sainsbury with 20 per cent.[30]

Hopes that Internet shopping would provide opportunities for new companies to challenge the dominance of the big stores appear to be sadly misplaced, for the established pattern of traditional shopping has been closely matched by the development of online sales. Tesco, the market leader in the conventional grocery business, has already emerged as the biggest online grocer in the world. At the beginning of 2000 it boasted annual Internet sales of £125m, and claimed it would treble the number of online stores by the end of the year.[31] Sainsbury, Asda, Waitrose and Iceland are investing heavily in the hope of catching up. Tesco's Internet sales are likely only to tip the balance further towards monopoly.

It may also be valid to consider the combined impact of the supermarkets. Some analysts have argued that Britain's biggest chains collectively meet the legal definition of a 'complex monopoly': a group of companies controlling between them more than 25 per cent of the market which 'whether voluntarily or not and whether by agreement or not, so conduct their respective affairs as to prevent, restrict or distort competition'. The five biggest chains shift 74.5 per cent of all the groceries sold in Britain.[32] This could be the most concentrated market of its kind on earth. Their profits have long been higher than those of similar chains anywhere in Continental Europe. The non-market advantages over smaller stores they enjoy appear to present a clear restriction or distortion of competition.

Moreover, as the Office of Fair Trading recognizes, a monopoly does not have to operate throughout the nation to be effective. It seems clear that a local monopoly is more likely to occur in retailing than in manufacturing or wholesaling, for ordinary people, unlike many companies, do most of their shopping close to home. There can surely be little doubt that some of the big chains operate what are, in effect, local or regional monopolies. Tesco and Sainsbury, for example, control 57 per cent of the grocery market in London and the south of England between them, and 58 per cent of the market in eastern England. But the superstores' market control is most clearly expressed through their relationships with their suppliers.

Tesco, according to its *Clubcard* magazine, is a robust defender of the local economy. 'You may be worried', its readers were told, 'that buying meat, fish, dairy, fruit and veg from a supermarket means local suppliers lose out. You needn't be. At Tesco we support local farmers wherever possible.'[33] It is not easy to see how Tesco can make this claim. A study of eighty-one small shops threatened by the opening of a new Tesco outside Saxmundham in Suffolk found that they stocked products from some two hundred local producers: farmers, smallholders, wine, cheese and jam makers, beekeepers and bakers.[34] The small shops, in other words, were a cornerstone of both the local retail economy and the local wholesale economy.

Tesco, by contrast, in common with the other superstore chains, buys most of its produce from a small number of very large suppliers. According to market analysts, the big chains are attempting to reduce the number of their horticultural suppliers to no more than three for each product: every company will buy from just three cauliflower producers, for example, or three apple growers, and their produce will be distributed all over the country.[35] As small shops close and the superstores tighten their grip, the great majority of British food producers will find their markets disappearing. The consequences are grave, not only for existing producers but also for anyone hoping to enter the market: most food producers start by selling their wares to local shops. Hundreds of wholesalers have also been driven out of business, as the superstores buy directly from producers. This is one of the reasons why so many livestock markets have closed down. Many of the sites they occupied are used, ironically, to build new superstores. But the prospects for those few farmers and manufacturers lucky enough to be chosen as suppliers to the superstores are scarcely brighter.

While the superstores routinely break the regulations and agreements which stand in their way, they impose the most draconian rules of their own. Several chains insist that farmers growing fruit for them belong to the nominally voluntary Assured Producers Scheme. This forces them to set higher standards than the superstores themselves apply.

They must, for example, replace their packhouses with buildings whose walls and ceilings are smooth, so that dust can't accumulate on them. Many superstores, by contrast, contain hundreds of possible dust traps. All the windows in the buildings in which the fruit is processed and packed must be replaced with shatterproof glass, even if they are nowhere near the processing areas, so that, in the event of a window breaking, shards do not enter the food. In the superstores, by contrast, fresh food is sometimes displayed beneath shelves of glass bottles and jars.

The superstores know that the farmers who sell to them have nowhere else to go: they can, therefore, make the most extortionate demands. They will specify the variety, age, size, feeding, drugs, pesticide or fertilizer treatments for the animals or crops the farmers supply. They will demand near-perfect uniformity in shape, size and colour. The supermarkets claim that they select certain breeds and specifications in response to consumer pressure. Suppliers say this is nonsense: the varieties they are asked to produce are generally those with the longest shelf life, irrespective of taste or texture. Draconian quality control, some argue, has more to do with the superstores' stock keeping and the engineering of holy terror among producers than with consumer preferences. If customers knew how many chemicals were required to grow fruit and vegetables of a consistent shape and size, they maintain, they would quickly opt for produce that is rather more diverse in appearance.

In 1999, the British Independent Fruit Growers' Association sent questionnaires to growers supplying the supermarkets. Sixty-six per cent of them reported that they had been forced to grub up productive orchards because the superstore chains had suddenly decided to change the varieties they sold. The whimsical demands of the stores, some believed, was driving British fruit farming to extinction.[36]

The position of the growers is, on the whole, too weak to demand that superstores sign contracts at the beginning of the growing season, and many have found that their produce is rejected for the flimsiest reasons: they suspect that the chains order far more food than they require, in order to keep the price down, then have to find excuses for rejecting much of the crop. The superstores pay nothing for the produce they turn away.

The growers also have to carry all of the costs of packaging and labelling the food they supply, according to the precise instructions they receive from the stores. The big companies may change their specifications at a moment's notice, forcing the producers to invest almost overnight in new machinery, cartons and labels. Some will even tell their suppliers which manufacturers they must buy from: this is because, the BBC's *Panorama* programme alleged, the supermarket chains get 'kickbacks' from the packagers.[37]

If the hapless farmers trying to respond to the big companies' ever-changing demands slip up, they can expect to be severely punished. A letter from Asda to a growers' cooperative at the end of 1998 complained that products arriving at its depot carried the previous week's prices. 'I ask that you focus your efforts on the processes that are in place,' it insisted, 'and must warn you that any further breach will result in the flat rate charge of £10,000 per product error, and potentially loss of business.'[38] Superstores have also threatened to banish suppliers who do not agree to their terms to 'death row': the top shelf, which customers seldom check. If suppliers want to ensure that their goods stay where people will find them, they must pay for the privilege.

In November 1999, Safeway sent the farmers it bought from a notice entitled 'Good News From Safeway'. Its 'new promotional strategy' would 'deliver a much improved level of availability for your product'. There was a catch, however. 'To take part in the programme we request a contribution from you per product line of £20,000 . . . We look forward to you joining us in this campaign, and anticipating a favourable response, we will take the liberty of sending you an invoice on Friday of this week. Thank you in advance for your support.'[39]

At the end of the year, both bakers and fruit growers supplying the superstores may be forced to pay a 'rebate' to the chain they supply: if they refuse they will not be asked to sell their produce to that company again.[40] The chairman of La Forneia, a firm that sells bread to one of the superstores, has revealed that when the chain he sells to is asked to make a donation to a charity, it will turn to him or one of its other suppliers and instruct them to hand over the money in the superstore's name.[41] The charity takes it in the belief that it had been provided by the superstore, and the grateful disabled children, cancer patients or injured pets are pictured in the local papers with the superstore's beaming manager.

While the supermarket owes nothing to the farmers, farmers often find themselves locked into selling food to the supermarket, simply because the collapsing wholesale market has left them with no choice. The supermarket can gradually reduce the price it pays until the farmer's business folds, whereupon it switches to a new supplier, who is less aware of the hidden costs of the relationship. A survey by the *Daily Mail* revealed that apples in the superstores were marked up by as much as 198 per cent, while eggs commanded prices up to 439 per cent higher than were paid to the farmers.[42] Some of the big chains ensure that the producer's options remain limited: in some cases manufacturers have been warned that if they also supply their goods to the discount clubs, they will lose their trade with the superstore.[43]

We hear little about practices like these because, as John Breach of the Fruit Growers' Association points out, 'farmers who dare to raise objections to terms and conditions run a very real risk of being delisted'.[44] After a meeting of livestock farmers convened to protest against the demands that Tesco was making on the way in which they raised their animals, one of the organizers complained: 'The fear factor was immense. Few people felt brave enough to put their head up and speak publicly.'[45]

While suppliers in Britain have little defence against the impositions of the superstore chains, workers in the developing world have even less. British supermarkets have been blamed for pesticide poisonings, exploitation, land alienation and water theft. In 1996 Christian Aid launched a campaign to persuade the chains to adopt verifiable codes of conduct. By 1999 it had little progress to report.[46] While Sainsbury had begun to take some of its responsibilities seriously, Safeway, Christian Aid found, had 'established a code relating to animal welfare standards before one relating to the conditions of its Third World suppliers'. Tesco told Christian Aid that it would commit £2m (0.5 per cent of its half-yearly profits) to ethical trading, but was later unable to say how this money had been spent. One year after informing Christian Aid that it was drawing up a code of practice, Asda had made no significant progress. 'Without clear targets and timetables,' Christian Aid concluded, 'the supermarkets' commitment to ethical trading cannot be taken seriously.'[47]

Wal-Mart, the American chain which moved into Britain in June 1999, has for many years been the subject of fierce criticism by human rights campaigners, who have accused it of buying goods in the past from companies using the forced labour of prisoners in China. A week after Wal-Mart secured its takeover of Asda, the US National Labour Committee reported that the American company's contractors in Bangladesh were paying workers as little as 5p an hour, a quarter of the Bangladeshi minimum wage. They were expected to work for up to eighty hours a week.[48] Wal-Mart insisted that it had been misled by the contractors, who had failed to abide by its code of conduct. Campaigners suggest that it should be doing more to ensure that human rights guidelines are followed.

In 1998, a report commissioned by the Office of Fair Trading found that the supermarkets' excessive 'buyer power' allowed them to wipe out smaller competitors, who could not force farmers to submit to such stringent demands. But their control over the producers has not led to lower prices for their customers. 'Retailers are increasingly able to retain the benefits from their increased bargaining power,' the report noted, 'rather than passing them to consumers.'[49]

*

With the exception of products selected by the stores as 'loss leaders', and those chosen for high-profile price campaigns, such as designer clothes and certain medicines, Britain's supermarkets appear to be considerably more expensive than many smaller shops selling similar products. Fruit and vegetables sold from market stalls tend to be around 40 or 50 per cent cheaper than the fruit and vegetables in superstores. Independent butchers, fishmongers and greengrocers generally undercut the big chains by 30 per cent or more. Potatoes seem, for some reason, to attract the biggest differentials: prices in the supermarkets may be six times as high as prices in specialist greengrocers. While conflicting evidence has been presented, several studies have found that British supermarkets charge significantly more for the groceries they sell than supermarkets on the Continent.[50]

Perversely, as a survey by the Citizen's Organizing Foundation discovered, the poor appear to be charged more for their food than the rich.[51] The cheapest available selection of a fixed list of groceries, it found, costs up to 69 per cent more in stores in some of the poorest parts of the country than in stores belonging to the same chain in richer places. In the poor areas, it seems, superstores encounter less competition, and the resident population is less mobile, so less capable of escaping the clutches of the local monopolist.

Britain's superstores insist that if their prices are higher than those of their European counterparts, it is because their expenses are greater. Land allocated for development is more expensive in Britain, and the strong pound has distorted the comparison. The currency argument is bizarre, for Britain is a major net importer of food, and the strong pound has enabled our superstores to trade on favourable terms. They are right about the price of land, but they have omitted to add that labour is considerably cheaper in Britain and that VAT is charged on food almost everywhere else in the European Union.

The superstores, in other words, enjoy low prices from

their suppliers and low labour costs and benefit from economies of scale unavailable to smaller shops, yet still they appear to charge their customers more for many goods than either their domestic competitors or their foreign counterparts. It is hardly surprising that they are massively profitable. In 1998, Tesco made £866m in profits, and Sainsbury £735m. British superstores, according to the report commissioned by the Office of Fair Trading, are roughly three times as profitable as similar companies in France, Germany, Italy and Spain.[52]

*

The Office of Fair Trading and the Monopolies and Mergers Commission have both examined the practices of the superstores in the past. In 1981 the MMC concluded that the superstores' insistence on special favours from their suppliers was 'beneficial to competition and to the consumer' and that its 'general effect . . . on the public interest' was harmless.[53] In 1985, the OFT decided that it 'was unable to identify any particular case which amounted to an abuse of buying power or other anti-competitive practice'.[54] In 1996, the OFT investigated a complaint filed by the National Association of Master Bakers about the predatory pricing of bread by superstores. Though bread prices in the big chains had clearly been marked down to way below the cost of production, the OFT decided to take no action.[55] In all cases, the public interest was deemed to be commensurate with low prices: extortionate practices which led to the elimination of suppliers and competitors were considered beneficial as long as the cost of the items in question fell as a result. Critics pointed out that the long-term effect of these strategies would almost certainly be a substantial rise in prices, as competitors were driven out of the market. The official reports, they charged, took no account of the wider costs imposed on society by the superstores.

By 1998, the demand for a full-blown inquiry had become irresistible. Parliament's Welsh Affairs Committee reported that the prices the supermarkets were paying to beef and lamb producers bore no relationship to the prices they charged their customers. A Liberal Democrat MP published a powerful report on competition in retailing.[56] Several national newspapers had run campaigns against high supermarket prices, and the wider social and environmental impact of the stores was at last being widely discussed. The Office of Fair Trading, which had, in its own words, 'previously taken the view that the growth of the major supermarket groups has been to the advantage of consumers in terms of amenity, choice and most crucially prices',[57] was forced to act. It launched an eight-month inquiry into competition in the sector.

At first, the OFT seemed characteristically reluctant to condemn the superstores. The man in charge of the inquiry, Bob Lawrie, told reporters, 'We have always taken the view that the growth of the supermarkets is broadly in the consumer interest. We have no specific intent to go back from that now.'[58] He was also relaxed about the fate of the farmers. 'We have started off with the assumption that retailers will screw suppliers for all they're worth – that's taken for granted.'[59] During the first round of his investigations, Mr Lawrie interviewed only representatives of the biggest four chains. This could have been because, as he conceded, 'including myself, there will be only four of us working on this – and that's along with the other cases we look at. We have to do this on a shoestring while the companies we look into have a hundred times more resources than we have. Someone like Sainsbury's can provide a Rolls-Royce while we've got a Raleigh bike.'[60] But gradually the scope of the inquiry opened up and, in April 1999, the Office of Fair Trading concluded that the superstores had a substantial case to answer. To many people's surprise, it referred the matter to the Competition Commission.

The superstores responded with alacrity. Having repeatedly assured the public that their prices were already as low as they could possibly go, they suddenly found room for massive reductions. Tesco slashed the price of over a thousand brands by more than 10 per cent. The cuts, it claimed, would amount to some £250m. Sainsbury marked down 1,500 lines, while Asda promised to reduce the price of 10,000 items by as much as 50 per cent by the end of 2000. Though he had previously argued that consumers were not being ripped off by the superstores, Archie Norman, the Chairman of Asda, finally admitted that they were. 'The industry is where it deserves to be, and we have brought it all on ourselves ... Nobody believes UK prices are lower – we have lost that argument already,' he conceded.[61] The other superstores were furious that he had broken ranks.

His company's advertised cuts were not all that they seemed, however. In December 1999, the Advertising Standards Authority ruled that Asda's promotional campaign, which claimed that prices would stay 'permanently low', was misleading: after a short period, many of them rose again.[62]

But the strategy seemed to work. In February 2000 the Competition Commission reported that there was 'only limited evidence of excessive profitability', as food prices had recently risen more slowly than general retail prices.[63] It did, however, conclude that the five biggest supermarkets were involved in two complex monopolies: the first relating to the pricing of groceries, the second concerning the power they wielded over their suppliers. But while it warned that it could force them to sell off some of their stores or could ban the use of loss leaders, the wording of its initial report made it clear to the superstores that it would do no such thing. One prominent retail analyst commented, 'This is as good as they could have hoped for. It is not ordering them to do anything but carry on.'[64] Critics of the superstores believe the Competition Commission has been fooled.

*

Someone had covered the lambs with graffiti. When they staggered to their feet from where they lay, small as litter in the grass, they seemed to be as much blue as white: huge numbers had been sprayed on their flanks. They tottered after the exhausted grey ewes with pathetic cries, and pushed and nuzzled at the udders.

It was a day on which the crimes of the winter were forgiven. Marsh tits chased each other through the March sunshine. A chaffinch sang from a hawthorn tree, and starlings rode on the backs of the sheep as proud and glossy as cavalry officers. The last snow shone on the slopes of the Brecon Beacons: pure white on the peaks and in the cwms, grey and stratified on the windward faces.

I walked along the River Usk, whose bumpy water rustled in the sun. An old fisherman, gaunt as a heron, stalked up the bank.

'Any luck?'

'No, I'm just watching the birds. It's too nice a day to

do any fishing. When it gets like this I think "Oh, sod the fish, I don't want them anyway."'

On the high ground above the river, a mile out of town, was a sea of churned maroon earth surrounded by plastic netting. Two men in yellow helmets sat on a girder, bolting a roof onto the new livestock market the county council was building. Already, it promised to become an eyesore of spectacular ugliness – vast hangars with glinting steel roofs – in the geographical centre of one of Brecon's most famous views.

Powys County Council had been trying to build this market for years. The old one, on the town centre site owned by the council, had been built in the 1950s, when cattle were smaller. Now the animals could jump over the pens. The site was tatty and neglected, and market days caused congestion in the town centre. The existing market could have been redesigned and rebuilt, but the council decided to demolish it and start again elsewhere. This would cost, it found, some £2.5m. It applied to the Welsh Office for a grant to move the market out of town, but the government turned it down. So it sold the town centre land to a property company working on behalf of Safeway. I was told by the council that it could not let me know how much money it had made, 'for reasons of commercial confidentiality'. But it used its earnings to move the market.

This seemed like a sensible, pragmatic solution to the problem the county council faced, and it might have been uncontroversial – had the county council not also enjoyed a powerful position on the planning authority. One third of the members of the Brecon Beacons National Park Authority, including its chairman and deputy chairman, are also members of Powys County Council, whose financial problems were solved by the sale of its land to Safeway.

Powys County Council, which is the highways authority in Brecon, also proposed that a new 'inner relief road' be built through Brecon, a plan which amazed many of the residents. The town already possessed a bypass, intended to remove much of its traffic. Why then did the council want to build a new road which was likely to pull it back in? Local people became even more perplexed when the county council announced that only the first two stretches of the road needed to be built – the third, which would have completed the loop through Brecon, was unnecessary.

From beside the old livestock market, I watched as the council's earthmovers destroyed, ironically, its own highways depot, and cleared a wide crescent of land from where I stood to the eastern edge of the town. The new road, whose construction involved the demolition of several old buildings and the effective reorientation of Brecon's traffic, came to a halt precisely where the superstore would begin. Far from relieving Brecon's traffic, it simply channelled it straight to Safeway, the purchaser of the county council's land. The council later told me that the road had been financed partly at public expense, and partly by the superstore.

The National Park Authority has several responsibilities, which reflect both the ordinary functions of a district council and the peculiar needs of an area of national conservation importance. It is responsible for protecting the environment, for ensuring that land use meets local people's needs, for boosting the tourist industry and enhancing the local economy. It has also been seeking to help local producers of food, investing in an annual 'Food Fest'. Its decision to grant planning permission for the supermarket contravenes every one of these functions. The store threatened the town's environmental quality, used land which local people insisted was badly needed for housing (houses would instead be built on greenfield land outside the town's boundaries), and would damage the tourism industry, hurt local shopkeepers, and thereby undermine the market for local produce.

Safeway made use of what planning consultants describe as the tried and tested technique of raising the stakes after planning permission has been granted. It applied at first for a moderately large store then, once that had been approved, requested an extension to the store. Crucially this would, it seemed, contain a substantial coffee shop, a feature which might have made initial permission harder to obtain had it been included, as it posed a threat to the town's many cafés. The National Park Authority, to local people's astonishment, approved the extension.

*

Brecon is one of many towns in which local authorities have supported superstore applications which appear to conflict with the interests of the public. In 1998 and 1999, Cheltenham, one of England's most genteel towns, became the scene of a major popular uprising after the borough council made the extraordinary decision to give to Waitrose the green fields, woodland and school playing fields it owned. This enabled the company to build an enormous edge-of-centre superstore, with 1,500 parking places.

Though councils are legally obliged to obtain the best possible value for the land they own, the site was handed, free, to Waitrose before any other developers had been able to bid for it. Barratt Homes later offered the council £6m for the land, but was turned down. Waitrose agreed to replace the three and a half acres of grass playing fields on which it was building with three-quarters of an acre of astroturf, which is inappropriate for a junior school as the harder surface can damage children's joints and bones.

The superstore offends both Cheltenham's local plan and national planning guidance, which insists that town-centre sites be investigated before permission is granted for edge-of-centre developments. Gloucestershire County Council opposed the store on the grounds that it would generate an insupportable volume of traffic. But the government refused to intervene, so the good burghers of Cheltenham built tree houses and dug tunnels on the site, to try to prevent the builders from moving in.[65]

The small market town of Romsey in Hampshire was forced to accept a deeply unpopular edge-of-centre Sainsbury's, after the land company acting on the supermarket's behalf advised Test Valley Borough Council that if the store did not receive permission it would take the application to inquiry, which could have cost the council a good deal of money. The site on which the superstore is due to be built was allocated in the local plan for sheltered housing, but residents were told, incorrectly, that if Romsey did not approve Sainsbury's proposal it would be forced to allow an out-of-town development. Approval for the store development breaches no fewer than thirty-nine council policies and will cause major traffic jams on some of Romsey's roads. Local people have been told that the council's traffic projections are confidential. Like Cheltenham's local authority, Test Valley Borough Council will make no money from the sale of its land to Sainsbury. It will spend the £500,000 it receives on providing car parking for the superstore.[66]

*

The supermarkets appear to have mastered the art of strategic payment. They are adept not only at avoiding the costs they could be expected to carry – for the land they build on and the infrastructure they require, for example – but also at offering payment when it might not be expected, in order to win support for their plans.

In Stockport in Greater Manchester, Tesco offered every allotment holder working the land it wanted a new plot, a greenhouse, a tool shed, a watering system, security services and five years without rent if they agreed to move. The allotments association would get offices, a lecture hall and toilets. Stockport Borough Council was offered an additional £6m for the land, which would have helped significantly to relieve its massive debts. The allotment holders turned the offer down and resolved to ask the Data Protection Registrar to find out how the company had obtained their addresses.[67]

In Pembury in Kent, Tesco offered to give £200,000 to the local authority's park-and-ride scheme and pay £300,000 for a community centre if it received planning permission for a new store.[68] In Witney, in Oxfordshire, the same company announced that it would pay £6.6m for a new road if its application were successful. The company, unusually, went to some lengths to persuade the authorities that its store would make Witney's traffic problems a good deal worse, in order to show that paying for the road bore a legitimate relationship to its planning application.[69] At Golden Hill in Bristol, Tesco received permission to build a new store on a greenfield site on condition that it paid for an all-weather football pitch.

In February 2000 the Cabinet Office minister Graham Stringer claimed that when he was the leader of Manchester City Council in the mid-1990s, Asda offered the authority hundreds of thousands of pounds for a piece of land it owned on which Kwik-Save was hoping to build a rival store.[70] In Cambridge, Sainsbury pledged an extraordinary £25.5m a year to pay for public transport measures, in return for planning permission for one of the biggest shopping centres in Britain.[71] In Merton, in South London, the company was less generous, however. It had proposed to build a leisure centre with a swimming pool for local children if it received consent for a major Savacentre store. The leisure centre was never built, however, and seven of the children who had hoped to make use of it attempted to sue Merton Council, to force it to persuade Sainsbury to honour the agreement. The judge ruled that the council's agreement with Sainsbury 'was so poorly drawn up it was unenforceable'. Residents complained that had they known the leisure centre would not be built, they would have raised so much opposition to the superstore proposal that it would never have received permission.[72]

Superstores frequently break the promises they make. The Tesco supermarket built on the green space at Golden Hill in Bristol was approved by a Conservative Environment Secretary after the city council had rejected the company's application and 16,600 people had objected in writing. In the hope of making its development more acceptable, the store promised to abide by tough restrictions, and to consult and listen to its neighbours. Since it opened, in 1993, it has failed to honour its promises. In 1994 it announced that it would expand the store, adding a forty-four-seat restaurant. By 1996 it had broken its pledge not to open on Sundays. Though residents complained that it would keep their children awake, in 1997 Tesco obtained permission to extend its opening hours to 10 p.m. and keep its car park floodlit until 10.30 p.m. In 1998, it asked the council to allow the store to take deliveries on Sundays. It succeeded, and they commenced in April 2000.

Planning permission for the Safeway superstore which opened in Plymouth in 1996 was granted on condition that it stayed closed on Sundays. Since then, the store has made three attempts to have that condition overturned. Local people believe that the chain is trying to exhaust their resistance: every time it applies for the restriction to be lifted, they have to launch a new campaign against it.

*

It would be wrong, however, to suggest that the public battle against the supermarkets is being lost on all fronts. In many parts of the country, public pressure has made planning permission much harder to obtain. In some places, small traders are managing to recover a little ground, especially by means of farmers' markets and organic box schemes. But not all the reported victories against the supermarkets are quite what they seem.

When, after three years of dithering, the Conservative Secretary of State for the Environment, John Gummer, finally imposed a moratorium on the construction of new out-of-town superstores, the companies swiftly found new means of expanding their operations. The first and simplest of these was to increase the size of their existing outlets. According to Andrea Barlow, Asda's Town Planning Manager, 'the extension of existing stores tends to face less opposition and tends to take a shorter time to be approved' than the construction of new supermarkets.[73] Both Asda and Tesco have spent the late 1990s upgrading and expanding their biggest shops, turning some of them into gigastores of 100,000 square feet or more.

The second tactic, which has so far met with less success, is to claim that shopping complexes which have already received planning permission are themselves new towns: adding extra stores to them is not, therefore, out-of-town development. Both the MetroCentre, near Gateshead, and the Merry Hill Centre, near Dudley in the West Midlands, have attempted to redefine themselves thus, but have been rejected. Bluewater Park, near Dartford in Kent, on the other hand, has been recognized as a new town in all but name, and the local authority intends to allow 25,000 new houses to be built around it. The superstores and the housebuilding lobby appear to have been coordinating their efforts in the hope of recasting these developments. For the housebuilders, new poles of development in the countryside enable them to capitalize on the price difference between farmland and development land; for the retail chains, a new town built around a superstore guarantees a captive market. In 2000, Wal-Mart purchased thirty-six acres outside Swindon, which was due to become the centre of a new town of 10,000 houses. The town, if Wal-Mart succeeds in obtaining planning permission, will be built around the superstore.

Supermarkets have shown some skill in attaching themselves to other developments. As Tesco has linked up with Esso, Safeway with BP and Somerfield with Elf, they have discovered in the service stations a new and largely un-regulated frontier of out-of-town development. Several companies have linked superstore proposals to plans for out-of-town football stadiums, arguing that the stadium will not be financially viable without the superstore, and hinting that anyone opposing their scheme is jeopardizing the success of the local team. *Estates Gazette* found that the plans for the Luton Town FC stadium 'could see the actual football aspect becoming almost incidental'.[74]

But perhaps most importantly, the supermarkets have been able to use the new out-of-town planning regulations to force through developments within town and village centres, in the face of tremendous local opposition. In Gerrards Cross in south Buckinghamshire, Tesco's application received 39 letters of support and 3,922 letters of objection. But the planning inspector ruled that refusing planning permission 'would be . . . a significant backtracking on encouragement given in published Planning Policy Guidance Notes to the promotion of new retail investment in established town centres'.[75] There is some evidence to back this assertion: the new planning guidance restricting out-of-town stores notes that 'The Government wishes local planning authorities to take a positive role in partnership with the private sector, in identifying additional sites for retail development'.[76] This could be interpreted to mean that new superstores *must* be permitted in town, whatever local opinion or local need might be.

*

The out-of-town restrictions appear to be negotiable for companies swinging sufficient political weight. In July 1997, John Prescott allowed a government inspector to overrule the local authority in Richmond, Surrey, and grant planning permission for a huge out-of-town Sainsbury's. Tony Blair denied that this decision had anything to do with the £2m David Sainsbury had donated to the Labour Party.

In March 1999, executives from the American retail chain Wal-Mart, which had at the time no significant commercial interest in Britain, visited 10 Downing Street for a meeting with Tony Blair. In keeping with its commitment to open government, the No. 10 press office won't reveal what they discussed. But Wal-Mart was well aware that if it were to come to Britain, the major impediment to its corporate strategy would be the planning system.

Three months after the meeting, Wal-Mart offered £6.7bn for the British superstore chain Asda. It is hard to believe that it would have made the bid if Mr Blair had told the executives that our planning restrictions were non-negotiable. All over the world, Wal-Mart operates almost exclusively out of town. Its success is contingent upon its size. It is able to stock ten times as many items as the biggest supermarkets in Britain, at lower prices, by building stores twice as large as any currently found on British soil. It was the first chain in the United States to discover that a town with a population of just 4,500 is large enough to support a gigantic out-of-town store, as long as most of the competition is eliminated. In the United States, where its tactics are deeply unpopular, it is widely known as 'Sprawl-Mart'. It chose to buy Asda, analysts believe, partly because that chain has a higher average store size than any other in Britain.

Wal-Mart's strategy, in other words, depends upon building enormous stores, which, in Britain, means building on virgin land. If it is unable to pursue this tactic, it loses much of its competitive edge. It knows that its lobbying power exceeds that of all our native superstores combined, despite their liberal representation in government. In 1998, its global sales equated to one tenth of Britain's entire economic output, and the new shopping space it opened in that year exceeded the total holdings of Tesco, Sainsbury, Safeway and Asda put together. Wal-Mart may have calculated that it could change the law.

The prospect that the government might repeal the out-of-town moratorium precipitated a public outcry, and the planning minister was forced to reassure parliament that he would not give Wal-Mart what it wanted. But the company soon began investigating other means of building its huge stores in Britain. In October 1999, it started negotiating to purchase entire out-of-town retail parks, in order, it seemed, to demolish the existing shops and turn the entire sites into Wal-Mart superstores.[77] Such schemes, it had discovered, would not require permission for a change of land use. Tesco was already pioneering the tactic: in the same month it bought an entire shopping centre in Coventry, in order to swallow up the other pitches and turn it into a single, gigantic supermarket.[78]

*

Tony Blair has done little to disguise his enthusiasm for out-of-town shopping. Four weeks after taking power, he told the Commons: 'There are certain elements of the development of out-of-town shopping centres, for example, that I think really accord with what people want to do ... we recognise there will be certain patterns of behaviour that will simply remain because people want them to remain.'[79]

If he does want to remove the out-of-town restrictions,

the Office of Fair Trading (OFT) could provide him with an appropriate excuse. In announcing his referral of the super-stores to the Competition Commission, John Bridgeman, the Director General of the OFT, pointed out that 'sites for new stores are dwindling and this gives the existing stores an advantage'. These 'barriers to entry . . . limit the impact new competitors could be expected to have'.[80]

He is quite right to suggest that the limitations on out-of-town development favour the companies which have already established themselves in Britain. But if the Compe-tition Commission, and the government it reports to, were to draw from this the obvious conclusion that in order to stimulate competition they should remove the restrictions, they would simply enable the existing stores to consolidate their monopoly. Planning law, quite rightly, forbids discrim-ination on the basis of an applicant's identity. Any lifting of the restrictions in order to allow new companies to enter the market, in other words, will also allow Tesco, Sainsbury, Asda and Safeway to build new stores. Britain's superstore chains have already lined up hundreds of planning applica-tions. They have the best planning consultants money can buy, and alarmingly comfortable relationships with planning authorities all over the country. Were the Competition Commission to recommend the removal of the restraint as a punishment for the superstores' abuse of their market dom-inance, it would give them even greater market advantages than they enjoy already.

In January 2000, the House of Commons Environment Committee reported that John Bridgeman's analysis posed grave dangers to the moratorium on out-of-town super-stores. It warned: 'We are concerned that the competition authorities and some Treasury and DTI [Department of

Trade and Industry] officials, who do not understand the planning system, may now be seeking relaxations in it and may hope such a policy can be introduced after the report of the Competition Commission. This would be disastrous.' 'We are appalled', it noted, 'that before referring planning matters to the Competition Commission, the OFT took no evidence from planning experts and did not consult the DETR [Department of the Environment]. In failing to take account of such expert evidence, it has behaved irresponsibly.'[81]

*

No commercial sector is better represented in British politics than the supermarkets. David Sainsbury, the chain's former chief executive and the richest man in Britain, is a minister at the Department of Trade and Industry (DTI), which oversees competition policy. Tesco executives inhabit no fewer than six government task forces, including the DTI's Competitiveness Advisory Group. A Tesco executive also sits on both the United Kingdom Eco-labelling Board and, alongside a representative of Marks and Spencer, the government's Advisory Committee on Packaging. The superstores have lobbied to ensure that regulations in both areas remain as 'flexible' as possible. Andrew Stone, Managing Director of Marks and Spencer, was made a life peer soon after Labour took office. The official spokesperson for the four biggest supermarkets at the British Retail Consortium is Baroness Thornton, a Labour peer and Director of the Labour Women's Network, and previously Chair of the Greater London Labour Party. Delegates to the 1998 Labour Party Conference wore identification badges sponsored and labelled by Somerfield. While Tesco gave £12m to the government's Millennium Dome, David Sainsbury (Lord Sainsbury of Turville) has personally donated a total of £5m to the Labour Party.

The Sainsbury family has long been blessed with a direct line to power. While David Sainsbury, a Labour peer, is one of the businessmen closest to Tony Blair, his cousin and predecessor as chairman of the firm, the Conservative peer Sir John Sainsbury (now Lord Sainsbury of Preston Candover), appears have been Margaret Thatcher's most frequent confidant. His brother, Sir Tim Sainsbury, another member of the Sainsbury board, was a Conservative MP who once held the same government post as David Sainsbury does today.

The opposition is unlikely to challenge the superstores' power. The shadow Secretary of State for the Environment, Transport and the Regions, who – if he took office – would be responsible for most of the decisions affecting the super-market chains, is Archie Norman, previously the Chief Executive of Asda. Francis Maude, the shadow Foreign Secretary, was one of Asda's non-executive directors.

The supermarkets conduct much of their lobbying through their trade association, the British Retail Consortium. According to its Director General, 'BRC is no longer an organization that simply reacts to Government proposed legislation or White Papers but sets out to help shape them. By creating significant links with special advisers, policy specialists and the leading think tanks, the intention is to work in a non confrontational way so we are involved at the beginning of any legislative process.'[82]

Its tactics appear to be successful. It has persuaded the government to allow 41-tonne lorries onto British roads and to consider its request for 44-tonne trucks to be permitted in a few years' time. It claims to have played an important role in the government's decision not to tax out-of-town car parking spaces.[83] Speakers at the BRC's annual dinner have included the Chancellor of the Exchequer, Gordon Brown, the Conservative Chancellor, Kenneth Clarke, John Major and Tony Blair. The Consortium's submission on the minimum wage 'was read by Chancellor Gordon Brown, the Treasury and the Bank of England' and was 'influential in persuading the Government and the Low Pay Commission' to hold the level down to £3.60 per hour and introduce a separate, lower rate 'not just for young people, but for returners to the labour market.'[84] The consortium successfully lobbied the government to introduce amendments to the Competition Bill to permit 'vertical agreements' of the kind the superstores strike with their suppliers.[85]

The BRC is also 'ready to shape the Brussels agenda in the same way it does the UK Government agenda'. In Europe it has lobbied for 'flexible' consumer guarantees and against the European legislation requiring companies to inform and consult their workers.[86] It has influenced European food safety standards and defended its members against the European requirement that the pesticides used on the foods they sell should be listed on the packaging. It has succeeded in keeping the definition of 'free range' as broad as possible.[87]

Government is not the only realm in which the influence of superstores and their employees raises public concern. Sainsbury, for example, is a sponsor of the Soil Association, which regulates organic standards in Britain. In 1998, the *Sunday Times* alleged that a chemist from Sainsbury's presented much of the case for the preservative sodium nitrite to the government's United Kingdom Register of Organic Food Standards. The chemical is banned from organic produce in Germany and Holland, partly because, in large doses, it has been linked to cancer. What the *Sunday Times* did not discover, however, was that one of the members of the register is Robert Duxbury, an employee of J. Sainsbury plc. Sainsbury was also one of the three sponsors of the Town and Country Planning Association's inquiry into the future of planning, a subject in which the superstore chain has more than a passing interest. The Chairman of the Post Office, Neville Bain, is also a non-executive director of Safeway. This causes alarm to some of the people campaigning to keep post offices on the high street and out of the superstores.

In 1999, the government published the first of its 'annual reports', which would tell the nation how well it was doing. It was launched not in Westminster, but in the Kensington Tesco's. The Prime Minister's office had given the supermarket chain an exclusive contract to sell it. It officially entered the public domain when Jack Cunningham, the Chancellor of the Duchy of Lancaster, handed a copy to the head of Tesco.

*

The end game is already being played, as the superstores seek to mop up the last pockets of retail resistance. When Tony Blair announced that he wanted to address the problem of 'food deserts' (the absence of good shops, caused partly by a relocation of middle-class trade to out-of-town superstores) in the poorest inner city areas, and called for a revitalization of corner shops in these places, Tesco, Sainsbury and Asda stepped forward to help, and received the government's blessing to move in on their own terms, with government subsidies.

In 1998 Sainsbury announced that it was riding to the rescue of beleaguered village shops by generously allowing their owners to buy goods (at normal retail prices) in its supermarkets, then sell them in their own shops. In 2000, Somerfield developed the idea, announcing that it had become 'the social conscience of the supermarketing industry', as it would now use its delivery fleets to supply independent grocers with its own goods. It was not motivated solely by altruism, however. 'This is a good business opportunity, allowing us to maximize our existing investment,' one of its executives explained.[88] The small shops would, to all intents and purposes, become branches of the supermarkets, but without any additional trouble or expense on the supermarkets' part. For the small shopkeepers it must have felt like the final humiliation, going cap in hand to their most menacing enemies.

The superstores insist that their expansion increases consumer choice. It is hard to see what that choice amounts to.

CHAPTER SIX

The Fat Cats Directory

All the appointments listed here were current after or made since the General Election of May 1997.

Fat Cat	Previous Gluttony	Subsequent Creamery
Lord Marshall of Knightsbridge	Chairman of British Airways, where he campaigned against proposals to introduce an aviation fuel tax, aimed at reducing the airlines' contribution to global climate change.[1] President of the Confederation of British Industry, where he warned Gordon Brown not to levy new taxes on corporations.[2]	In charge of Gordon Brown's energy tax review, which investigated the case for new fuel taxes on corporations, aimed at reducing their contribution to global warming.
	His company's 1999 holiday brochures warned travellers: 'We will not cover claims arising from equipment or any computer program failing to recognize, interpret or process any date changes for example the year 2000.'[3]	Helped promote the government's Action 2000 campaign, encouraging businesses to ensure that their computers recognized, interpreted and processed the year 2000 date change.

Fat Cat	Previous Gluttony	Subsequent Creamery
Ewen Cameron	President of the Country Landowners' Association, where he fought the government's proposal for a right to roam.	Chairman of the government's Countryside Agency, responsible for implementing the right to roam.
	Owner of 3,000 acres of Somerset.	Also responsible for tackling social exclusion in rural areas.
	Twice blocked a footpath across his Somerset estate with crops, failing to restore the surface after cultivation. Reported to the highway authority by the Ramblers Association.	The Countryside Agency's guidance on public footpaths warns that 'Farmers and land managers have a responsibility to ensure they are not blocked by crops or obstructed, and that the route is identifiable and the surface condition restored after cultivation. If you find a public right of way blocked or impassable, you should report it to the highway authority.'[4]
Lord Rogers of Riverside	Architect of Heathrow's Terminal 5, the biggest greenfield development ever proposed in Britain. Architect of the Montevetro Tower, London's most exclusive building, whose flats are priced at up to £4.5m, with private sports facilities and secure grounds, from which the public are excluded.	Chairman of the government's Urban Task Force, whose principal tasks were to find means of reducing the pressure on greenfield land, and to 'encourage social cohesion and participation' in Britain's cities.[5]

Fat Cat	Previous Gluttony	Subsequent Creamery
Lord Sainsbury of Turville	Chairman of J Sainsbury plc, one of the superstore chains referred to the Competition Commission for alleged anti-competitive practices.	Minister in the government's Department of Trade and Industry, which regulates competition policy, and to which the Competition Commission reports.
	Chairman of the Food Chain Group, which represents food retailing interests on the government's Foresight Programme.	Minister with responsibility for science and technology. In overall charge of the government's Foresight Programme.
	Principal backer of the biotechnology company Diatech.	As Science Minister, he led a delegation of the BioIndustry Association, which represents Diatech, among other companies, to the United States. The Department of Trade and Industry paid some of the lobby group's costs.[6]
	Funded the construction of the Sainsbury Laboratory at the John Innes Centre, a genetic engineering centre in Norwich.	Has ultimate control of the Biotechnology and Biological Sciences Research Council, a government funding body which helps finance the Sainsbury Laboratory.
	Widely criticized, as head of J Sainsbury, for undermining skilled jobs in the independent retailing sector and replacing them with unskilled shelf-stacking and checkout assistant positions.	Chairman of the government's University for Industry, whose purpose is to boost young people's skills.

THE FAT CATS DIRECTORY

Fat Cat	Previous Gluttony	Subsequent Creamery
Lord Simon of Highbury	Chairman of BP, the oil and gas company, where he lobbied against oil taxation.[7] Vice-chairman of the European Round Table of Industrialists, the powerful lobby group which drafted the Single European Act.	Minister for Trade and Competitiveness in Europe at the Department of Trade and Industry (DTI) and the Treasury. Responsible for Britain's single market action plan. Responsible for negotiating with European ministers over a common energy tax and the liberalization of the gas market.[8] The DTI is responsible for the UK's energy policy.
	BP, under Lord Simon's chairmanship, was accused of evicting peasants from their lands in Colombia, and, in a Colombian government report, of handing over photographs and video footage of local campaigners to the military. BP has paid millions of pounds to the Colombian army, units of which are accused of torturing and killing trades unionists and protesters against the oil industry. It has given money to the notorious 16th Brigade, accused by the government's report of murder, kidnapping, torture and rape.[9]	Among the ministers responsible for implementing Britain's 'ethical foreign policy'.
Jack Cunningham MP	Paid adviser to Albright and Wilson (UK) Ltd, an agrochemicals company and member of the Chemical	Secretary of State for Agriculture. Chair of the Cabinet committee on biotechnology which

Fat Cat	Previous Gluttony	Subsequent Creamery
	Industries Association, which lobbies for the deregulation of pesticides.	coordinates government policy on pesticide-resistant crops.
Sir Peter Davis	Chairman and chief executive of Reed International, where he sent 900 employees from work to welfare. Chief Executive of Prudential Corporation plc, the company condemned by the Treasury for mis-selling more pensions than any other firm. Ordered by the Securities and Investments Board to retrain its entire sales staff, due to 'continuing and persistent breaches' of the standards of training for its sales force.[10]	Appointed by the Treasury as chairman of the New Deal Task Force, responsible for finding ways of getting people to move from welfare to work, partly through appropriate training.
John Bowman	A director of Commercial Union, which was named and shamed by the Treasury for 7,900 possible mis-sold pensions.	On the board of the Occupational Pensions Regulatory Authority, which protects pensioners from being exploited.
Lord De Ramsey	President of the Country Landowners' Association, which repeatedly warned the government against imposing 'unjustified' environmental 'burdens' on agriculture. Sold part of his 6,500 acre Cambridgeshire estate for the construction of 3,000 new houses, doubling the size of the village of Ramsey and destroying a pond that contained great crested newts,	Chairman of the Environment Agency, the government body responsible for protecting the environment.

Fat Cat	Previous Gluttony	Subsequent Creamery
	a protected species. Has grown genetically modified sugar beet on his land for the biotechnology company Monsanto. Employed a chauffeur to drive from Reading to London in the mornings in order to pick him up from King's Cross and take him the two miles to Millbank.[11]	
Paul Leinster	Director of Smithkline Beecham (SB) plc, which has polluted streams in Sussex and Gloucestershire.[12] Previously employed by BP and Schering Agrochemicals Ltd, part-owner of the biotechnology company AgrEvo. In 1998, AgrEvo was named and shamed by a government body for failing to comply with the environmental regulations governing the testing of genetically engineered crops.[13]	Head of the Environment Agency's Environmental Protection Directorate. In October 1999, Dr Leinster proposed that companies should be allowed to monitor their own pollution and that the Environment Agency's regulatory policies be redesigned by the industries it is supposed to be regulating.[14]
Justin McCracken	Managing director of ICI Katalco, based on Teesside. In 1996 ICI factories occupied second, fifth, sixth, and fourteenth places in the Environment Agency's list of plants emitting cancer-causing chemicals.[15] In 1999 ICI came first in the Environment Agency's 'hall of shame', its table of the companies fined	Regional General Manager of the Environment Agency, North West region.

Fat Cat	Previous Gluttony	Subsequent Creamery
	most for pollution incidents in England and Wales.[16] ICI is allowed by the Agency to release 20 tonnes of hormone-disrupting chemicals into the Tees estuary every year, though the Teesmouth marshes are one of Europe's most important wildlife habitats.[17] ICI was fined £300,000 in 1998, after 150 tonnes of chloroform escaped into groundwater at Runcorn, in the Environment Agency's North West region.[18] The Agency has been criticized by Friends of the Earth for 'utterly failing in its duty to control pollution from this disgustingly filthy factory'. The pressure group recorded 244 unauthorized pollution incidents from ICI's Runcorn plant in 1996 and 1997.[19]	
Dinah Nichols	Non-executive director, Anglian Water plc, the company which in 1999 came sixth in the Environment Agency's 'hall of shame', after being prosecuted six times for pollution incidents.[20]	Director-General of Environmental Protection at the Department of the Environment.
Ian McAllister	Chairman and Managing Director, Ford UK. Until December 1999, Ford was a member of the Global Climate Coalition, which lobbies	Chairman of the government's Cleaner Vehicles Task Force.

Fat Cat	Previous Gluttony	Subsequent Creamery
	against attempts to reduce carbon dioxide emissions. President, Society of Motor Manufacturers and Traders. The society has objected to the Department of the Environment's standards on ozone, lead and sulphur dioxide pollution from cars.[21] It has lobbied against European Directives aimed at reducing exhaust gases,[22] against moves to remove lead from petrol and against laws forcing motor manufacturers to install catalytic converters in their cars.[23]	
Chris Fay	Chairman and Chief Executive of Shell UK, the British company with the most controversial environmental record, due to pollution incidents at home, its contribution to global climate change and the activities of its sister company in Nigeria, where the lands of the Ogoni people have been damaged by crude-oil pollution. Executive Director of BAA plc, which is attempting to double the size of Heathrow Airport with the largest greenfield development ever proposed in Britain. President of the UK Offshore Operators Association, the oil	Chairman of the government's Advisory Committee on Business and the Environment.

Fat Cat	Previous Gluttony	Subsequent Creamery
	industry lobby group which has fiercely resisted attempts to introduce new environmental regulations.	
Brian Riddleston	Chief Executive of the open-cast mining company Celtic Energy, which destroyed the Selar Grasslands Site of Special Scientific Interest in South Wales, a remarkable wildflower habitat and home to the extremely rare marsh fritillary butterfly.	Member of the government's Countryside Council for Wales, which looks after Sites of Special Scientific Interest.
Stephanie Monk	Human Resources Director, Granada Group plc, which appealed against an industrial tribunal's order to reinstate workers who had gone on strike after their pay was cut from £140 to £100 a week.[24] Is paid £230,000 a year by Granada, with £205,000 of share options.	Member of the Low Pay Commission, which determines the level of Britain's minimum wage. Member of the New Deal Task Force, charged with boosting people's incomes by moving them off welfare and into work.
Graham Hawker	Chief executive of the Welsh utilities company Hyder. In 1996 the company spent £42.2m on redundancy, compared to £700,000 on research and development.[25] Publicly opposed the windfall tax on privatized utilities, which provided initial funding for the New Deal.	Chair of the New Deal Taskforce in Wales.

THE FAT CATS DIRECTORY

Fat Cat	Previous Gluttony	Subsequent Creamery
Martin Taylor	Chief Executive of Barclays plc, earning £976,000 a year, plus £762,000 in bonuses, with share options worth £1,020,000. Barclays reduced its workforce by 21,000 in the ten years to 1997.	Chair of the government's Tax and Benefits Taskforce, whose remit is to find ways of reducing poverty and welfare dependency. Offered the post of Minister for the Welfare State.
Lord Haskins	Chairman, Northern Foods plc. Member of the Hampel Committee on corporate governance, which was fiercely criticized by Margaret Beckett, President of the Board of Trade, for failing to recommend substantial improvements to the ways in which companies regulate themselves.	Chair of the government's Better Regulation Task Force.
Peter Salsbury	Managing Director for Corporate and External Affairs at Marks and Spencer.	Head of the Better Regulation Taskforce's Consumer Affairs Group, whose duties include ensuring that consumers are properly protected from the superstores. The group concluded that voluntary measures and 'consumer education' are preferable to regulation.[26]
Geoffrey Robinson MP	Director of Central and Sheerwood plc, a property company owned and chaired by the fraudster Robert Maxwell, who raided his own companies' pension funds in order to obscure his embezzlement and false	Paymaster-General.

217

Fat Cat	Previous Gluttony	Subsequent Creamery
	accounting. C&S merged with Geoffrey Robinson's company TransTec, to form Transfer Technology plc. Robinson became chairman with a 28% stake, Maxwell became a director, with 27%.[27] TransTec later collapsed, with debts of £170m.	
Sue Clifton	Executive at Group 4, a security company with a financial interest in the incarceration of young people, as it runs two private children's jails in Britain. It has been strongly criticized for the mishandling of child offenders, following escapes, bullying, a riot and attacks on staff.[28]	Adviser to the government's Youth Justice Board on the handling of juvenile offenders.
Keith McCullagh	Chief Executive of British Biotech, the company censured by the Stock Exchange for serious rule breaches, including the failure to reveal that its leading drug product wasn't working. When the news finally emerged, the company's stock value fell by 94 per cent.	Chairman of the government's Finance Advisory Group, set up to help high-tech companies win the confidence of financial investors.
Sir Robin Biggam	Non-executive director of British Aerospace, which sells assault rifles, grenade launchers and missiles to Turkey, some of which are used to attack Kurdish separatists.[29]	Chairman of the Independent Television Commission, which revoked the licence of the Kurdish satellite station Med T.V., after Turkish complaints that it provided a forum for Kurdish separatists.

THE FAT CATS DIRECTORY

Fat Cat	Previous Gluttony	Subsequent Creamery
Neville Bain	Non-executive director, Safeway. Safeway is one of the supermarkets which, controversially, have been swallowing local branches of the Post Office.	Appointed by the government as Chairman of the Post Office.
Robert Osborne	Head of the Special Projects division at the construction company Tarmac, one of the major builders of the privately financed hospitals commissioned by the Department of Health.	Chief Executive of the Department of Health's Private Finance Unit. In 1998, Robert Osborne returned to Tarmac, to run its Private Finance Initiative division.
David Steeds	Corporate Development Director of Serco Group plc, one of the most successful bidders for privately financed government projects.	Chief Executive of the government's Private Finance Panel.
Tony Edwards	Director of the TI group, which owns Matrix Churchill, the company which provided machine tools for arms manufacture to the Iraqi government. The subsidiary of which he is Chief Executive is engaged in 150 military operations around the world.	Head of the government's Defence Export Services Organisation, which advises the government on whether or not licences for the sale of British weapons to foreign countries should be granted.
Neil Caldwell	Director of PTBRO, the organization which distributes the government's landfill tax money, and receives 10 per cent of the amount it handles in administration fees.	Director of Entrust, the government's regulatory body overseeing the distribution of landfill tax money.

Fat Cat	Previous Gluttony	Subsequent Creamery
Judith Hanratty	Company Secretary, BP Amoco plc. The BP–Amoco merger was among the most controversial of the 1990s, as it brought together two of the world's biggest oil companies.	On the board of the government's Competition Commission, which regulates corporate mergers.
Jonathan Rickford	Director of Corporate Strategy, BT, a company which has frequently been in trouble with the government's competition authorities for having too great a share of the market.	On the board of the Competition Commission.
Sir Alan Cockshaw	Chairman of the construction company AMEC plc.	Chairman of the government's Commission for New Towns, which designates places for new construction. Chairman of the government agency English Partnerships, which helps ensure that new construction and property development meets public needs.
	Watson Steel, part of the AMEC group, won the contract to build the Millennium Dome's masts and cables.	On the board of the New Millennium Experience Company, the firm set up by the government to oversee Britain's millennium celebrations, including the Millennium Dome.
Michael Mallinson	President of the British Property Federation, the lobby group representing property developers.	Deputy Chairman, English Partnerships.

THE FAT CATS DIRECTORY

Fat Cat	Previous Gluttony	Subsequent Creamery
Peter Mason	Group Chief Executive, AMEC plc. In 1997/98, AMEC was the seventh largest recipient of support from the government's Export Credit Guarantee Department, receiving £80m for construction work in Hong Kong. The trade body to which AMEC belongs – the Export Group for the Constructional Industries – has lobbied against the imposition of environment and human rights conditions on the Export Credit Guarantee Department's loans.[30]	On the Export Guarantees Advisory Council, which guides the disbursement of government money by the Export Credit Guarantee Department. Another member of the Council is Liz Airey, a non-executive director of AMEC.
Professor Sir John Cadogan	Research Director of BP.	Director-General of the Research Councils. The research councils are supposed to fund the scientific work which does not have an obvious or immediate application for corporations.
Sir Anthony Cleaver	Chairman of Atomic Energy Authority Technology plc. Oversaw the organizational changes at the Dounreay nuclear power station which, according to the Health and Safety Executive, 'have so weakened the management and technical base of Dounreay that it is not in a good position to tackle its principal mission, which is the decommissioning of the site'.[31]	Chairman of the government's Medical Research Council. The government has been repeatedly criticized for failing to provide research funds for sufficient investigations into the medical effects of radiation. Also sits on the government's Panel on Sustainable Development.

Fat Cat	Previous Gluttony	Subsequent Creamery
	Dounreay is considered by some critics to be the most dangerous nuclear installation in Western Europe, threatening the health of workers and neighbours. Executive director of the pharmaceutical company Smith and Nephew plc.	
Peter Doyle	Executive Director, Zeneca Group plc. Zeneca is a major biotechnology firm, and was the foremost British developer of genetically engineered crop plants. The company is engaged in a ten-year collaboration with the John Innes Centre in Norwich, aimed at finding profitable applications of biotechnology.	Chairman of the Biotechnology and Biological Sciences Research Council, the government body channelling state funds to biological research. The BBSRC gives substantial funding to the John Innes Research Institute. The BBSRC has seven specialist committees. Employees of Zeneca, according to the council's Web site, sit on all seven of them.[32]
	Zeneca was prosecuted four times in 1998 for pollution. Environment Agency figures place its Huddersfield plant as the third largest emitter of solid toxic waste in Britain.	Member of the government's Advisory Committee on Business and the Environment.
Professor Nigel Poole	External and Regulatory Affairs Manager of Zeneca Plant Science, which has had six applications to release genetically modified organisms approved by the Advisory	Member of the government's Advisory Committee on Releases to the Environment.

Fat Cat	Previous Gluttony	Subsequent Creamery
	Committee on Releases to the Environment. Sits on five of the taskforces run by EuropaBio, the lobbying organization which seeks to persuade European governments to deregulate the release of genetically modified organisms.	
Professor John Hillman	Board member of the BioIndustry Association, whose purpose is 'Encouraging and promoting the biotechnology sector of the UK economy' by lobbying to 'enhance the status of the industry within government'.[33]	Director of the government's Scottish Crop Research Institute, which is charged with overseeing government-funded research projects and providing impartial advice on biotechnology to the government.
Antony Pike	Director General of the British Agrochemicals Association Ltd., and Managing Director of Schering Agrochemicals/ AgrEvo UK Ltd.	Chairman of the government's Home Grown Cereals Authority (HGCA), which carries out and funds research into cereal crops. It has so far failed to fund any projects aimed at improving organic cereal production.
Professor P. J. Agett	Head of the School of Medicine and Health, University of Central Lancashire. His department has received research support from three companies producing baby milk. Professor Agett has himself received fees from two companies which produce baby milk, including Nestec, the technical service division	Chair of the Department of Health's Committee on the Medical Aspects of Food and Nutrition Policy (COMA). Three other members of COMA have either benefited directly from payments by baby milk manufacturers (one is an executive at Nestlé) or belong to academic departments which have received payments.[35]

Fat Cat	Previous Gluttony	Subsequent Creamery
	of Nestlé.[34] Nestlé's promotion of baby milk powder in poor countries is one of the world's most controversial issues involving the medical aspects of food and nutrition policy.	
Professor Peter Schroeder	Director of Research and Development, Nestlé.	Director of the government's Institute of Food Research.
Sir Alastair Morton	Chairman of the Channel Tunnel construction consortium Eurotunnel, whose debts rose to £8bn.	Advises John Prescott on the financing of the Channel Tunnel Rail Link. Chairman of the government's Strategic Rail Authority, the body responsible for 'influencing the use of the significant amounts of public funds which we provide to the industry' and ensuring that rail transport 'constitutes good value for money'.[36]

CHAPTER SEVEN

Monsanto's Magic Potion

On a scorching day in the middle of July 1999, a ghost army lined up on the edge of a field in the agricultural heart of Oxfordshire. For a moment, no one spoke or stirred. The pennants snapped and slackened in the wind, and the five hundred revenant warriors, white suited, white cowled, white masked, rippled, broke and reunited in the heat haze without stirring a limb. Someone, somewhere along the line, must have shouted, for all at once the horde surged forward, half walking, half running, banners streaming, sticks raised, yelling and cheering. The handful of black-clad men who opposed them – the infantry of the British Crown – gave way, and the army poured into the field.

It marched for two hundred yards then stopped. No opposing force stood in its way: the ranked ghosts confronted an enemy even more spectral than themselves. They raised their sticks and struck, slashing not at the air in front of them, but at the ground beneath their feet. The battlefield was not merely the scene of combat, but the enemy itself.

For four hours the eco-warriors, shrouded in their decontamination suits, hacked their way across five hectares of rape. The enemy fell like corn; the rape was pillaged. Columns of police marched into the crop, stopped, stood and stared, then marched out again. A police helicopter battered the hot air far above, filming the protesters, but as everyone was dressed identically, the film was useless. The suits made the warriors as invulnerable as ghosts.

By early evening, just a couple of tattered corners of the crop remained. The police drew up on horses, but at the first Battle of Watlington the cavalry had arrived too late: the spectral roundheads, hooded and muffled, pushed past the horses' flanks into a crowd of cheering followers, where they immediately disrobed and were absorbed.

The protesters had terminated one of Britain's first 'farm-scale' trials of genetically modified crops. They had left five hectares of unmodified rape – the experimental control – untouched, and all but eliminated the five hectares of rape engineered for resistance to the weedkiller glufosinate. The campaigners claimed victory. The field was theirs.

*

When I started researching this book, in May 1997, few people in Britain had heard of genetic engineering. By the time I began writing it, two and a half years later, few people had not. The technology had become the subject of controversies of all kinds – scientific, economic and political – and the focus of much of the growing public unease concerning the proximity of the British government to the interests of big business.

But the story we have heard is fragmentary and confused. The issues have frequently been muddled: even government ministers, for example, have managed to conflate human health and environmental concerns. My purpose here is to explore just one of the issues behind genetic engineering, the subversion of government by the biotechnology companies.

This is the story of one of the most audacious business strategies ever launched, a daring attempt by a handful of multinational companies to turn the food chain into a controllable commodity, to manoeuvre themselves into a position from which they can determine not only what the people of the world eat, but also whether they eat. It is the story of a strategy which has, so far, been only partly successful. In Britain in particular, public pressure has forced the government to reconsider some of its policies.

To help explain what has been happening in Britain, I have started my account elsewhere. In this chapter, I will tell the story of the attempt by the American company Monsanto, and its accomplices in the Canadian and US governments and the United Nations, to impose an allegedly dangerous genetically engineered product on the people first of their own countries, then on Britain and Europe.

In the following chapter, I will show how the British company SmithKline Beecham helped engineer the approval of new legislation, granting corporations rights over the blueprints of human life. I will also tell a story which has, as far as I am aware, never been fully told before: of how the British government raised by 200 times the permitted residues of a pesticide linked by some scientists to the rapid spread of a once-rare cancer, in order to allow a genetically modified crop to be introduced. The Labour government then ensured that consumers had no means of knowing whether or not these residues were present in the food they bought. I document the extraordinary web of contacts linking biotechnology companies, government ministers and government agencies, and the misrepresentations and public relations strategies the government has deployed as a result. But this story starts in Canada, in the stainless environment of an obscure public health laboratory.

*

In most of the world's temperate agricultural countries, dairy farmers suffer from an oversupply of milk. New breeds of cattle and better feeding techniques have doubled in less than a century the amount each animal can produce. Farmers have discovered that there are, as a result, simply too many herds in the market. As competition has intensified, each has striven to reduce the costs of his or her production, and this, inevitably, means cutting the size of the herd while increasing the productivity of its animals. If a farmer can produce the same amount of milk with fewer cows, he or she need spend less on labour, housing and feed.

In the 1980s, the American biotechnology company Monsanto devised an ingenious means of helping farmers to get ahead of the competition. It found that bacteria could be genetically engineered to produce a chemical almost identical to the naturally occurring growth hormone which regulates the amount of milk a cow produces. When cows are injected with this chemical, they produce up to 15 per cent more milk. In 1993, the US government's Food and Drug Administration licensed the artificial hormone for commercial use. It was soon widely deployed on American farms.

Injecting cows with rBST (the hormone's full name is recombinant bovine somatotropin) was controversial in some quarters but, until 1999, most Americans were either unaware of the practice, or largely unconcerned. The crisis which pushed rBST onto the American and then the British political agendas began not in the United States, but in Canada.

In 1997, rBST was on the verge of gaining official approval in Canada. Senior managers at the Health Ministry's Bureau of Veterinary Drugs had concluded that its use 'posed no human health risk'. They were about to grant it a 'notice of compliance'.[1] But then an extraordinary thing happened. To the astonishment of their bosses, six of the researchers who had studied the drug on behalf of the ministry mutinied. They filed grievances against the bureau, claiming they were being forced to approve rBST before its safety had been established. They wrote an internal report detailing flaws in the bureau's research. The ministry instructed them to rewrite it, removing any references to wrongdoing by the bureau's managers, but at length the original report leaked out.[2] Soon afterwards, as two Canadian senators started investigating, the whole horrifying tale of the government's attempts to approve a drug whose safety had not been assured began to come to light.

*

In February 1990, Monsanto filed its application to have rBST licensed for sale in Canada. Within two weeks, the Bureau of Veterinary Drugs reported that there was 'no hazard to man consuming milk or meat' from animals treated with the drug.[3] The head of the bureau's Human Safety Division wrote to Monsanto to inform it that the product was acceptable. Four months later, however, researchers at the bureau pointed out that there was no basis for making this assumption. They insisted that the data were incomplete and the design of Monsanto's experiments was flawed. In August 1990, Monsanto admitted to a 'shortage of Canadian data'. The drug's approval was delayed for several years, during which Monsanto worked hard to persuade the Canadian authorities that it was safe.

By 1995, evidence of devastating effects on the health of dairy cattle treated with rBST had begun to accumulate. There were increased instances of lameness and birth defects and severe reactions in the parts of the body where the drug was injected. An analysis of Monsanto's own data by researchers at Sussex University in England showed that use of the hormone increased the incidence of mastitis (inflammation of the udders) by 39 per cent.[4] Monsanto tried to prevent publication of the researchers' results on the bizarre grounds that use of its data constituted 'plagiarism'.[5] When cows contract mastitis, they require antibiotics. The widespread use of antibiotics on farms leads to an increased risk that certain dangerous bacteria could become immune to them, posing a threat to human health.

By 1997, serious concerns about rBST's direct effects on human health had begun to emerge, and it had still not been approved for sale in Canada. However, Monsanto had not given up. In August, a manager at the Bureau of Veterinary Drugs, Dr Ian Alexander, received a phone call from Dr David Kowalczyk, Director of Regulatory Affairs at a subsidiary of Monsanto. Dr Kowalczyk, according to a leaked e-mail from Dr Alexander, was anxious to know how the bureau's review of rBST was progressing. He was also keen to discover whether 'Canada would have someone' on the rBST panel of the United Nations Joint Expert Committee on Food Additives, 'as Dr Ritter had been on it last time'.[6]

This UN committee is critical to Monsanto's hopes of receiving approval for rBST worldwide. If it rules that the drug is safe, then other governments can be forced by the World Trade Organization to license it and allow its sale.

Dr Len Ritter was formerly the Director of the Bureau of Veterinary Drugs. During his tenure there, he spoke to the Parliamentary Agriculture Committee, on behalf of companies manufacturing rBST.[7] He also sits on the hormone advisory panel of a lobby group called the Chemical Manufacturers' Association. He secured a place too on the committee advising the Canadian government in its attempt to force the European Union to import beef from cattle treated with growth hormones. He concluded that residues of the hormones are 'not considered to pose a risk to consumers of meat or meat products'.[8] Controversially, he has also claimed that there is no 'increased risk of cancer' from 'any increased intake of pesticide residues' in fruit and vegetables.[9] Dr Ritter was, as Monsanto clearly desired, reappointed to the United Nations Joint Expert Committee on Food Additives, in time for its key meeting on rBST in February 1998.[10]

Monsanto's Dr Kowalczyk appears to have been well acquainted with Dr Alexander, the bureau manager. In March 1998, he sent Dr Alexander a handwritten fax. Under the heading 'BST', he warned him: 'Ian, Note: That it appears that Michael Hansen is not completely on board. Dave K.'[11] Michael Hansen is head of the Consumer Policy Institute, a voluntary organization defending consumers, which, at the time, was considering its response to the use of rBST.

The researchers employed to review rBST could take it no longer. They drew up a list of their bureau's failings, circulating their report to other members of the department in 1998. The Bureau of Veterinary Drugs, they maintained, had accepted Monsanto's assurances that rBST did not cause cancer in man or animals 'without providing a rationale'. The bureau had failed to ask Monsanto to find out whether the drug caused cancer or reproductive problems in people or animals drinking the milk. 'There was no discussion ... of possible deleterious effects' on human babies, 'the sub-population at greatest risk'. The researchers found that 'The usually required long-term toxicology studies to ascertain human safety were not conducted. Hence, such possibilities and potential as sterility, infertility, birth defects, cancer and immunological derangements were not addressed.' They alleged that 'The only short-term toxicology study, for three months in rats, was improperly reported, to conclude that rBST ... was not and could not be absorbed into the blood stream.'[12]

*

As news of the researchers' report spread, the bureau's failure to investigate rBST properly became a national scandal. The Senate Committee on rBST invited the researchers to testify, but they responded that they might lose their jobs if they did. So the senators spoke to the Minister of Health, who promised the researchers that they would not be punished. At the same time, however, an internal memo revealed that the Health Ministry would 'try to engineer' the appearance of a senior manager before the committee at the same time as the researchers.[13] The senators, concerned that the manager might intimidate his employees, refused to allow him to attend.

The Health Ministry announced that it would send the rebel researchers' report to a panel of experts for a 'completely objective and arm's length review'.[14] One of the experts, however, turned out to be a researcher who had worked as a consultant to Monsanto for the previous five years and who, with the help of a grant from a lobbying group partly financed by Monsanto, had previously published a paper recommending that rBST be approved.[15]

Eventually the Ministry of Health saw that it could no longer sustain the fiction that rBST could be guaranteed to be a safe and healthy product. In December 1998, the government announced that it would not be approved in the foreseeable future.

This was not, however, the end of the matter. In October 1999, one of the researchers complained to senators that 'the harassment and retaliation toward me by Health Canada [the Ministry of Health] management is worsening by the day'.[16] Among his complaints was that a health ministry employee had been 'removing or shredding large amounts of BVD [Bureau of Veterinary Drugs] documents for several weeks under the supervision of a newly appointed Manager'. 'This same man', he and his colleagues noted, 'has obtained duplicate keys for the individual filing cabinets used by each Drug Evaluator . . . we are concerned that critical documents and background information may have been and is being eliminated.'[17]

As Canada closed its doors on rBST, the focus of concern about the drug began to shift. If, as the Canadian researchers claimed, the experiments Monsanto had conducted were insufficient to show that the chemical was safe, and if evidence of serious implications for animal welfare had already arisen, then how had the drug been approved in the United States? In seeking to find out, investigators and health campaigners unearthed one of the murkiest known episodes in American corporate history.

∗

The United States is, at the time of writing, the only First World nation in which rBST has been licensed (it is also sold in several Third World countries). Monsanto, the manufacturer, has been pushing hard for its adoption in Europe, but has so far been unsuccessful. The hormone is used in dairy farms all over America, however, with the result that nearly everyone in the States consumes milk or milk products from animals injected with it. In 1998, sales of rBST made some $200m for Monsanto. The American Consumers Union estimates that the hormone costs the US taxpayer a similar amount every year, as the government has to buy the surplus milk produced by US farmers.[18]

In 1985, eight years before it gave rBST final approval, the United States Food and Drug Administration (FDA) had taken the unprecedented step of claiming, in public, that a drug it had not yet fully evaluated was 'safe for human consumption'.[19] In 1999, two Food and Drug Administration researchers published an article in *Science* magazine, in which tables of experimental data, taken from an unpublished study by Monsanto, purported to show that rBST 'is not orally active in rats', meaning that it has no ill effects on the animals eating it. It 'presents', the researchers maintained, 'no increased health risk to consumers'.[20]

The FDA's analysis was flawed. The Canadian researchers who re-examined the data discovered that rBST 'was absorbed intact' by the guts of rats fed with high doses, causing 'a primary antigenic response'. It had, in other words, entered the blood.[21] When the City of New York's

Department of Consumer Affairs reviewed the paper published in *Science*, it concluded that the data showed 'clever deviations from standard and well established safety practice which would be detected only by an experienced scientist'.[22]

In October 1998, when, following publication of the Canadian report, the FDA was challenged to explain its analysis, its representative told reporters 'we do not have data from that study'.[23] In violation of its own procedures, the agency had relied instead on a summary provided by Monsanto.

Between 1990 and 1998, the Food and Drug Administration had been presented with plenty of opportunities to change its opinion about rBST. Evidence of devastating impacts on the health of cows and significant threats to the health of humans had begun to accumulate in universities and government departments in America, Canada and Europe. The most disturbing findings involved a by-product of rBST injection called Insulin-like Growth Factor One, or IGF-1.

rBST works by forcing the cow to produce increased quantities of IGF-1, which in turn stimulates milk production. IGF-1 is identical in cows and humans. All milk contains traces of it, but studies have shown that concentrations of the chemical are higher in milk from cattle injected with rBST.[24] When milk is swallowed, a protein called casein protects IGF-1 from being broken down by digestion, and some 67 per cent of the chemical passes, undamaged, across the gut wall and into the bloodstream.[25]

In 1996, Professor Samuel Epstein of the University of Illinois published evidence in the *International Journal of Health Services* suggesting that increased concentrations of IGF-1 in milk could cause breast and colon cancers in humans.[26] He also cited a 1992 study showing that Tamoxifen, the most effective of the drugs used against breast cancer, works by reducing the levels of IGF-1 in the bloodstream.[27] In January 1998, a paper in *Science* published by a team of medical researchers from Harvard suggested that men with the highest levels of IGF-1 in their blood were four times more likely to contract prostate cancer.[28] In May 1998, a study published in *The Lancet* showed that premenopausal women with high levels of IGF-1 in their blood were seven times more susceptible to breast cancer.[29] The study also referred to experiments showing that IGF-1 encourages the growth of cancerous breast cells in mice.

*

Far from revoking its decision to approve rBST, the FDA has repeatedly reinforced it. Its commissioner, David Kessler, reassured Americans that 'The public can be confident that milk and meat from BST-treated cows is safe to consume' and that 'There is virtually no difference in milk from treated and untreated cows'.[30] In 1999, Donna Shalala, the US Secretary of State for Health, to whom the FDA reports, claimed that the critics of rBST had raised 'no new scientific concerns': she 'does not intend to remove the product from the market'.[31]

But above all, the Food and Drug Administration has ensured that American people have no means of telling whether or not they are drinking milk from cows injected with the hormone. The FDA has warned shops not to label the milk they sell as free from rBST. Its biotechnology coordinator revealed that the administration would not 'require things to be on the label just because a consumer might want to know them'.[32]

In 1994, when two retailers disregarded the FDA's advice and labelled the milk they sold as 'BST-free', Monsanto sued them. In the same year it sent letters to thousands of dairies and grocery shops, warning them that 'Dr David Kessler, the Commissioner of the FDA, has stated publicly that the FDA "looked carefully at every single question raised, and we are confident that this product is safe for consumers, for cows, and for the environment". There is no significant difference between milk from cows supplemented with [rBST] and other milk. The milk is equally wholesome, nutritious, and safe ... Signs or labels placed on or near milk and other dairy products that are false or mislead consumers about bovine somatotropin, either by what they say or fail to say, are unlawful.'[33]

*

As the researcher John Verrall has pointed out, government bodies regulating a drug intended to treat a disease usually require evidence that even when three times the recommended dose is used, it has no ill effect on the person or animal receiving it. Yet here is a drug which cures no disease and is used not occasionally but regularly throughout a cow's milking life, which shows serious side effects not only at three times the recommended dose, but also at the recommended dose itself. Far from banning it, the United States Food and Drug Administration has been actively promoting it. As the Canadian findings began to come to light, American consumers wondered how on earth the agency which was supposed to protect them from dangerous foods had come, instead, to force them to consume milk which appeared to threaten the health of both animals and humans. By 1999, an answer had begun to emerge.

In 1988, Dr Richard Lehmann from the FDA's Center for Veterinary Medicine wrote to Monsanto to inform the company that its experimental procedures were inadequate. His deputy, Dr Richard Burroughs, commissioned much longer and more thorough trials of the drug. Within a few weeks of authorizing them, he was summarily dismissed. The trials he had ordered were discontinued.[34]

By 1993, in order to approve rBST, the FDA had invented a wholly new category of approvals. While hitherto it had insisted that a food additive should pose 'no risk' to consumers, it now argued that rBST was acceptable in that it posed a 'manageable risk'. Dr Burroughs later explained why he had been sacked by the FDA. 'I was told that I was slowing down the approval process. It used to be that we had a review process at the FDA. Now we have an approval process. I don't think the FDA is doing good, honest reviews any more. They've become an extension of the drug industry.'[35]

There is evidence to support his contention. The Deputy Commissioner for Policy at the Food and Drug Administration was, until recently, a lawyer called Michael Taylor. Until 1991, Mr Taylor worked for a law firm called King and Spaulding, during which time he specialized in food labelling issues and personally represented Monsanto. In 1991, Mr Taylor joined the FDA. It was he who signed the FDA's notice in the Federal Register that it would not require the labelling of milk from cows injected with Monsanto's drug.[36]

Margaret Miller was the head of the FDA branch responsible for reviewing the human safety aspects of Monsanto's rBST. In 1992, she signed the human safety approval for the drug. Before she joined the FDA, she was a senior scientist at Monsanto, working on rBST.[37]

The person responsible for reviewing the data on rBST for the FDA was a researcher called Suzanne Sechen.[38] Before joining the Food and Drug Administration, she was a graduate student at Cornell University supervised by a consultant for Monsanto called Dr Dale Bauman. She carried out studies on rBST commissioned and funded by Monsanto at Cornell, while simultaneously helping the FDA to develop its rBST guidelines. In 1987, she left Cornell to work full time for the FDA, where she reviewed her own, Monsanto-funded data on rBST, as well as that of her ex-superviser, Dr Bauman.[39] The United States General Accounting Office noted that this extraordinary position 'raises questions about the objectivity that she would be able to bring to the review of the data'.[40]

The FDA is not the only arm of government well disposed towards Monsanto and industrial milk producers. Donna Shalala has appeared on adverts placed by the milk industry's trade associations, promoting milk as a health food. In 1994, the White House published a report on rBST which insisted that 'BST-treated milk is safe because it is indistinguishable from normal milk'.[41] Congress was to have debated a bill ensuring that milk and milk products from cows injected with rBST were labelled. The bill was considered and rejected by the Dairy, Livestock and Poultry Committee. Four of the committee's twelve members received campaign contributions from Monsanto.[42]

Monsanto is one of the companies most closely associated with President Clinton's administration. It has made substantial legal contributions to Mr Clinton's presidential campaigns. In 1997, the President singled out the company for special praise in his State of the Union Address. In 1999, he appointed Arnold Donald, head of Monsanto's Nutrition and Consumer sector, to the President's Export Council.

One of Monsanto's board members is Mickey Kantor, previously the US Trade Representative and chairman of Clinton's 1992 presidential campaign. Another is Marcia Hale, who was formerly the President's assistant and his Director for Intergovernmental Affairs. She now runs Monsanto's Corporate Strategy Department. William Ruckelshaus was the Chief Administrator of the United States Environmental Protection Agency before he, too, became a director of Monsanto. Linda Fisher was the US Environmental Protection Agency's Assistant Administrator for Pesticides before becoming Vice-President of Government Affairs for Monsanto. Josh King, previously the Director of Production for White House events, is now Monsanto's Director of Global Communication. When Michael Taylor, the lawyer who had helped oversee the Food and Drug Administration's approval of rBST, left the FDA, he became head of Monsanto's Washington office.[43]

Contacts like this have enabled biotechnology companies to achieve an extraordinary degree of access to the US government. When Monsanto flew a group of Irish journalists to the United States in the hope of reversing the flow of bad news about its genetically engineered crops, it took them on a tour of the White House, including, remarkably, the Oval Office itself.[44] When American consumers began to respond to a series of food scandals involving genetically engineered products by turning to organic food instead, the US Department of Agriculture sought to widen the statutory definition of 'organic' to include genetically engineered crops, and to outlaw higher organic standards than those it set. It withdrew the proposal only after receiving 270,000 letters of protest.

*

The Food and Drug Administration has been as generous in its approval of genetically engineered plants as it has been in its licensing of rBST. In 1992, the FDA announced that foods derived from engineered plant varieties would be regulated like those from conventional plants. No labels would be needed to tell consumers which were which. The administration's approach caused disquiet among some of its own research staff. Dr Linda Kahl, one of its compliance officers, for example, complained that the administration was 'trying to fit a square peg into a round hole' by 'trying to force an ultimate conclusion that there is no difference between foods modified by genetic engineering and foods modified by traditional breeding practices'. She pointed out that 'The processes of genetic engineering and traditional breeding are different, and according to the technical experts in the agency, they lead to different risks.'[45]

The US Food, Drug and Cosmetic Act insists that new food additives are proven safe before they are marketed. The FDA argues that genetically engineered crops are exempt from this provision because they are 'generally recognized as safe'. As several of its own scientists have pointed to potential hazards peculiar to the engineered crops, it is hard to see how it could have arrived at this conclusion.

*

So what does all this have to do with Britain, which is, of course, supposed to be the subject of this book? Well, it is partly because of determined lobbying by the United States that Britain and Europe have committed themselves to supporting certain technologies. Britain has a large biotechnology sector of its own, armed with powerful lobby groups. Tony Blair and some of his ministers foresee a new technological revolution, as high-tech industries replace heavy manufacturing as an important source of national income. Both these factors have contributed to the government's support for genetic engineering. But there is no question that intense pressure from the United States has reinforced the British government's reluctance to yield to the public demand that new genetic technologies be treated with great caution.

On 18 May 1998, the European Union was due to discuss several crucial biotechnology issues, among them the labelling of genetically engineered food. A few hours before the European meeting began, President Clinton visited Tony Blair in London. At the time there was speculation that the issue of genetic engineering had been raised, but it was impossible to confirm. In November 1998 the MP Norman Baker asked Tony Blair for details of the discussions he and his staff had conducted with the United States government about biotechnology. Mr Blair refused to answer the question, arguing that 'By convention it is not the practice of governments to make information on such meetings or their content publicly available.'[46]

But in February 2000, the *Observer* used US Freedom of Information legislation to obtain President Clinton's briefings for the day of 18 May 1998. The documents reveal that he was briefed to warn the Prime Minister that 'the EU's slow and non-transparent approval process for genetically modified organisms has cost US exporters hundreds of millions in lost sales ... In the spirit of increased US–EU regulatory cooperation, we urge the EU to take immediate action to ensure that these products receive a timely review.'[47]

The lobbying worked. On 18 May, Britain, which at the time held the presidency of the European Union, insisted that the EU should weaken its labelling requirements for genetically modified ingredients.

Two months earlier, I have found, when a key European Council of Ministers decision on whether or not to approve Monsanto's modified maize was about to be made, the United States government exerted similar pressure on Ireland. The European vote would be a close one, and Ireland was wavering. The EU meeting happened to be taking place the day after St Patrick's Day, which the Irish Prime Minister Bertie Ahern was celebrating in the United States. He was briefed on biotechnology not by the agriculture or trade secretaries but, astonishingly, by Sandy Berger, the Director of the National Security Council. 'In this post-Cold War era,' a Security Council official explained, 'America's national interests have changed, and crises aren't always military crises.'[48] As Mr Ahern was led around Washington by his hosts in the US government, he encountered a massive and well-orchestrated lobbying effort by US officials, congressmen and senators. As Toby Moffett, Monsanto's head of international business, recorded, 'Everywhere he went, before people said "Happy St Patrick's Day," they asked him, "What about that corn vote?" I'm fifty-four years old and I've been in a lot of coalitions in my life, but this is one of the most breathtaking I've seen.'[49]

Ireland voted to license Monsanto's maize. In October 1999, the Irish people found out why. Ireland's Minister of the Environment, Noel Dempsey, admitted that the Prime

Minister, or Taoiseach, had told him to instruct his officials at the European talks to vote in favour of Monsanto's crop, as a direct result of the US government's lobbying. 'During the Taoiseach's visit to the United States in March 1998,' he told the Irish Parliament, 'the issue of Ireland's attitude to genetically modified products on the EU market was raised ... This was conveyed to me by the Taoiseach's office in the context of Ireland's position on four marketing proposals which were considered at a meeting of EU member states.'[50]

In July 1999, the US Freedom of Information Act revealed another interesting item. Reporters from the *Sunday Telegraph* asked US government agencies whether they held any files on British ministers. They did. The US Environmental Protection Agency had a file on Michael Meacher, the minister at the Department of the Environment who – to the discomfort of several more senior members of the British government – has urged that Britain respond warily towards genetic engineering. The Environmental Protection Agency regretted that it could not reveal the file's contents, because it 'originated within the Central Intelligence Agency'.[51]

*

Despite its energetic efforts to influence the European political process, the United States achieved only some of its objectives. Thwarted by European campaigners and consumers, who applied pressure on their own governments not to buckle to the biotech companies, the US began to threaten a trade dispute.

Most of the trade legislation that Britain has to adhere to is formulated by the European Union. This is where the United States launched its attack. In June 1999, Charlene

Barchefsky, the US Trade representative, complained that 'The EU approval process on GMOs [genetically modified organisms] is completely broken'.[52] Referring to France's refusal to import genetically engineered maize, she commented, 'This is very serious and threatens a very substantial trade row if these corn varieties are not allowed to be marketed fully.'[53] Soon afterwards, Dan Glickman, the United States Agriculture Secretary, spoke of an 'impending train wreck between the United States and Europe on biotechnology'.[54]

The United States singled out France because it had, after some indecision, banned imports of Monsanto's genetically altered maize, arguing that the crop threatened both human health and the environment. After the French Agriculture Minister, Jean Glavany, accused US corporations of trying 'to flood the world with their products, genetically modified or not, and to spread their own agricultural and food model', Dan Glickman slapped a hamburger and fries in front of him and told him 'Enjoy'.[55] M. Glavany politely declined his kind offer.

Glickman's subtle diplomacy was accompanied by lobbying at higher levels. In July 1999, Al Gore, the US Vice-President, phoned Lionel Jospin, the French Prime Minister, to remind him, a US spokesman revealed, 'how important this issue is to our government, our farmers and in particular our corn growers'. Jospin was urged 'to come to a quick and positive decision on the matter'.[56] Ten days later, the French surrendered, and approved Monsanto's maize.

In 1999, the United States government executed a series of extraordinary diplomatic manoeuvres. In August 1999, it managed to persuade the European Commission to remove responsibility for genetically engineered crops from its

Environment Department and hand it instead to a new 'Consumer Affairs' Department. This was precisely what the biotechnology corporations wanted, having failed repeatedly to persuade the Environment Commissioner that their products were socially and environmentally beneficial. This was only a step towards the American government's ultimate goal, however. For months it had been lobbying the European Commission to surrender the regulation of genetically modified products completely, and hand it over to the World Trade Organization, an international body heavily influenced by US interests. European governments had resisted. In December, however, without consulting European ministers, Pascal Lamy, the European Commissioner for Trade, quietly yielded to the American proposal. 'This is intolerable, totally unacceptable and unprecedented,' Michael Meacher observed. 'The commission did not have the competence to give this away.'⁵⁷

*

The United States was, at first, confident that it could force Britain and Europe to start using Monsanto's drug rBST. While most British farmers, and those consumers who had heard about rBST, wanted nothing to do with it, the previous, Conservative government had gone to some trouble to prepare the ground for its introduction to Britain. In 1985, the government secretly granted Monsanto a licence to test rBST on British dairy herds. For three years the hormone was used on thirty-eight British farms.⁵⁸ Extraordinarily, instead of being compelled to dispose of the milk, the farms were secretly allowed to sell this product on the open market, even though it had been neither tested for its effects on human health nor licensed for sale in Britain. Consumers had no means of telling whether or not they were drinking milk from rBST treated cows. The experiments remain shrouded in secrecy. When the British Agriculture Minister, Jeff Rooker, was asked about the trials in 1999, he refused to tell Parliament precisely what had happened, arguing that details of the experiments were 'confidential to the manufacturers'.[59]

Britain had also sought to undermine the position of other European nations. In 1994, the United Kingdom was the only country to vote against the EC Council of Ministers' decision to impose a moratorium on sales of the drug until the end of December 1999. In January 1997, the British Ministry of Agriculture informed the public 'the product is safe for use'.[60]

The United States government believed it possessed the means of forcing European consumers to drink rBST treated milk. The United Nations runs an international food standards agency called Codex Alimentarius. On matters such as rBST, Codex Alimentarius is advised by the UN's Joint Expert Committee on Food Additives (JECFA), the body to which Dr Ritter, the Canadian researcher named in Monsanto's memo to the Bureau of Veterinary Drugs, had been reappointed. If Codex and JECFA decide that a food additive poses no danger to human health, then countries are forbidden by international trade rules to prevent it from being sold within their borders.

If, in other words, the US could persuade JECFA to approve Monsanto's drug, it could then insist that both milk from cows in the US which had been injected with rBST and rBST itself could be sold in the European Union. It might also have been able to prevent European retailers from labelling the milk as containing or not containing the chemical. Had JECFA and Codex Alimentarius both ruled in Monsanto's favour, and had Europe then refused to import America's tainted milk and dairy products, the US could have lodged an appeal with the World Trade Organization, which would then have allowed punitive sanctions to be levied against all the countries in the European Union. This is precisely what happened in the similar, but separate, case of hormone-treated beef.

JECFA investigated rBST in February 1998. 'The potential for IGF-1 to promote tumour growth', it reported, 'will not increase when milk from rBST-treated cows is consumed.' It recommended approval of rBST on the basis that it 'does not represent a hazard to human health'.[61]

European MPs immediately began to question the basis on which JECFA's decision had been made. 'There is a strong suspicion', the Belgian MEP Paul Lannoye noted, 'of improper outside influence and selective use of scientific studies' by JECFA.[62] According to the Italian MEP Gianni Tamino, the 'decision-making process requires complete overhaul . . . proceedings were dominated by industry representatives either as members of their national delegations or as observers'.[63]

There certainly appeared to be grounds for suspicion. The researcher John Verrall has shown that the JECFA meeting at which the decision to back rBST was made was dominated by the meeting's two rapporteurs, both of whom happened to be officials at the US Food and Drug Administration. One of them was a man named Dr Nick Weber. The other was his manager at the FDA, Dr Margaret Miller: the scientist who had previously worked for Monsanto.[64]

Dr Weber provided the delegates with a summary of rBST issues. It insisted that 'there was no significant difference between milk labelled as having been produced from cows that were not treated with rBST and milk from cows whose treatment was not disclosed'.[65] Though he referred to one study which appeared to suggest that rBST and IGF-1 were not getting into milk, he failed to refer to several others suggesting that they were. He also appears to have either glossed over or ignored scientific papers showing that IGF-1 is not destroyed by digestion, and crosses the gut wall intact.[66]

To understand what was happening, we need to return to Canada, and that cordial exchange of messages between Dr Ian Alexander, the manager at the Bureau of Veterinary Drugs, and Dr David Kowalczyk, Director of Regulatory Affairs of a subsidiary of Monsanto. You will remember that Dr Kowalczyk had been anxious to know whether Canada would have a representative on JECFA's rBST committee and had also informed Dr Alexander that the consumer advocate Michael Hansen was 'not completely on board'. The minutes of a Bureau of Veterinary Drugs meeting in October 1997 also reveal that 'I. Alexander had received word from Monsanto that N. Weber, FDA ... would be residue ... reviewer' for JECFA's evaluation in February 1998.[67] Monsanto, in other words, appeared to possess information about the composition of the UN committee ahead of the Canadian government. But a leaked e-mail sent six weeks later by Dr Alexander to some of his staff is far more explosive.

'I received a call from David Kowalczyk, Monsanto U.S. this morning,' Ian Alexander's memo revealed. Dr Weber from the FDA had sent Dr Kowalczyk a package. David would 'send a copy to us overnight'.[68] The package arrived on 12 December, with a covering note from David, informing

Ian that it contained 'one copy of the material that has been submitted on bovine somatotropin by others for review at the 50th JECFA meeting'.[69]

This material consisted of the submissions handed in confidence to JECFA by seven people and organizations, including the European Commission, the Toronto Food Policy Council, the researcher John Verrall and the consumer advocate Michael Hansen. JECFA had told everyone submitting information that it would not be seen by other applicants, so that no one had a lobbying advantage over any other. Its members had all signed confidentiality agreements. But JECFA's own rapporteur, the FDA official Nick Weber, had sent the confidential information to Monsanto.

JECFA's approval of rBST seemed to be based both on Dr Weber's report and on new papers submitted by one of the authors of the FDA's 1990 report in *Science* magazine, which New York's Department of Consumer Affairs had claimed showed 'clever deviations from standard and well established safety practice'. The committee sent its summary and conclusions, but strangely not the main body of the report itself, to Codex Alimentarius. The Codex panel, in other words, had to make its decision without access to the data on which JECFA had drawn.[70] Its chairman did not seem particularly worried about this. At its meeting to discuss the issue in September 1998, the panel was precisely split, with most of the European delegates expressing grave reservations. The chair used his casting vote to rule that steps towards the worldwide approval of rBST be taken. It is worth noting that the Chairman of the Codex panel is also the Director of Veterinary Medicine at the United States Food and Drug Administration.

The European delegates objected in the strongest terms.

In March 1999, the European Union's Scientific Committee on Animal Health reported that rBST 'causes substantially and very significantly poorer welfare' for the cows injected with it, including 'painful and debilitating' conditions such as 'foot disorders', mastitis and 'reproductive disorders'.[71] Its Scientific Committee on Veterinary Measures Relating to Public Health noted that levels of Insulin-like Growth Factor-1 in the milk rose by up to five times in cows treated with rBST and cited 'experimental evidence for an association between IGF-1 and breast and prostate cancer'.[72]

In June 1999, the United States acknowledged that it could not win the battle simply by battering other countries into submission. It executed a tactical and, most campaigners believe, temporary withdrawal. In October 1999, the European Union extended its ban on the sale of rBST in Europe.

*

The international fight over rBST and genetically engineered crops has been characterized by some observers as a simple case of the American government's domination of the global economy. But this suggests a misunderstanding of what is happening. The US government is, in cases like this, simply a channel for corporate power, a vehicle for the global ambitions of multinational companies. It has been able to exercise little judgement of its own. This is, as I hope this book is beginning to show, a problem that is not confined to the United States. As the next chapter will explain, British biotechnology companies have also exercised a formidable power to steer public policy.

CHAPTER EIGHT

A Padlock on the Food Chain

Genetic engineering is not the only means of radically altering the way plants grow. Conventional breeding has become so sophisticated that crops can be selected for frost tolerance, for a precise starch or vitamin content, even for resistance to certain herbicides. So why have biotechnology companies invested so much in genetics, when other methods could achieve similar results?

There are two main reasons. The first is that gene splicing enables companies to move a characteristic belonging to one species into another one. They can cross almost any biological boundary, shuffling genes between plants, animals, bacteria and fungi. The second reason is just as important. By patenting the technology required to make the gene transfer, or, better still, by patenting the genes themselves, companies can lay claim to the variety they have engineered as if it were no more than a mechanical invention. They can, in other words, claim ownership of life.

This grants corporations a monopolistic power they have never been able to obtain before. They can control the use of crop plants from the sowing of seed to the sale of food.

They can begin to execute the takeover of the biggest and most widely dispersed commodity market of all: food. In 1996, Robert Fraley, then the President of Monsanto's Ceregen Division, explained the company's strategy of taking over scores of plant-breeding institutes and smaller biotechnology firms to the American magazine *Farm Journal*. 'What you're seeing,' he boasted, 'is not just a consolidation of seed companies, it's really a consolidation of the entire food chain.'[1]

In 1999, a survey of 1,600 patents for genetically modified crops and the technologies associated with them found that 81 per cent resided in the hands of just thirteen companies.[2] Some of these patents are extraordinarily wide. In 1994, for example, the biotechnology company Agracetus became the official European owner of all possible present or future modifications of soya beans. Its rival Monsanto was furious and demanded that the patent be revoked. Monsanto then bought Agracetus and its patents, and quietly dropped its complaint.[3] Monsanto also owns a patent on all genetically engineered cotton: any cotton treated with any gene, by any company, for any purpose, now and in the future, belongs to Monsanto.

Monsanto was one of the corporations to demand that the General Agreement on Tariffs and Trade, the forerunner of the World Trade Organization, incorporate a worldwide patents regime, in order to protect what it claimed were its inventions. This enables the US government to levy punitive sanctions against countries which allow their farmers to use seed Monsanto has patented without paying royalties to the company. James Enyart, a senior Monsanto employee, described his sector's lobbying thus: 'Industry identified a major problem for international trade. It crafted a solution, reduced it to a concrete proposal, and sold it to our own and other governments.'[4]

Having acquired a patent on a genetically engineered plant or animal, a company can then control precisely how and by whom its seeds are used. Monsanto's licence to American farmers buying soya beans engineered to resist the herbicide glyphosate, for example, insists that the grower may not save seed from his or her crops for further plantings. 'If the Grower uses any glyphosate . . . herbicide in connection with the soybean crop produced from this seed,' it continues, 'the herbicide will be a ROUNDUP® branded herbicide (or other Monsanto authorized glyphosate-containing herbicide).' If any farmer breaches this agreement, he or she must 'pay Monsanto as liquidated damages a sum equal to 100 times the then applicable fee for the Roundup Ready gene, times the number of units of transferred seed, plus reasonable attorneys' fees and expenses . . . Nothing herein shall be deemed to limit the amount of damages that Monsanto might recover for any violation of this Agreement.'[5] Monsanto is as good as its word – hundreds of US farmers have been forced to pay ruinous fines.

*

In the early 1990s, biotechnology companies began lobbying for a European directive which would enable them to patent individual genes throughout the European Union. While the corporations engineering new crops were actively involved, the firm which led the effort in Europe is mostly concerned with the medical uses of gene technology.

SmithKline Beecham is a vast pharmaceutical company based in Harlow, in Essex. It was one of the first large companies of its kind to recognize that the sale of proprietary medicines and equipment is not the only way to make money from medicine. 'Genes,' its Research Director George Poste foresaw, 'are the currency of the future'.[6]

The pharmaceutical industry and the British government argued that wide-ranging patents on genetic research were essential if the private sector was to be encouraged to invest in new cures. Without 'a favourable climate for investment, based on the security of a firm legal framework',[7] laboratories, the Conservative government warned, would flee Europe for the United States and Japan, whose patent laws were more generous. Most importantly, companies could not be expected to invest millions of pounds in developing treatments if they were not confident that the benefits of this research would accrue to them, rather than another company pirating their work. Being allowed to patent all the outcomes of their genetic research, it was argued, would give corporations the incentive to make dramatic medical advances.

Many doctors and scientists disagreed, however. While they had no problem with the patenting of medicines or treatments derived from genetic research, ownership of the genes themselves, British scientists argued, 'would not foster research, it would kill it'.[8] Doctors at St Mary's Hospital in Manchester, for example, were painfully aware of the implications of the proposed European directive. The hospital's laboratory had devised a test of its own for discovering whether or not someone possessed the cystic fibrosis gene. This helped to speed up the diagnosis and treatment of patients suspected of suffering from the disease. In 1994, the hospital was contacted by a company from Toronto, claiming to own the gene and demanding a licence fee and royalties every time the hospital carried out its tests.[9] Luckily, the hospital discovered, the Canadian company did not yet possess a patent in the United Kingdom, so it had no obligation to pay. But it also knew that, if the European directive became law, North American patents would be valid in Europe, under an international agreement.

'Licence fees and royalties', doctors at the hospital warned, 'will have to be paid on all patented genes. In the future genetic tests for heart disease and breast cancer may involve the testing of fifteen or more genes each ... This will make genetic testing much more expensive and more inaccessible.'[10] A corporation which owned a gene would have no need to develop any tests or treatments of its own. It could merely sit on its patent and claim money every time someone wanted to use it. As a result, the doctors pointed out, other researchers, hospitals and companies would be discouraged from looking for cures involving that gene, as profits from the therapies they devised would belong not to them, but to the person or company which owned it.

The patenting of genes, scientists argued, would discourage research not only by removing financial incentives, but also by restricting academic freedom. Companies and laboratories seeking patents on their work tend to be secretive and to subject their staff to gagging orders. As nine eminent scientists pointed out in a letter to *Nature*, 'instead of helping biotechnology to make a responsible and useful contribution to medicine and agriculture, the present directive from Brussels succeeds only in threatening the very basis of scientific research – free access to material and freedom to pursue promising lines of enquiry'.[11]

*

These were the arguments deployed against the European Commission's attempt to obtain approval for its 'Directive on the Legal Protection of Biotechnological Inventions'. In March 1995, European MPs defied the Commission for the first time in history by decisively rejecting it. In July 1997, the European Commission resubmitted the directive to Parliament. It had scarcely changed. 'An element isolated from the human body,' it proposed, 'or otherwise produced by means of a technical process, including the sequence or partial sequence of a gene, may constitute a patentable invention, even if the structure of that element is identical to that of a natural element.'[12] The directive also allowed companies to patent plant and animal genes and varieties and even isolated human body parts. 'To say that the combination of a technique and newly isolated gene represents an inventive step,' the researchers at St Mary's Hospital commented, 'is like saying that America could have been patented when Columbus discovered it using the technique of sailing in a ship.'[13]

The directive's opponents were confident of success. Few of the pressing concerns raised by MEPs in 1995 had been addressed in its re-drafting. But the campaigners against the patenting of genes had reckoned without the persuasive powers of the biotechnology companies. The corporations launched the biggest lobbying effort in the European Union's history. SmithKline Beecham alone spent 30m ecus on its campaign. It also pursued a strategy which had seldom been tried before outside the United States.

*

The Genetic Interest Group is a coalition of organizations representing the victims of genetic disorders. In the early

1990s, when the directive was first being considered, it had publicly opposed the patenting of genes. Alastair Kent, its director, who is not himself disabled, warned that 'there is something fundamentally unacceptable about any institution, corporation, or individual having ownership over part of a human being'.[14] 'The granting of patents on gene sequences,' the group told a parliamentary inquiry in February 1995, 'imposes an unnecessary barrier and we want it removed ... costs will mount if payments have to be made to each and every discoverer of a gene.'[15]

But by the time the new draft was being considered, the Genetics Interest Group seemed to have executed a remarkable pirouette. In March 1997, Alastair Kent's name appeared on a pamphlet called 'Patents for Life'. 'MEPs', it instructed, 'must ... vote to pass the gene patenting directive into law as soon as possible. Or else you will have to explain to families how it was that you had the opportunity to create significant progress in the search for cures, but you chose not to take that step.' Like the biotechnology corporations, the pamphlet argued that companies wouldn't invest in genetic research unless the profits accrued to them.[16]

When, on 16 July 1997, the MEPs arrived at the steps of the European Parliament in Strasbourg to vote on the directive, they were confronted by a sight which would have struck terror into the heart of any delegate: a dozen wheelchair-bound people wearing T-shirts printed with the slogan 'Patents for Life' were noisily protesting that they were about to be denied the chance of a cure. They were being organized and assisted by Alastair Kent. Several MEPs were visibly affected by the sight, and later confessed that the demonstration had influenced their decision. The directive was passed.

No one was more astonished by Alastair Kent's change of heart than some of the members of the Genetic Interest Group. 'Our names were taken in vain,' the director of one of the groups GIG was supposed to represent later complained. 'GIG in the UK has always been against the idea of exclusive patenting of a gene or gene sequence.'[17] The directive, she added, 'will cost the NHS dearly, probably restrict access to genetic tests and create a field day for biomedical companies and lawyers'.[18] 'We were not aware,' another association represented by GIG commented, that 'we were part of an aggressive lobby to influence MEPs ... Can anyone help our members to highlight the fact that the human gene sequence must not be patented?'[19] Seventeen of the groups GIG claimed to be speaking for signed a statement raising serious concerns about the directive, pointing out that 'there is nothing novel or innovative' about the discovery of gene sequences, and arguing that 'gene sequences should not be patentable'.[20] The people in wheelchairs, some campaigners suggested, 'did not even realize what all this was about'. They were being 'misused in order to put emotional pressure on MEPs'.[21] Unrepresentative, unsanctioned, Alastair Kent's stooges had handed to the corporations the means to secure exclusive rights over human life.

Only after the directive was passed did MEPs and many of the members of the Genetic Interest Group discover that, since mid-1995, GIG had been receiving expenses and 'gifts in kind' from SmithKline Beecham. The company confirms that it gave the group 'money and expenses for getting there and back' and to 'help them to find their way around Brussels', as well as 'direct grants' and 'access to our consultants'.[22] Though there is no suggestion that Alastair Kent himself made any financial gain, his 'expenses for the vote' were covered by SmithKline Beecham.[23]

Writing in GIG's annual report, Simon Gentry, Smith-Kline Beecham's Director of External Affairs, enthused that 'GIG is a highly effective and articulate advocate for the interests of the people and groups it represents ... People with genetic disorders should be encouraged by recent scientific developments and reassured that, by working together, industry and GIG will ensure that the research imperative is not threatened.'[24] Mr Gentry later told me that his company's funding for GIG had 'done democracy a good turn' as 'patients are never included in the debate at all'.[25]

MEPs might have approved the directive, but they also introduced a number of important amendments, whose purpose was to protect hospitals, researchers, human rights and the environment. One by one, these were either dropped or diluted by the European Commission and the Council of Ministers. By the time the bill was presented to Parliament for a second reading in 1998, it had reverted to a text almost identical to that which had been considered in 1997. But the MEPs, battered by lobbyists, confounded by technicalities and threatened by a restriction of the parliament's powers, passed it without a fight. Life is now patentable in the European Union.

*

The directive's opponents have, regrettably, been vindicated. In January 2000, an American company called Myriad Genetics claimed that the directive had enabled it to become the European owner of two key human genes, certain of whose mutations predispose people to contract breast cancer. Now that Myriad owned the genes, public health laboratories testing women for the mutations in Britain would, the company warned, no longer be permitted to carry out their own tests. They would have to use the procedure developed and licensed by Myriad. This, British health researchers pointed out, would double the cost of the tests, reducing their availability. Doctors and scientists were outraged, not least because, they claimed, much of work identifying the genes had been carried out by British laboratories, at public expense. Myriad had filed its patent applications a few hours before Britain's Institute of Cancer Research reported its own discovery of one of the genes in the scientific journal *Nature*.[26]

In March 2000, Tony Blair and Bill Clinton took the extraordinary step of begging the biotech companies not to use the powers they had been granted. Research on human genes, their joint statement argued, 'should be made freely available to scientists everywhere'.[27] But they offered no legislative means by which this could be achieved, and the biotechnology companies, empowered by the rules the two men had helped to implement, understandably ignored them.

*

In opposition, current Labour ministers campaigned against the European patents directive. In March 1995, after the European Parliament had rejected the first attempt by the commission to have the directive approved, Kim Howells, Alan Meale, Jeff Rooker and Elliot Morley all signed an Early Day Motion congratulating 'the European Parliament on the stand it has taken on the patenting of life' and urging 'the European Commission to reassess its policy on biotechnology and genetic engineering to ensure proper respect for human life, animal life and the integrity of the natural environment'.[28]

In 1997, when the European Parliament approved the same directive, Jeff Rooker and Elliot Morley were ministers of agriculture, Alan Meale was an environment minister and Kim Howells was the minister at the Department of Trade and Industry responsible for patenting. None of them raised a squeak of protest against the British government's enthusiastic support of the European Parliament's vote. When the Dutch and Italian governments subsequently sought to challenge the decision, it was the British administration which led the counterattack. 'Provision of a secure and effective intellectual property regime is paramount for biotechnology industries,' the government noted. 'That is central to the UK's approach.'[29]

This position is consistent with the British government's approach to many of the key European biotechnology issues. It was Britain which blocked the attempt by France and Greece, in June 1999, to introduce a moratorium on genetically engineered crops in the European Union. It was Britain which lobbied and voted at the European Commission to prevent Austria and Luxembourg from shutting their doors to genetically modified maize. But most importantly, it was Britain, influenced by the US, which used its presidency of the European Union in 1998 to break the resolve of the nations which wanted all products derived from genetically engineered crops to be labelled.

*

If you buy a can of genetically modified tomato paste, both the modified DNA and the altered proteins it gives rise to are likely to be present in the can. But if you buy a processed meal containing genetically modified tomatoes, which has already been partly cooked by the manufacturer, the DNA and its proteins are likely to have been broken down. The GM tomato in the meal will be, as a result, chemically identical to similarly treated non-GM tomato. Indeed, most of the end products of genetically engineered crops have, by the time they reach our shelves, been processed to the extent that they are no longer chemically distinguishable from the products of conventional crops. As up to 85 per cent of all processed foods contain either soya or maize derivatives, processed GM ingredients could be present in much of the food we eat.

Denmark, Sweden and Italy wanted all foods derived from GM plants to be labelled as such, whether or not they still contained engineered DNA and proteins. They had discovered that their consumers were not solely concerned with the final chemical composition of their food, but also wanted to know whether or not its production threatened wildlife, or granted control over the food chain to multinational companies. A survey in Britain found similar concerns: 89 per cent of respondents said that food should be clearly labelled as containing GM ingredients whether or not chemical changes were demonstrable.[30]

But Jack Cunningham, when he was the British Agriculture Minister, argued fiercely against inclusive labelling. In May 1998, a few hours after President Clinton had, as documented in Chapter 7, lobbied Tony Blair, he used the British presidency to force through a new European law, ruling that only foods in which engineered DNA or proteins had survived intact should be labelled as containing genetically modified ingredients. He described the law as 'a triumph for consumer rights to better information'.[31] The

British government argued that once the altered DNA has been broken down, GM foods pose no new threats to consumer health or safety.

At first sight, the British (or American) position makes sense: ingredients labels are, after all, meant to tell you what the food contains, rather than what it would have contained had it not been processed. But the ruling acquires a new significance when viewed in conjunction with the scarcely noticed events of just over a year before.

In April 1997, just before the General Election, Britain's Conservative government quietly agreed to raise the permitted levels of a chemical called glyphosate in soya beans destined for human consumption. The decision was an extraordinary one, not only because permitted levels of chemical residues are usually reduced over time rather than raised, but also because this particular one was raised by a staggering 200 times, or 20,000 per cent. Glyphosate is an organophosphate, and the active ingredient of Roundup, the world's best-selling herbicide, manufactured by Monsanto.

Glyphosate is also said by some medical authorities to pose significant dangers to human health. In 1999, the *Journal of the American Cancer Society* reported that exposure to glyphosate led to increased risks of contracting a type of cancer called non-Hodgkin's lymphoma, or NHL.[32] NHL has increased in the United States by 80 per cent since the early 1970s. This has been linked to long-term exposure to pesticide residues. Studies by researchers at the University of California, Berkeley, suggest that the chemical is also the third most commonly reported cause of pesticide illness among farm workers, and the commonest among gardeners.[33]

Monsanto's biggest genetically modified crop is its

'Roundup Ready' soya bean. The bean has been engineered to resist applications of glyphosate. It allows farmers to spray their fields with this total herbicide not only before the crop has been planted, but also while the crop is growing. The genetically engineered soya plants are unaffected, but all the weeds are wiped out. It might help the farmer, but at a cost: the soya plants may absorb some of the glyphosate sprayed on them.

Throughout the late 1990s, Monsanto had been lobbying to raise the permitted glyphosate levels in soya beans. It persuaded Codex Alimentarius and the American and UK governments to agree to its request to lift the level to 20 milligrams per kilogram of beans. The Labour Agriculture Minister in Britain's House of Lords, Lord Donoughue, later explained that 'The low level prevented the import of soya treated in this way from, say, the United States. When that issue was raised, the level was increased by 200 to make it a more relevant level.'[34] But he could not reveal any details of how Monsanto had won this extraordinary concession 'because the matter was conducted under the previous administration and all such information is kept secret'.[35]

When the soya products derived from 'Roundup Ready' beans are processed, the DNA and proteins which distinguish them from conventional beans are broken down. Thanks to Dr Cunningham's interventions during Britain's presidency of the European Union, they are, therefore, exempt from labelling. But while their DNA and protein content might be identical, they could contain significant quantities of glyphosate. Jack Cunningham's legislation, in other words, ensures that the consumer is unable to distinguish between food which is likely to be largely free of glyphosate, and food which might contain high concentrations of the chemical. It is worth noting that until he became Secretary of State for Agriculture, Jack Cunningham was retained as a paid consultant to an agrochemicals company called Albright and Wilson. Albright and Wilson is a member of the Chemical Industries Association, which lobbies for the deregulation of pesticides.

*

During the twenty months following the 1997 General Election, Monsanto representatives met ministers and officials from the departments of Agriculture and the Environment on twenty-two occasions.[36] Its ease of access has been linked by some newspapers to its contacts with some of the Labour Party's most influential strategists and advisers. Stanley Greenberg, one of Tony Blair's key tacticians before the election and the Chairman of Greenberg Research, is a consultant to Monsanto. He was commissioned by the company to find out why its public relations strategy was not working in Britain, and what could be done to improve it. David Hill, formerly Labour's chief spokesman, is now a director of the lobbying company Bell Pottinger Good Relations, where he works as Monsanto's media adviser. He insisted: 'I do not introduce people to Ministers or MPs. My role is one of media handling – how do Monsanto present themselves, do you rebut, how do you put your point across positively?'[37]

In October 1998, Cathy McGlynn, formerly Jack Cunningham's special adviser, also started work for Bell Pottinger Good Relations. During the same month, Dr Cunningham, who had been transferred from agriculture to the Cabinet Office, became chairman of the committee coordinating government policy on GM foods.

Bell Pottinger's appointments are not confined to the ruling party. It pays up to £10,000 a year to the Tory MP Peter Luff, who is Chairman of the Agriculture Select Committee. Mr Luff argued that he had never had any dealings with Monsanto, but the Liberal Democrat MP Norman Baker insisted that his connections were still too close for comfort. 'How can the chair of the Agriculture Select Committee be seen to be neutral in an investigation into GM food,' he wondered, 'when he is paid by a company which services Monsanto?'[38]

The government is evasive about its contacts with Monsanto. When Jack Cunningham's deputy at the Cabinet Office was asked in Parliament to list 'the trips, facilities, gifts and other offerings of a financial value provided by Monsanto to civil servants', he replied: 'The information requested in respect of all civil servants is not held centrally and could be obtained only at disproportionate cost.'[39] When a minister at the Department of Trade and Industry was asked to list the benefits provided by Monsanto to ministers and civil servants in his department, he replied: 'Departmental hospitality records show that ... DTI officials have had working lunches with Monsanto on two occasions.' He failed to reveal whether or not officials or ministers had met Monsanto outside the department, and had dined or been entertained at the company's expense.[40]

*

While Dr Cunningham was running the Cabinet Office, two intriguing documents leaked out. The first, dated 19 February 1999, was an internal memorandum questioning the government's own policies. 'Why', it wanted to know, 'don't we require a pharmaceutical type analysis of the safety of these foods with proper trials?'[41] This is a question that some doctors and health campaigners have also asked, arguing that the chemical changes in some crops amount, in effect, to the introduction of new drugs into the food chain, and pointing to the absence of long-term feeding trials which would determine whether or not they are safe for human consumption.

The leaked memo went on to note that the cabinet committee on genetically modified foods had asked the Chief Medical Officer and the Chief Scientific Adviser for 'a paper ... on human health implications of GM foods. Will we publish this when it is ready (c. April) and use it as a means to explain that GM foods on the market are safe? What if it shows up any doubts? What can we do? We will be pressured to ban them immediately. What if it says that we need evidence of long term effects? This will look like we are not sure about their safety.'[42]

We will never know what the Chief Medical Officer and the Chief Scientific Adviser initially recommended. For, three months later, the second leaked document, a letter from the Cabinet Office to other departments, revealed an extraordinary exercise in information control. It covered the minutes of a committee of whose existence no one outside government had previously been aware, called the Biotechnology Presentation Group. The group was chaired by Jack Cunningham. 'With regard to media interest,' the minutes began, 'the Group concluded that: it had been a relatively quiet week in media terms – with the most significant story being the Christian Aid/Action Aid report on GM foods in the third world on 10 May. Although the Government had not been able to identify an independent scientist to appear on the *Today* programme in the morning, Dr Greerson from

Nottingham University had given a very effective interview.'[43] (Dr Greerson had argued in defence of the biotechnology companies and against the Christian Aid/Action Aid
position.)

The minutes went on to discuss the government's media
'handling strategy'. 'It would be better', the meeting had
decided, 'to present the Government's stance as a single
package by way of an oral statement in the House. This
would allow the Government to get on the front foot ...
The package should include the CMO/CSA [Chief Medical
Officer and Chief Scientific Adviser] paper on GM foods
and public health ... The CMO/CSA paper should be
revised to make sure that it was intelligible to the lay reader
and so that it contained clear recommendations, but Ministers needed to guard against the charge that the Government
was seeking to influence the findings of the paper. The
revised draft should be cleared by a future meeting of the
Presentation Group ... Departments would have to start
working now to line up third parties to author articles in the
media in the days before the announcement.'[44]

In the House of Commons, Jack Cunningham was asked
to publish both the initial drafts of the medical and scientific
advisers' reports and the amendments made by the Biotechnology Presentation Group. He refused.[45] He was asked to
give a public account of the work of the Biotechnology
Presentation Group and to publish all its minutes. He
refused.[46] He was asked to explain why, in giving evidence
to the House of Commons Environmental Audit Committee,
which was studying the coordination of government policy
on genetic engineering, he failed the mention the existence
of the presentation group. He replied: 'It is not Government
practice to announce or discuss' the existence of such

groups.[47] 'There is,' Dr Cunningham explained, 'a great danger that we could seriously damage important United Kingdom industrial and commercial interests. We are one of the world leaders in the biosciences, and it would be a terrible error to allow that to be damaged or undermined in any way.'[48]

In line with this approach, the Cabinet Office appears to have been coordinating its public relations policies with those of the biotechnology companies. In July 1999, a reporter at the *Daily Express* contacted AgrEvo, a corporation hoping to be among the first to secure consent for the full-scale commercial planting of engineered crops in Britain. The newspaper's call was returned, not by AgrEvo but, to the journalist's amazement, by the Cabinet Office. The official who rang back was able to answer the reporter's questions before he was asked: AgrEvo had rung the government, and the government had taken on the task of answering the tricky questions the *Express* had put to the company.[49]

*

But the most controversial contacts between biotechnology companies and the government concern a man who has featured in this book already, the Minister for Science and Innovation at the Department of Trade and Industry, Lord Sainsbury of Turville. Before becoming a minister Lord Sainsbury was, of course, Chairman of the supermarket group J. Sainsbury plc. He was also a major investor in genetic engineering.

Until he became a minister, Lord Sainsbury was the principal backer of the biotechnology company Diatech. Among other patents, Diatech owns some of the key technologies and processes surrounding a series of genes called the Omega sequence. The Omega sequence, researchers have found, can enhance the expression of other genes, making genetic engineering much more effective. It is likely to be useful to gene splicers all over the world, generating large profits for Diatech and its investors.

When he became a minister, Lord Sainsbury placed all his investments in a 'blind trust': an agency administered by other people, who might buy or sell assets without the owner's knowledge. This, in principle, relieved the minister of potential conflicts of interest, as he would not be aware whether or not the decisions he made would favour a company in which he had money.

On 20 July 1998, eight days before he became a minister, Lord Sainsbury lent Diatech £2m to buy a building in Westminster. The loan arrangements were not completed until 14 August, seventeen days after he became a minister.[50] While Lord Sainsbury points out that the deal was finalized by his blind trust, it is hard to see how he could have failed to know that the completion was taking place.

In May 1999, nine months after Lord Sainsbury assumed his ministerial duties, the *Observer* revealed that Diatech was helping to pay for the renovation of a grand house in Buckinghamshire called Turville Park. Turville Park is Lord Sainsbury's country home.[51]

'It's possible that I may still have some commercial interest in biotech firms,' he wrote later that year. 'I simply don't know.'[52] We are asked to believe that his trustees might have taken it into their heads to sell a company with which Lord Sainsbury has long had the closest of associations, and which has not yet made much money but which promises to become enormously profitable in the future.

The Chief Executive of Diatech is a man called Christopher Stone. His biographical details describe Diatech as 'the private office of Mr. David Sainsbury (Lord Sainsbury of Turville)'. Mr Stone 'serves as trustee of the Social Market Foundation, the Sainsbury Centre for Mental Health, the Sainsbury Centre for Visual Arts ... and several other Sainsbury family grant-making charities ... Stone participated in the establishment, in 1987, of the Sainsbury Laboratory for Plant Molecular Pathology in Norwich.'[53] The activities of the Chief Executive of Diatech, in other words, cut across many of Lord Sainsbury's interests.

Mr Stone is a close personal friend of the noble lord. In March 1999, the Secretary of State for Trade and Industry told Parliament that Lord Sainsbury 'has met with Christopher Stone of Diatech Ltd. on a number of times on a personal basis'.[54] Yet officially Lord Sainsbury has no idea whether or not Diatech is prospering as a result of the science policies for which he is responsible.

Christopher Stone is also a trustee of the Gatsby Charitable Foundation, an organization funded by Lord Sainsbury, through which the supermarket boss paid for the construction of the Sainsbury Laboratory at the John Innes Centre, a genetic engineering centre in Norwich. The Gatsby Foundation also funds the promotional campaign run by the institute, called Biotechnology in Our Future. The Gatsby Foundation is not the only substantial backer of the John Innes Centre: another is the Biotechnology and Biological Sciences Research Council, the government funding body which Lord Sainsbury oversees. During Lord Sainsbury's first year in office, the council gave the Sainsbury Laboratory a total of £1.1m to finance research into genetically engineered food. Lord Sainsbury is not responsible for the allocation of individual BBSRC grants, but the research council is in safe hands. Its Chairman, Peter Doyle, was, when he first took the post, also an executive director of the biotechnology company Zeneca. Like the Gatsby Charitable Foundation, Zeneca has invested heavily in the John Innes Centre. The centre carrying out research on behalf of Zeneca and Lord Sainsbury, in other words, also benefits from public grants administered by a director of Zeneca and Lord Sainsbury.

Until the day before he became a minister, Lord Sainsbury was also the chairman of an organization called the Food Chain Group, set up by the Department of Trade and Industry's Office of Science and Technology (which Lord Sainsbury now controls) in order to help make the government's science funding 'relevant to our colleagues in food chain companies'.[55] The report it produced under Lord Sainsbury's chairmanship praises Zeneca for 'becoming the first company in the UK to achieve competitive advantage with a genetically modified product – tomato paste produced from Zeneca seeds'.[56] Zeneca achieved its 'competitive advantage' by selling its tomato purée through Sainsbury supermarkets.

*

'I have', Lord Sainsbury claims, 'not taken part in any government decisions or discussions relating to GM food policy.'[57] According to the government's Chief Scientific Adviser, Lord Sainsbury 'always leaves the room whenever GM food is being discussed'.[58] According to the Secretary of State for Trade and Industry, 'neither I nor my friend the Minister for Science have held any meetings to specifically discuss genetically modified food policy'.[59] According to the

Minister of Agriculture, 'My noble friend . . . is in no way involved in the regulatory process in decisions relating to novel foods.'[60] However, since Lord Sainsbury became a minister, he has travelled to the United States with the BioIndustry Association, a lobby group representing genetic engineering companies, including Diatech. The Department of Trade and Industry paid some of the lobby group's costs.[61] He has met Monsanto to discuss, among other issues, GM crops and food. He is in charge of a government programme to 'help scientists and policy makers understand the attitudes of the general public' towards genetic engineering, and has chaired at least one of its meetings.[62] He has publicly defended the government's position on GM foods on the BBC.[63]

He oversees the work of the Office of Science and Technology's Foresight programme, including that of the Food Chain Group, of which he was once Chairman. He is a member of the cabinet committee established to coordinate the government's biotechnology policy. He was responsible for promoting the growth of 'biotechnology clusters': places in which several companies come together for mutual advantage. Among his tasks were 'looking for any barriers to their further development; and considering what needs to be done, by government and others, to ensure that biotechnology clusters in the UK continue to flourish'.[64] 'It is,' he maintained, 'vital that we create the conditions which allow companies to grow and prosper.'[65] Among these conditions, he insisted, was a 'supportive policy environment' for biotechnology.[66]

*

The establishment of a 'supportive policy environment' appears to be the government's priority when deciding whether or not genetic engineering should be promoted. It claims to make its decisions only on the basis of science. But there is plenty of evidence to suggest that commercial and corporate considerations take precedence over others.

In 1999, for example, demand for organic food in Britain outstripped domestic supply by 200 per cent, and was growing exponentially. Demand for genetically engineered food was approximately zero – in fact there was sustained consumer pressure for GM ingredients to be removed from food wherever possible. One might have imagined that if the government were to invest in agricultural research, it would favour those sectors in which demand was unmet, rather than those in which existing supplies could not be sold. But in 1999 government funding for research into the agricultural applications of biotechnology amounted to £52m, while its funding for research into organic farming totalled just £1.7m.[67]

In the same year, the government allocated £13m 'to improve the profile of the biotech industry'.[68] Its 'Bio-Wise' programme asked companies for 'examples of biotechnology at work within industry'. It would 'publicise these as Case Studies or in press articles' in order to 'provide information on the financial and environmental benefits of biotechnology.'[69] The government has also awarded grants to 'promote better exploitation of intellectual property' in the biotechnology industry[70] and has allocated £15m to help British researchers build up 'gene libraries' which can be commercialized by biotechnology companies.[71]

*

The government is just as supportive when deciding how biotechnology should be regulated, and the extent to which the public and the environment should be defended against its potentially adverse consequences. In order to help the sector expand, the Department of Trade and Industry tried to engineer the relaxation of planning constraints in those parts of the country in which biotechnology companies were strongly represented. This threw the DTI into direct conflict with the Department of the Environment. When the Wellcome Trust tried to act on the DTI's advice and build a vast 'Human Genome Campus' on greenfield land in Cambridgeshire, the local authority, citing massive environmental damage, told the trust that it would have to submit a smaller application, whose components were all related to biotechnology (it seems that the trust had taken the opportunity to throw in a few lucrative developments not directly connected to genome research). In September 1999, John Prescott endorsed the council's decision, to the fury of the Secretary of State for Trade and Industry, Stephen Byers. But in November 1999, under pressure from other ministers, he announced that in future he would relax planning permission to 'promote competition' in the biotechnology sector.[72]

The Department of Trade and Industry, its Web site reveals, 'works to ensure that industry's voice is heard throughout government. To help in that process, it set up a key advisory group for industrialists and regulators to discuss new and existing biotechnology regulations and other concerns with a view to influencing future UK policy.'[73] The government, the DTI reveals, will 'continue to work for a supportive regime throughout Europe to assist biotechnology development'.[74]

The DTI's Invest in Britain Bureau informs potential foreign investors that 'the country has a clear and supportive regulatory environment' and 'strong and effective industry groups representing the interests of industry sectors'[75] (the government, in other words, is boasting about the competence of the organizations set up to lobby it). The United Kingdom, the bureau reports, 'leads the way in Europe in ensuring that regulations and other measures affecting the development of biotechnology take full account of the concerns of business'.[76] Britain, it continued, was the first country in Europe to give biotechnology companies a general permit 'to cover release of more than one GMO at more than one site'.[77] This was still official policy, according to the Invest in Britain Bureau's Web site, in May 1999, a month after the government admitted in court that it was illegal.

*

The government's boasts of taking 'full account of the concerns of business' were not idle ones. In 1998, a study by Friends of the Earth found that eight of the thirteen members of the government's Advisory Committee on Releases to the Environment, which decides whether or not it is safe to let new GM crops be planted in Britain, either worked for academic departments receiving funding from biotechnology companies, were employed by biotechnology companies, or were members of organizations directly involved in releasing GM crops into the environment.[78] By April 1999, it had approved 160 applications for experimental planting, and rejected none, despite concerns among ecologists about the dangers of cross-pollination and the emergence of herbicide-resistant 'super-weeds'.

Following a public controversy over the composition of this committee, the Environment Minister, Michael Meacher, agreed to flush it out in 1999. He appointed a largely new panel, whose members had few direct connections to the planting of GM crops. But the neutrality of its new Chairman, Professor Alan Gray, was soon questioned. He works for the Institute of Terrestrial Ecology, the organization contracted to carry out the large-scale trials of crops developed by the biotechnology company AgrEvo. He is also a fierce critic of alternative farming methods, claiming, controversially, that organic food is more likely to cause food poisoning than conventional crops, because of its reliance on manure as a fertilizer.[79] (Organic standards, however, insist that manure is properly composted. Conventional arable farmers, by contrast, are subject to fewer restraints when spreading human sewage on their fields.) He also claims that GM crop regulation in Britain 'is incredibly thorough ... It is the most regulated aspect of our agriculture and is admired by many other countries.' The restoration of public confidence in GM crops is, he believes, of pressing concern.[80]

The independence of the Advisory Committee on Novel Foods and Processes, which is responsible for ensuring that genetically engineered foods are safe to eat, has also been challenged – in this case by one of its own members. In 1999, Dr Kate Venables argued that the committee's members were so deeply involved in genetic engineering that they were unlikely to stop to ask all the questions they should. 'Scientists who are desperately excited by the idea of genetic modification', she maintained, 'are not going to be deflected from this as an interesting and exciting research tool.'[81] There seems to be some evidence for this proposition. When Professor Janet Bainbridge, chair of the committee and an outspoken enthusiast for GM crops, was asked whether the public should be able to choose between GM and non-GM food, she observed that 'most people do not even know what a gene is. Sometimes my young son wants to cross the road when it's dangerous – sometimes you have to tell people what's best for them.'[82]

*

Concerned that sentiments like this are hard to reconcile with either the scientific principles of rigour and caution or the democratic principles of representation and public participation, thousands of British people have continued to protest against the biotechnology companies' consolidation of the food chain. They have enjoyed some success.

In January 2000, public pressure encouraged the Environment Minister, Michael Meacher, to confront US attempts to disrupt a global 'biosafety protocol'. The United States was not party to the protocol's negotiations, having refused to sign the convention which governed them. But when Third World nations tried to use the talks to introduce firm rules on genetically engineered crops, the US government began persuading other countries to undermine them. Michael Meacher managed to rally the other European states in support of the developing world, with the result that nations are now permitted to ban crops which might threaten the environment or human health.

A few weeks later, Tony Blair acknowledged for the first time that 'the jury is still out on the application of this new technology to food and crops . . . there is cause for legitimate public concern'.[83] But perhaps the most significant reversal of fortune concerns the company whose name has featured prominently in these chapters, Monsanto. Until the middle of 1999, Monsanto appeared to be conquering the world. It had, in the past two years, initiated $8bn worth of mergers, cornered much of the global market in seed and farm chemicals, and boosted its share price several times over. By December 1999, however, it had been all but buried.

Consumers on both sides of the Atlantic had become suspicious of its products. Farmers were reluctant to plant, and financiers were wary of investing. As its share price plummeted, the company was forced to merge with the drugs company Pharmacia and Upjohn. A month later, the name Monsanto disappeared from all but one of the new corporation's divisions. The behemoth has been swallowed.

This is not, of course, the end of the story. Big biotechnology corporations are still attempting to take over the food chain and turn the genes of plants, animals and humans into private property. Their investments in genetic engineering have already earned them hundreds of millions of pounds. Their investments in social engineering have, so far, been less successful.

CHAPTER NINE

Silent Science –
The Corporate Takeover of
the Universities

Number 15 Buccleuch Place is one of the most sedate Victorian buildings in one of Edinburgh's most sedate Victorian squares: quiet, cobbled and fronted by weatherstained limestone terraces. The plaque beside the forbidding black door announces that it is Edinburgh University's Faculty of Arts Postgraduate Centre. This is a recent designation. Until 1996, the building housed another department, with a rather more controversial mandate.

The Centre for Human Ecology studied the interactions between people and the environment. It developed a reputation for working on issues of the utmost political sensitivity. Its staff investigated, for example, the effects of Scotland's concentration of landownership and the social and environmental impacts of the massive quarry a major roadstone company was proposing to dig on the Isle of Harris. Its Head of Teaching, Alastair McIntosh, raised questions in both the scientific and the popular press about the Conservative government's science policies. But while its work was controversial, its standards were widely acknowledged to be high. The external examiner for the master's degree it taught reported that the Centre for Human Ecology had 'developed an intellectually innovative, creative and exacting approach to issues of mounting public significance, in important respects helping blaze a trail'.[1]

Edinburgh University, however, appears to have viewed the centre's staff as an unruly nuisance. In April 1996, the university's Principal, Professor Sir Stuart Sutherland, announced that the master's course had been 'suspended': which meant, in effect, that the centre was to be closed down.

The reason the university gave for the closure was that the centre's Director had resigned after failing to receive 'the support and cooperation necessary' from Alastair McIntosh and the rest of the staff.[2] There was no question that the relationship between the staff and the university authorities had broken down. But the centre's problems appear to have been exacerbated by the hostility of some of Scotland's most powerful commercial interests. A mineral rights holder and a mining consultant who supported the proposed quarry had written to the centre complaining of 'mendacious fanaticism'[3] and 'deliberate misrepresent[ation]'[4] on the part of Alastair McIntosh. The hundreds of eminent academics who rose to his defence took a very different view of his work. A later letter from the director of a company of consulting engineers instructed the head of the centre: 'You really will have to gag Alastair McIntosh. His hard hitting article in the *Glasgow Herald* debunking the Government's Science and Technology White Paper will alienate most, if not all, wealth creators.'[5]

Many observers felt that the centre had been closed because its radicalism was incompatible with the ethics of a university receiving an increasing proportion of its money from corporations. They contrasted the decision to shut it with another announcement, made on the same day: that the university would not suspend a lecturer in psychology who insisted that the IQ of black people was lower than that of whites. Explaining this decision, the Principal noted that: 'The concept of academic freedom is sometimes treated as an inconvenience to be waived if statements made or conclusions reached by a member of academic staff at this or another university attract widespread condemnation. It is nothing of the kind, but an important precondition for learning and research.'[6]

The demolition of the Centre for Human Ecology has come to symbolize, for many academics, the erosion of the freedom the Principal of Edinburgh rightly celebrates. For Britain's universities have swiftly and silently been colonized by corporations.

For most of the twentieth century, scientists in British universities were discouraged from engaging with industry, for fear that such contact would persuade them to concentrate on immediate technological needs rather than on the more profound scientific questions. In the 1970s and 1980s, however, industrialists and some academics began to argue that the funding of research should be reoriented to meet the needs of business. Britain, they pointed out, was renowned for generating scientific breakthroughs, but these seldom translated into economic success, as our discoveries were commercialized elsewhere. Unless British science could be tailored to meet the needs of British industry, our global economic position would continue to slide.

This may, in the short term, be true. Much of our recent economic growth has emerged from the development of high-tech industry, stoked by scientific innovation and discovery. But it is also clear that this approach leads to a narrowing of scientific horizons, as researchers pursue precise technological outcomes, rather than spending decades on the speculative quests, inspired or quixotic, which lead to major scientific breakthroughs. In the long term, this constriction could damage not only scientific success but also economic competitiveness.

Moreover, a key component of the academic freedom which every university claims to defend is surely the freedom to explore that which has no immediate application. Academic freedom is a guarantor of our wider liberties. Science tells us who we are and how we can live better. It is the glass through which we perceive the world. If distorted, it twists our understanding of the ways in which we might progress, of the alternatives to existing models of development. If companies want research conducted, it is hard to see why this work needs to be carried out at government expense in the universities, rather than at corporate expense in their own laboratories.

Today, there is scarcely a science faculty in the United Kingdom whose academic freedom has not been compromised by its funding arrangements. Contact between government-funded researchers and industry, having once been discouraged, is now, in many departments, effectively compulsory. This chapter shows how our universities have been offered for sale, with the result that objectivity and intellectual honesty are becoming surplus to requirements.

*

In 1993, the Conservative government published a White Paper on science called *Realizing Our Potential.*[7] Its purpose was 'to produce a better match between publicly funded strategic research and the needs of industry'. The research councils, which distribute most of the money for science, would be obliged to develop 'more extensive and deeper links . . . with industry'. They would be required 'to recruit more of their senior staff from industry', and would each be given a chairman who would 'bring in relevant experience from the industrial and commercial sectors'.[8] In 1994, the government established its 'Foresight Panels', teams of business people and academics who would 'identify . . . emerging opportunities in markets'.[9] Their decisions would guide the allocation of government money. In 1995, the Office of Science and Technology was moved from the government's Cabinet Office to the Department of Trade and Industry. 'What the change means,' the Science Minister explained, 'is that we in Government recognize the vital need to bring industry and academe closer together.'[10]

These reforms were extended by the Labour administration. Its 1998 White Paper on competitiveness launched a 'reach-out fund', to encourage universities to 'work more effectively with business'.[11] The role of the higher education funding councils, which provide the core money for the universities, was redefined 'to ensure that higher education is responsive to the needs of business and industry'.[12] The LINK programme, which diverts government money into projects jointly funded by business, was expanded. In 1998, the government resuscitated the dormant Council for Science and Technology, its most important source of scientific advice. Appointed by the Prime Minister, the council contains seven university academics and six industrialists. Among the academics is Sir Stuart Sutherland, the Principal of Edinburgh University and the man who signed the death warrant for the Centre for Human Ecology.

Science budgets have not only been diverted, they have also been cut. Between 1983 and 1999, public research funds in Britain declined in real terms by 20 per cent.[13] In 1999, the Higher Education Funding Council for England reported that its budget had been reduced by 35 per cent in real terms over the previous eight years. As a result, 30 per cent of universities would fall into debt over the following year.[14] In December 1999, the government set aside an extra £320m for university science. Welcome as it was, this money, the campaign Save British Science calculates, represents less than half the annual extra spending needed to bring university research funding in Britain up to the global average.

The result of all these changes is that universities and research institutes seeking to keep their heads above water have little choice but to turn to business for help. And the companies – recognizing that publicly funded labs, whose researchers are paid a fraction of the wages of those working in the private sector, offer them value for money, prestige and political support – are only too happy to oblige.

*

In December 1998, the Committee of Vice-Chancellors and Principals announced that the universities they ran would no longer take money for cancer research from the tobacco industry. The companies' backing, they had decided, 'is not likely to be viewed as disinterested and will consequently damage the university's standing and reputation'.[15] It seems astonishing that they had been taking this money in the first place. But while this, the most controversial source of industrial funding, was discontinued, the business sponsorship of other areas of research has expanded. Why funding from other corporate sectors should 'be viewed as disinterested' and not likely to 'damage the university's standing and reputation' has never been satisfactorily explained by the vice-chancellors. But I have been unable to find a university anywhere in the United Kingdom which does not accept corporate money for research in which the companies involved have an immediate interest.

Business now inhabits the cloisters of even the biggest and richest institutions. The University of Cambridge, for example, possesses a Shell Chair in Chemical Engineering, BP Professorships in Organic Chemistry and Petroleum Science, an ICI Chair in Applied Thermodynamics, a Glaxo Chair of Molecular Parasitology, a Unilever Chair of Molecular Science, a Price Waterhouse Chair of Financial Accounting and a Marks and Spencer Chair of Farm Animal Health and Food Science. Before the acceptance of new tobacco money was banned, it accepted a £1.6m endowment from BAT Industries to establish the Sir Patrick Sheehy Chair of International Relations. (Sir Patrick Sheehy was British American Tobacco's Chairman.) Rolls-Royce, AT&T, Microsoft and Zeneca have all set up laboratories in the university.

In June 1999, BP gave the university £25m, to fund work across five departments. In November 1999, Cambridge set up an £84m joint venture, funded largely by the British government, partly by industry, with the Massachusetts Institute of Technology. Its purpose is to 'change the face of business and wealth creation in the UK',[16] by stimulating 'research spin-offs' and 'training the business leaders of the future'.[17] Cambridge's Vice-Chancellor explained, 'We may once have been thought of as an ivory tower – today we are a tower of hi-technology and business prowess.'[18]

Oxford University has accepted £20m from Wafic Said to build a business school which will bear his name. Mr Said was named in the Commons inquiry into the sale of a 'supergun' to Iraq, as the agent responsible for brokering Britain's £20bn arms deal with Saudi Arabia.[19] In 1998, he reached a £2m settlement with the Inland Revenue after investigators found that his companies had not paid the necessary British taxes.[20] Mr Said has appointed six of the business school's ten trustees.[21] Lord Jenkins, the Chancellor of the University, announced that the gift would place Mr Said among those 'to whom Oxford has given immortality'.[22] The university has allowed Rupert Murdoch, a man whose contribution to the language has been, shall we say, resourceful, to endow a chair in English and a visiting professorship in the broadcast media. The first beneficiary of the professorship is David Elstein, who used to run Mr Murdoch's channel Sky One.

The independent researchers Greg Muttitt and Chris Grimshaw have examined the influence of oil companies on British universities.[23] They identified nearly 1,000 research projects being conducted for oil and gas firms. Some university faculties, they discovered, have become largely dependent upon industrial money. Aberdeen's Geology Department, for example, boasts that 'Industrial contracts and sponsorship now account for more than two thirds of our research income, support over one third of our lecturing staff, fund nearly all our postgraduates, and even provide appropriate components of our undergraduate training'.[24] There are BP professorships, fellowships or lectureships at seven British universities, including both Oxford and Cambridge. A director of BP sits on the Council for Science and Technology. Until the end of 1998, the Director General of the UK's Research Councils was Sir John Cadogan, formerly BP's Research Director. The Chairman and Chief Executive of Esso UK sits on the Higher Education Funding Council for England. Lord Oxburgh, the Rector of Imperial College, is a director of Shell.

The result of such corporate involvement, the researchers found, was a significant distortion of the research agenda. Five times as much money is spent in British universities on research into oil and gas as on research into renewable sources of energy. Not only does this 'strengthen the competitive position of the industry against its alternatives', which conflicts with the government's aim of bringing down carbon emissions, but it also establishes an inverse relationship between research needs and research funds.[25] Renewable energy, which is an emerging industry, requires a great deal of research as it approaches its take-off phase. Oil and gas extraction, a mature industry, could be expected to need far less.

David Whyte, of the Centre for Criminal Justice Research at Liverpool John Moores University, recorded a conversation with a health and safety researcher at a university department partly funded by oil companies. The researcher had discovered that one of the companies had been falsifying its own accident figures. 'When I ask these guys [the senior managers of oil companies] about why the accident rates are changed for their own records,' the researcher revealed, 'they tell me to shut up. Of course I do. Because you can't challenge what they say if you want to keep credibility.'[26]

Some government funding bodies appear to share this belief. After exposing the way in which university departments funded by the oil industry have adapted their work to suit the needs of their patrons, David Whyte was called into the office of a senior manager at the Health and Safety

Executive, a government body which funds university research into safety on the oil rigs. He accused Dr Whyte of 'misrepresenting the truth' and lectured him on the importance of the North Sea oil industry to the British economy. 'We have a large pool of research funds,' he revealed. 'Six million pounds is a lot of money, you know ... It would be very difficult to win this money for Merseyside.' 'Obviously,' he warned, 'you would have to be very careful about the way you put things.'[27]

Money buys influence throughout the scientific community. A team of Canadian researchers studied a series of contributions to academic journals on the subject of a class of drugs called 'calcium channel blockers'.[28] The drugs, which are used to treat high blood pressure and heart disease, are controversial: some doctors believe that at least one of them is dangerous, increasing the risk of heart attacks. The researchers examined seventy articles in medical journals by scientists studying these drugs. They found that 96 per cent of those who supported their use had financial relationships with the manufacturers, as opposed to just 37 per cent of those who criticized them. Disturbingly, only two of the authors of these papers divulged their connections.[29] But while the acceptance of corporate money might encourage researchers to change the way they view the world, the acceptance of public money is now scarcely less hazardous.

*

The main source of funds for the biologists working in Britain's universities is the Biotechnology and Biological Sciences Research Council, or BBSRC, a government body with an annual budget of £190m. Its chairman is Peter Doyle, who, as Chapter 8 showed, was when he became

Chairman an executive director of the biotechnology company Zeneca. Among the members of its council are the Chief Executive of the pharmaceutical firm Chiroscience; the former Director of Research and Development at the controversial food company Nestlé; the President of the Food and Drink Federation; a consultant to the biochemical industry; and the general manager of Britain's biggest farming business. The BBSRC's strategy board contains executives from SmithKline Beecham, Merck Sharpe and Dohme and AgrEvo UK, the company hoping to be the first to commercialize genetically engineered crops in Britain. The research council has seven specialist committees, each overseeing the dispersal of money to different branches of biology. Employees of Zeneca, according to the council's Web site, sit on all of them.[30]

When the BBSRC was established in 1994, it took over the biological funding programme previously run by the Science and Engineering Research Council, or SERC. SERC's purpose was to advance knowledge of all kinds, whether or not it had an immediate commercial application. The BBSRC's purpose, it maintains, 'is to sustain a broad base of interdisciplinary research and training to help industry, commerce and Government create wealth and improve the quality of life'.[31]

Public statements by the research council's Chief Executive, Professor Ray Baker, suggest that he is taking this mandate seriously. The council's press releases fall into three categories: news about the research grants it allocates; news about the findings resulting from those grants; and fierce attacks on the critics of genetic engineering.

When the medical journal *The Lancet* announced its intention to publish a paper by the controversial geneticist

Arpad Pusztai, who was to claim that genetic engineering could endanger human health, Ray Baker used a BBSRC press release to condemn the publication as 'irresponsible'.[32] When Friends of the Earth and the BBC's *Newsnight* programme released the results of research showing that pollen from genetically modified rape plants was being carried four and half kilometres by bees, Professor Baker issued a statement claiming that the finding was 'a distraction from the key issues'.[33] When the trustees of a farm carrying out a field trial of GM rape decided to stop the experiment, Professor Baker used the BBSRC press office to complain that 'there is absolutely no scientific justification for this destruction', as there was 'no risk of cross-pollination' with 'organic oilseed rape, as it is not grown in the UK'.[34] Unfortunately he forgot to add that there was a near certainty that the GM rape would cross-pollinate with non-organic, unmodified, rape plants, as well as a clear possibility that it would exchange genetic material with its wild relatives. Professor Baker, in other words, has been using a government research body as a platform for contentious and, in some cases, misleading political statements, which appear to favour the interests of the biotechnology companies. It is worth noting that one of the tasks of the Chief Executive of the BBSRC is to provide impartial scientific advice to the government.

The Chief Executive's worldview is, unsurprisingly, reflected in the way the research council distributes its funds. Large sums of public money that might otherwise have been spent on blue skies biological research have been diverted to genetic engineering. In January 1999, the council set aside £15m for 'a new initiative to help British researchers win the race to identify the function of key genes'.[35] In July of that year, it announced that it was spending £19m on new research facilities to 'underpin the economic and environmental sustainability of agriculture in the UK' through 'work on genetically modified crops'.[36] In October, the BBSRC allocated £11m for projects which would enable the UK 'to remain internationally competitive in the development of gene-based technologies'.[37] Every year, the council gives the John Innes Centre in Norwich, the genetic engineering institute which houses the Sainsbury Laboratory and has formed a research alliance with the companies Zeneca and DuPont, over £10m in grants.

The BBSRC also funds the secondment of academics into corporations. The companies are invited 'to select both the project and the academic partner'.[38] Such schemes, the council enthuses, help 'companies establish long-lasting personal and corporate linkages with academics/Higher Education Institutions' and to 'influence basic research relevant to company objectives'.[39] The council has launched a Biotechnology Young Entrepreneurs Scheme, 'aimed at encouraging a more entrepreneurial attitude in bioscientists'.[40] It has paid for researchers to work for Nestlé, Unilever, Glaxo Wellcome, SmithKline Beecham, AgrEvo, Dupont, Rhone Poulenc, and, of course, Zeneca.

Unlike Professor Baker, the scientists working in university departments receiving BBSRC grants are formally gagged to prevent them becoming 'involved in political controversy in matters affecting research in biotechnology and biological sciences'.[41] In practice, the gagging order is used against scientists who rock the corporate boat, rather than against those who suggest, rightly or wrongly, that the technologies they are developing pose no threat to people or the environment. This became clear when Dr Arpad Pusztai, a geneticist working at an institute funded by the research council, challenged the safety of genetically engineered foods. His claims may not have been supportable, but nor were some of those made by the scientists from BBSRC-funded laboratories who spoke out against him. Unlike Dr Pusztai, none of them was suspended for speaking to the media. 'Political controversy' appears to mean positions with which the BBSRC disagrees.

*

The BBSRC is not the only research council with strong corporate affiliations. The Chairman of the Natural Environment Research Council (NERC), James Smith, was formerly Chairman and Chief Executive of the Eastern Electricity group. Like just about every other committee overseeing national science policy in Britain, NERC contains a representative of Zeneca. The Natural Environment Research Council helps to fund studies for the UK's oil and gas companies, identified by many environmentalists as the foremost threats to the natural environment.

The Chairman of the Medical Research Council is Sir Anthony Cleaver, the former Chairman of AEA Technology plc, who was responsible for the organizational changes at the Dounreay nuclear power station which, the Health and Safety Executive reported in 1998, 'have so weakened the management and technical base of Dounreay that it is not in a good position to tackle its principal mission, which is the decommissioning of the site'.[42] One result is that the health of some of the site's workers and neighbours has been endangered. He was also an executive director of the pharmaceutical company Smith and Nephew plc.

Far more disturbing than the activities of the research

councils, however, are the priorities of the Office of Science and Technology's sixteen Foresight Panels. The Foresight Panels scarcely pretend to promote either academic objectivity or the wider public interest. Though they are official sources of scientific advice to both central government and to the research councils, they are largely controlled not by scientists but by business people.

The Food and Drink Foresight Panel, for example, is composed of eight representatives of food companies and trade bodies, and three members of university departments, as well as members of the BBSRC and the Medical Research Council, who are expected to respond to its demands. It has several sub-committees, whose purpose is to identify 'research priorities'. One is called the Alcoholic Drinks Panel. The report it produced was drawn up in consultation with five trade associations, three industry-sponsored research institutes, fifteen drinks companies and no one else. It called for 'a sophisticated understanding of individuals' eating and drinking behaviour' to assist 'product development'.[43] It demanded research which would help drinks companies to resist 'unnecessary barriers to innovation and burdens on the industry' caused by regulation.[44]

The report of the Fruit and Vegetables sub-committee suggested that 'Irradiation may be re-examined for extending shelf life' and hoped that new research would allow 'Personnel levels in the sector' to 'be reduced'.[45] The Dairy sub-committee concluded that 'More effort should be put into publicising the health benefits of milk in the human diet.'[46] The Meat sub-committee complained that 'criticisms of meat production from an animal welfare and environmental impact perspective, and of high levels of red meat consumption as potentially damaging to human health, gained credence from some scientific work'.[47] Apparently referring to injectable growth hormones, it lamented that 'sensitivity to current concerns will cause us to be "left behind" in development of potentially beneficial technologies'. It called for research into 'manipulation of the immune system' and the 'application of physical or chemical treatments of carcasses'. 'Concern that the outcome may not be acceptable in the current climate', it asserted, 'should not ... hold back the related basic research.'[48]

Until the day before he became Minister for Science and Technology, another sub-committee, called the Food Chain Group, was, as I mentioned in Chapter 8, chaired by Lord Sainsbury. His report, published like all the others by the government's Department of Trade and Industry, expressed the hope that in the future 'the expensive precautionary principle is abandoned'[49] (the precautionary principle declares that if there is scientific doubt about the safety of a product or practice, it should not be deployed until that doubt has been dispelled). 'The most progressive farms', the report suggested, would be those on which 'herbicides are applied by robots under the management of satellites'.[50]

Lord Sainsbury and John Battle, then a minister at the Department of Trade and Industry, attended a Food Chain Group Summit in March 1998, which concluded that this government-funded research programme should involve 'Influencing and anticipating future behaviour of consumers'.[51] The summit went on to lament, without a hint of irony, the 'falling consumer confidence in science'. Summing up, Lord Sainsbury told the delegates, 'It is important for food chain companies to establish better contact with scientists and the people that provide public funds for research –

OST [the Office of Science and Technology] and MAFF [the Ministry of Agriculture] can help you make contact with the right people.'[52]

The Food and Drink Foresight Panel's recommendations are already bearing fruit. 'The Ministry of Agriculture, Fisheries and Food', the panel notes, 'has undertaken a comprehensive review of its programmes in the light of the panel's report. Much of the research it supports is closely aligned with the panel's recommendations.'[53] It has also, it claims, been able to influence the agenda of several of the research councils. The BBSRC, for example, now has 'a much more explicit emphasis on consumer science, a priority topic identified by the panel'.[54]

The Agriculture and Forestry Foresight Panel has made a similarly selfless contribution to scientific inquiry. It is responsible for identifying research priorities in, for example, 'the effects of land use on the environment' and rural employment.[55] Yet, while the National Farmers' Union, the Pig Improvement Company and, needless to say, Zeneca Agrochemicals are all represented on the panel, it contains just one member of a university department and no one from a trades union, an environmental group or any other voluntary body. Perhaps unsurprisingly, its answer to most agricultural issues is more investment in the genetic modification of crops, whose 'products will be accepted by the public over the timescale considered here'.[56]

The Retail and Consumer Services Foresight Panel, chaired by Sir John Banham, the head of Tarmac, warns of the 'potentially dire' impact of growing concerns about the environment. The consequences of these concerns, such as 'increasing difficulty in carrying out green field developments coupled with attempts to restrict traffic and reduce congestion', would result, inexplicably, in 'fewer women . . . working', 'cuts in state pensions' and a collapse in living standards.[57] It has drawn up an 'Agenda for Social Science Research': the taxpayer was asked to finance studies into 'the patterns of choice and behaviour which affect the consumption of certain goods'.[58]

*

The Foresight Panel's recommendations to government are likely to continue to fall upon fertile ground. Until February 1999, Lord Sainsbury was Chairman of a government-funded outfit called the 'University for Industry', 'a new kind of public–private partnership which will boost the competitiveness of business and the employability of individuals' by tailoring adult education to meet the needs of business.[59] Until 27 July 1998, as Chairman of both the Foresight Panel's Food Chain Group and the superstore chain J. Sainsbury plc, he was charged with helping food manufacturers and retailers ensure that government science policy met their needs. On 28 July, he became responsible for ensuring that science meets the needs of all British people, overseeing the allocation of most of the government's spending on scientific research.

Lord Sainsbury's former interests continue to feature prominently in the department he runs. He presents the prizes to the winners of his ministry's Bioscience Business Plan Competition, which is sponsored by Glaxo-Wellcome and the Gatsby Charitable Foundation, the science-funding body he established before he became a minister. The Chairman of the Institute of Arable Crops Research, appointed by the BBSRC, was previously Chairman of the

Sainsbury Laboratory. An employee of J. Sainsbury plc sits on the Food and Drink Foresight Panel.

At the end of 1998, as public concern about the government's science policies began to emerge, Lord Sainsbury announced a 'nationwide consultation' to 'explore the wider implications of scientific progress.' Lord Sainsbury explained that: 'Our long-term aim is to build public confidence in the government's use of scientific information.'[60] The consultation was designed by an advisory group of six people. One of the members of the group was, of course, a senior manager at Zeneca. Another was an employee of J. Sainsbury plc.

*

Some of the consequences of the corporate takeover of science are immediately obvious; others are harder to identify. The first and most evident outcome is that the scope of research necessarily contracts: business is less interested in the big questions, whose answers might not lead to technological outcomes for many years, than in the small questions with marketable answers. Science in Britain is in danger of being reduced to a search for new applications of existing knowledge.

Moreover, there is often a conflict between the needs of large companies and the needs of the rest of the world. Expensive cures for non-lethal diseases in the First World are pursued enthusiastically, while the search for a malaria vaccine has been neglected. Poor farmers in remote parts of the world are offered costly technological solutions to their problems, rather than strategies they can deploy with their own resources.

As big business infiltrates the research agenda, ever wider

zones of enquiry are placed off-limits. In 1999, the government published a White Paper on public health called *Saving Lives: Our Healthier Nation*.[61] The only atmospheric pollutant named in the report is radon. It also happens to be one of the only pollutants in Britain which does not result from the activities of large corporations: it is naturally occurring. The report warns us about the dangers of cancer resulting from 'exposure to radon gas in certain homes or excessive sunlight', but nuclear power stations are not mentioned, and nor are any other chemicals, even though the paper concedes that 'Pollutants in the environment may cause cancer if inhaled or swallowed'.[62] The language in which this warning is given is interesting: it creates the impression that breathing or ingesting pollution is something we can avoid. The paper informs us that the government hosted 'the largest ever Ministerial conference on environment and health' in 1999.[63] It fails to tell us that the links between cancer and industrial pollution were dropped from the agenda soon before the meeting began.

The key questions are left for amateurs and voluntary organizations to investigate. Friends of the Earth and *Newsnight* studied the pollen flow from the government's GM test sites only because government researchers were not examining the issue.[64] It was a retired GP called Dr Dick van Steenis who discovered that the number of primary school children using asthma inhalers was directly proportionate to the levels of pollution to which they were exposed.[65] In both Britain and the United States, the funding for studies of corporate crime has all but disappeared. Edinburgh's Centre for Human Ecology has sustained its radical research programme and relaunched its master's course, but only by re-establishing itself as an independent charity in a farmhouse in Fife and scraping together the necessary funds from well-wishers and trusts.

While openness has long informed the ethics of science, corporations demand confidentiality. Information that the companies find uncomfortable can be withheld, even when it arises from projects half-funded by the government: the LINK programme, for example, grants discretion over whether or not to publish results to the corporate partners. The free flow of ideas is further impeded by the need to secure corporate intellectual property.

Perhaps most importantly, the corporate takeover of science leads directly to the corporate takeover of science teaching. The research agenda necessarily influences the teaching agenda. Universities hire staff likely to attract corporate money, and these staff import perspectives which are inevitably transmitted to their students. In both universities and schools (as Chapter 11 shows), corporate teaching materials, advertisements and even, in some cases, educational programmes appear designed subtly to influence the way in which the student views the world.

Business now stands as a guard dog at the gates of perception. Only the enquiries which suit its needs are allowed to pass.

CHAPTER TEN

Government in Exile –
The Corporate Bid for World Domination

In April 1998, a ragged band of protesters inflicted the first of a series of defeats on a coalition of the most powerful interests on earth. The twenty-nine richest nations had joined forces with the world's biggest multinational companies to write, one of the chief negotiators boasted, 'the constitution of a single global economy'.[1] Proposed and drafted by businessmen, secretly discussed by governments, the Multilateral Agreement on Investment would, had it succeeded, have granted corporations the right to sue any country whose laws restricted their ability to make money. The treaty was, its opponents claimed, a charter for the corporate takeover of the world.

The secret treaty was leaked in 1997. The protesters posted it on the Web and held demonstrations wherever its negotiators met. They exposed a scheme conceived and gestated in the dark to the light of day, whereupon it shrivelled and sickened. In April 1998, the negotiating governments were forced by both internal disputes and public pressure to delay their signing of the agreement for six months, providing the scheme's opponents with more time in which to contest the proposals. By October 1998, when the Multilateral Agreement on Investment was to have been approved at a meeting in Paris, the French government had received the results of a study it had commissioned into the implications of the treaty. The report showed that the agreement threatened the nation's health, safety and environmental laws, and would criminalize the government's attempts to protect the French film industry. The French Prime Minister promptly refused to host the discussions and the treaty collapsed. The governments of the developed nations assured their people that they would attempt no such venture again.

They broke their promise. The European Commission, with the active support of the British government, immediately began to shift the proposals into another forum: the World Trade Organization. Again they were thwarted, once more by a combination of internal disputes and external opposition. In November 1999, protesters blocked the streets of Seattle, where the negotiators were meeting, helping to create political space into which the weaker nations opposing European and American plans could move.

But the governments and corporations which had attempted to broker both the Multilateral Agreement on Investment and a new world trade agreement at Seattle had already begun to implement a fallback plan. A 'Transatlantic Economic Partnership' linking the markets of the European Union and the United States would be the first of several agreements struck between the world's major trading blocs. The blocs would, eventually, be connected and 'harmonized' to establish a single, deregulated global market, in which, opponents feared, the laws protecting

human rights and the environment would be progressively
unpicked.

*

There is, in principle, nothing wrong with a global agreement governing trade. Fair, transparent rules are essential to
prevent rich nations from crushing poor ones: the powerful
have long insisted on freedom for their own traders and
restrictions on the traders from weaker countries. But negotiations on such agreements appear, time and again, to
conform to a certain pattern: they are conducted in private
by committees far removed from democratic scrutiny and
control, providing splendid opportunities for lobbyists to
infiltrate and direct them. Corporations have repeatedly
steered and controlled such negotiations to ensure that they
respond to their needs. On every occasion, the negotiators
insist that they are devising a formula for a fairer world. On
every occasion they emerge with a prescription for corporate
rule.

The General Agreement on Tariffs and Trade was established, like the World Bank and the International Monetary
Fund, with the best of intentions. The world which had just
emerged from the horrors of global warfare would be a fairer
place, in which the strong would have to abide by the same
rules as the weak. But the three institutions, established in
the late 1940s, all succumbed, at length, to the interests of
the strong. Expert panels of the General Agreement on
Tariffs and Trade were stuffed with corporate nominees, key
decisions were taken by trade bureaucrats with startling
conflicts of interest. By the time the agreement was replaced,
in 1995, by the World Trade Organization, it had become
the means by which corporations force governments to open

their borders to the crudest forms of exploitation. By conflating the protection of human beings and the environment with trade protectionism, by setting maximum standards for world trade rather than minimum ones, by overriding any national or international law with which they conflict, trade agreements have become the greatest threats to representative government on earth.

One might have imagined that the governments of rich countries would have resisted these attempts to transfer power away from national parliaments and concentrate it instead in the hands of remote and unaccountable committees of corporate lawyers. Curiously, however, they have found ever more enterprising means of speeding the passage of such agreements, in the face of sustained resistance from their own populations. In a straight fight between the electorate and big business for the affections of government, big business appears to possess all the heavy weapons. This chapter documents its strategies, its failures and its successes. It shows how governments in general, and the British government in particular, have worked on behalf of corporate lobbyists to exclude their people from decision-making.

*

Until the eve of the Multilateral Agreement on Investment's defeat, the British government was promising that the agreement posed no threat to democracy. 'MAI obligations', the government was telling aggrieved constituents in 1997 and 1998, 'will not affect a country's right to maintain its own internal regulations.'[2] This was simply not true.

At first sight, the aims of the Multilateral Agreement on Investment seemed sensible. It would create a predictable, reliable legal framework governing investments made by foreign companies. The countries which signed it would not be allowed arbitrarily to seize the property of a foreign company, or to pass laws whose purpose was to discriminate against certain investors.

Unlike any other international agreement to which the UK is party, however, the MAI would have allowed corporations directly to challenge laws passed by national or local governments, through a special tribunal. If the tribunal decided in favour of the corporation, the offending country would be obliged both to remove the law in question and to compensate the company for any losses it had sustained as a result of that law. When, at length, a draft was leaked, it became clear that the Multilateral Agreement on Investment could allow corporations to remove some of the key regulations intended to protect the workforce, the environment and consumers from some of the ill effects of international trade.[3]

If, for example, a local authority insisted that any company to which it gave a public contract would have to employ a certain percentage of local people, or use local contractors, it would soon have found itself facing a major international lawsuit. Any law which happened to fall more heavily on the foreign suppliers of goods and services could also have been struck down. The British local authorities which banned genetically engineered foods from school meals, for example, could have been sued by biotechnology companies on the basis that as no GM crops are grown commercially in Britain, their ban amounts to unfair discrimination against foreign food producers.

The agreement would have prohibited national or local governments from refusing to deal with companies which, for example, were operating in Burma, or using the labour of political prisoners in China, or destroying endangered forests in Brazil. A country signing the treaty, the draft agreement insisted, 'shall not prohibit outside its territory, directly or indirectly' a company from acting as it wishes in another country, as long as it does not break that country's laws.[4] The international boycott which helped to bring down South Africa's apartheid regime would, under the Multilateral Agreement on Investment, have been illegal.

The MAI's negotiators insisted that though the draft agreement contained clauses which appeared directly to challenge some of the laws protecting both people and places, the environment and workers' rights would be protected by the 'Guidelines for Multinational Enterprises' which the signatory countries would be asked to implement. But these guidelines were first approved by the world's rich countries in 1976. Since that year, corporations have been expected to 'respect the right of their employees to be represented by trade unions' and to introduce 'a system of environmental protection at the level of the enterprise as a whole'.[5] It's not hard to see how effective the guidelines have been. Unlike the MAI, they would remain voluntary.

But perhaps most alarming was the scope of the powers multinational companies would be able to wield over democratically elected governments. They would be allowed to sue them, not only for losses already suffered, but also for the loss of the profits they might have made had the law in question not existed. The draft agreement, remarkably, defined these imaginary profits as the companies' inalienable property.

The right to sue would be confined to 'investors',

which, in practice, means multinational companies. Governments, communities or ordinary citizens would have no new reciprocal rights to hold corporations to account. The draft agreement listed three potential tribunals which could hear the cases corporations brought, none of which was subject to direct democratic scrutiny. One of them was the arbitration panel of the International Chamber of Commerce, an industrial lobby group composed of the chief executives of the world's biggest companies.[6] The tribunals' rulings could be overturned only with the agreement of every national signatory to the MAI. The public would have no right to be heard or even to see the details of the ruling.

The International Chamber of Commerce appears to have had some influence in the drafting and preparation of the Multilateral Agreement on Investment. The draft agreement the chamber drew up in 1996 bears striking similarities to the draft text of the MAI which was leaked a few months later.[7] The idea may have been initiated by another lobby group, called the European Round Table of Industrialists. In its 1991 report, *Reshaping Europe*,[8] it calls for 'a solid framework for foreign direct investment' worldwide. The measures it proposes ('rules ... to allow foreign-owned businesses to establish themselves on the same basis and with the same degree of security as locally-owned companies'; 'the OECD concept of National Treatment'; 'consultation on all the issues that can distort the value of investment, including subsidies and competition policy')[9] accurately prefigure what was to become, six years later, the intended MAI. The OECD, or Organisation for Economic Co-operation and Development, is the body through which the MAI was negotiated.

The charges of undue corporate influence and threats to democracy were, at first, robustly denied by the British government. But by 1998 the treaty's opponents no longer needed to rely on theoretical impacts to support their case. A working model of the Multilateral Agreement on Investment was already proving to be a major hazard to representative politics.

*

The MAI's 'investor protection provisions' were almost identical to those of another international treaty, the North American Free Trade Agreement, implemented in 1994. This was no coincidence: the provisions appear to seek to 'harmonize' regulations in the rest of the world with those of North America. A single global trading regime would have allowed the largest companies to reap economies of scale: they could sell the same product everywhere without having to adapt it. This would present them with a significant advantage over smaller firms, trading locally. Were the Multilateral Agreement on Investment to have been approved, then big business could have been expected to become still bigger, while small business may have been squeezed out of some sectors.

When the North American Free Trade Agreement was negotiated, protesters argued that it would undermine environmental, health, safety and consumer protection rules. North American governments replied, just as the British government would later counter criticism of the MAI, that this was nonsense. The treaty would simply allow foreign companies to compete on equal terms with domestic firms within the North American trading bloc: it would challenge only those laws designed to discriminate against foreign investors. In 1998, a US company became the first to test the free trade agreement.

The Ethyl Corporation makes a chemical called methyl-cyclopentadienyl manganese tricarbonyl, or (and I think we can embrace the abbreviation) MMT. MMT is a fuel additive, which is mixed with petrol in order to prevent engine knocking. Some scientists believe that it is also a dangerous neurotoxin. Manganese entering the body through the lungs has been blamed for nerve damage leading to psychosis, memory loss, and early death.

Until 1997, Canada was the only country on earth in which MMT was bought and sold as a reformulated petrol additive. In the United States the Environmental Protection Agency had banned its use for this purpose. Canadian MPs began to question why their citizens were, uniquely, exposed to this chemical. After a long and intelligent debate, Parliament voted to ban it in April 1997.

Had the vote taken place three years earlier, the Ethyl Corporation would have had to abide by the decision. A sovereign parliament had decided to protect its citizens from a suspected nerve poison, and that would have been the end of the matter. But Ethyl decided to sue the Canadian government for the expropriation of its property (namely its anticipated profits) and the damage to its good reputation caused by the parliamentary debate. It took its case to the officers overseeing the North American Free Trade Agreement. They appointed (just as the MAI's enforcers would have done) a secret tribunal whose records are not disclosed and whose decisions cannot be appealed, to assess the case.

In July 1998, the Canadian government, realizing that its

chances of success were approximately zero, settled with Ethyl. It agreed to allow the corporation to resume its sales of MMT in Canada. It agreed to pay Ethyl US$13m by way of compensation. It agreed, too, to mislead its citizens, by suggesting a scientific consensus which did not exist. Upon settling the suit, it announced that 'MMT poses no health risk'.

It is worth recording that MMT was banned in Canada irrespective of who produced it: the rules were precisely the same for foreign and for domestic investors. This, as campaigners predicted, offered no protection to the sovereignty of the Canadian Parliament.

The Ethyl case was soon followed by others. For example, two days after the Canadian government conceded to Ethyl, another US company, S. D. Myers Inc., filed notice of its intent to sue Canada over its decision to ban the export of waste contaminated with PCBs, which are among the most dangerous and persistent of environmental pollutants. Myers claimed that the Canadian government had imposed the export ban in order that Canadian companies could win the contracts for disposing of the waste. Canada countered that it was simply taking sensible precautions: trucking large volumes of a deadly poison over long distances increased the chances that it could escape into the environment. The US Environmental Protection Agency seemed to agree with the Canadian position: a few months after Canada banned the export of PCBs, the US authorities banned their import. Despite this, NAFTA obliged the Canadian government to lift its ban. Myers was able to sue Canada for the profits it had lost before the US had banned imports of the waste.

It is hard to see what anyone has gained from NAFTA,

except, of course, the region's multinational companies. Before the agreement was signed, the US government promised that it would create 200,000 new American jobs a year. Four years later, government departments conceded that only 1,500 new jobs had been generated by the agreement,[10] while 204,000 had been lost as a direct result of its implementation.[11]

Right-wing US protectionists claim that these jobs have been unfairly transferred by NAFTA to Mexico, where wages are lower, but this is quite untrue. Between 1993, when Mexico signed the agreement, and 1997, unemployment there rose by two million, while wages fell by 29 per cent.[12] The truth is that jobs on both sides of the border simply evaporated. It is not hard to see why.

NAFTA enabled big business to expand the scale of its operations. Companies in Mexico were taken over by US firms, plants were merged and shut down and any workforce which refused to accept the harsher terms the expanding corporations offered was told that they would take their business elsewhere. In Mexico alone, the agreement resulted in the destruction of 28,000 small firms within four years of the treaty's execution.[13]

*

While British voters began to discover what was happening only through the agitation of protesters, the government's Department of Trade and Industry appears to have made little effort to inform other ministers. On 29 April 1998, the government's attempt to negotiate away many of its own powers through the MAI was spectacularly stalled. On 30 April the British Home Secretary, Jack Straw, appeared on the BBC's *Question Time* programme. A member of the audience asked him whether he supported the MAI.

'MAI?' Mr Straw replied. 'I don't know what that is.' 'Multilateral Agreement on Investment,' the questioner explained, 'which vetoes local countries being able to decide what investment goes in their area.' 'When I find out about it,' Mr Straw answered, 'I'll let you know.'

The Department of Trade and Industry's covert diplomacy was assisted by an absence of interest from the official opposition. In contesting the swifter integration of the European Union, the Conservatives have insisted that theirs is the party of national sovereignty. But when the Multilateral Agreement on Investment, which threatened to override many of the sovereign powers of its signatory governments, was debated in the House of Commons in February 1998, the Conservative benches were completely empty.

This is not to suggest, however, that there was no parliamentary opposition to the treaty. It was heavily criticized by Labour and Liberal Democrat backbenchers. The House of Commons Environmental Audit Committee concluded that the proposed MAI was 'a prime example of the failure [to address] the economic, environmental and social impacts of policy'.[14]

*

Only when the French government pulled out at a critical stage of negotiations, in response to public pressure and the results of its own analysis, did the first corporate masterplan for world domination collapse. Governments immediately sought to replace it.

In November 1998, after the MAI had failed, Brian

Wilson, a minister at the Department of Trade and Industry (and the man who denied that Labour had pledged to abolish tolls on the Skye Bridge), promised that the government had learnt valuable lessons from its defeat. 'The MAI negotiations,' he conceded, 'were dogged by the perception that they were secret and unaccountable. I am determined that we should not make this mistake again.'[15] There was no question, he stated, of 'resurrecting the MAI' through the World Trade Organization.[16] Just nineteen days after he made that second statement, and twelve days after the MAI was officially abandoned, the promise was comprehensively broken.

On 15 December 1998, a confidential document was presented by the European Commission for discussion by the Council of Ministers' committee on external trade.[17] The paper proposed that the main elements of the failed Multilateral Agreement on Investment be shifted onto the agenda for talks at the World Trade Organization (WTO). New WTO rules, the Commission's proposal suggested, should allow corporations 'to enforce their rights in specific cases where they want to make a claim against the host country, typically for damages arising from a specific government action or decision'.[18] In other words, just as the Multilateral Agreement on Investment had proposed, companies would be able to sue a government if they didn't like what it was doing.

Rather than trying to implement this policy immediately, the Commission would proceed with stealth. 'Some, if not all, of these issues will be controversial,' the leaked document observed. 'Thus, the "ideal" result sketched out above may well not be the final deal. But even if a perfect result is not achieved in a first agreement, the main point is to get investment rules firmly implanted in the WTO. Further improvements of these rules ... can be part of future agendas, once we have the basis from which to work.'[19]

The paper made no attempt to disguise the origins of these proposals. 'The European Business community,' it reported, 'has made clear its position in favour of multilateral rules on investment both through its representative bodies (UNICE, ERT) and through informal direct contacts with investment decision-makers.'[20] UNICE is the Union of Industrial and Employers' Confederations of Europe (not a trades union, but a business lobby group). ERT is the European Round Table of Industrialists.

This document was never published, but a few weeks after it was circulated within the Commission, another paper bearing the same title and the same code was released to the public and the European Parliament. The two papers differed only in that the controversial sections of the original report had been cut from the public document. References to UNICE and the ERT, as well as the plans to allow corporations to sue governments, had been removed. When the Commission was challenged to explain the discrepancies, it insisted that the report had been updated. This explanation failed to inspire confidence, not least because the public document was listed A, B, C, D, G: the most revealing chapters had simply been excised.

Of all the nations and trade blocs arriving in Seattle in November 1999 to negotiate a new World Trade Agreement, the European Union was proposing the most extensive treaty. Within the European Union, one nation was pushing harder than any other: the United Kingdom.

*

The World Trade Organization's rules were, its critics maintained, already among the foremost threats to equitable development, human rights and the environment. United Nations figures show that the previous round of world trade talks, completed in 1993, had cut the export earnings of the poorest countries by up to $265m.[21] It had also failed to address some of the ancient injustices levied against the poor. Europe, for example, continued to levy devastating tariffs against cotton goods from India. Rich countries were still destroying the livelihoods of farmers in the Third World by dumping subsidized grain onto their markets. Multinational companies had used the last round of negotiations to lay claim to the exclusive ownership of plant varieties: this, the Organization of African Unity and several Asian countries have argued, facilitates the theft of national resources and poses a serious threat to food security.

In 1998, the state of Massachusetts was forced to drop its boycott of companies trading with the murderous military regime in Burma. The decision was made by a US federal judge, but he cited an appeal to the World Trade Organization by the European Union, which argued that the sanctions were an unfair barrier to trade.[22] The state's lawyers suggested that if current world trade rules had been in force during the 1980s, Nelson Mandela would still be in prison.

In 1997, the European Union, following powerful corporate lobbying, dropped its proposed bans on cosmetics which had been tested on animals and on fur from animals caught in leghold traps, for fear that the legislation would conflict with WTO rules. The same statutes will prevent Europe from banning imports of eggs from battery chickens, allowing US producers to undercut European farmers when battery cages are proscribed. The European Union has had to suspend its ban on noisy and polluting aircraft, and may have to drop its plans to make electronics manufacturers responsible for recycling their products. In 1997, France banned the sale of asbestos. In 1999, Canada, which mines the mineral, appealed to the WTO. World trade rules could, in principle, be used to dismantle the Montreal Protocol protecting the ozone layer, the Basel Convention on the shipment of hazardous wastes, and the Convention on International Trade in Endangered Species.

In May 1999, the United States sought to oblige Europeans to eat beef contaminated with six injected hormones, one of which has been identified as a potent cause of cancer in children. Europe refused, so the WTO allowed the US to levy $117m worth of sanctions every year. Despite the concessions it has already extracted from the European Union (see Chapters 7 and 8), the United States has threatened to use world trade rules to forbid European nations from labelling any food as containing genetically engineered ingredients.

These decisions and positions are, in practice, impossible for citizens or voluntary organizations to challenge. The World Trade Organization's meetings are strictly private. The cases brought to the organization are resolved at undisclosed times and secret locations. Its decisions are binding and unappealable outside the organization. Most of the judges are corporate lawyers. There are no rules on conflict of interest.

The new world trade talks, which should have begun in the American city of Seattle in November 1999, could have been an excellent opportunity to redress some of these problems and distortions. As the negotiating positions of the world's powerful nations emerged, however, it became clear that this was not their primary concern.

*

In preparing her government's position for the talks in Seattle, Charlene Barchefsky, the US trade representative, took advice from an American lobby group called the Coalition of Service Industries. The coalition told her it wanted 'the opportunity for US business to expand into foreign health care markets'.[23] As 'health care services in many foreign countries have largely been the responsibility of the public sector', it was 'difficult for US private sector health care providers to market in foreign countries'.[24] Barchefsky took up their call: one of her aims at Seattle would be 'encouraging more privatization'.[25]

The World Trade Organization appeared to be receptive to this approach. Where private as well as public health care is available in the same country, it maintained, 'It seems unrealistic in such cases to argue ... that no competitive relationship exists between the two groups of suppliers'. Member governments, it suggested, should 'reconsider the breadth and depth of their commitments on health and social services'.[26] The European Union, backed by Britain, had already approved the means by which the World Trade Organization could be used to enforce privatization. 'Horizontal negotiations', it had agreed, would be used to ensure that a liberalization approach pioneered in one service sector, such as telecoms, could be applied automatically to any other, such as health.[27] Britain, in other words, was helping to prepare a new trade agreement which could force the eventual privatization of the NHS.

Indeed, though few British people knew it, the government was hoping to use the WTO to deregulate the services provided by several commercial sectors. A consultation document prepared by the Department of Trade and Industry identified both restrictions on the foreign ownership of the media and planning laws as potentially unfair restraints on trade.[28] Countries hoping to join the World Trade Organization, it suggested, should be required to 'liberalise' their education services, to allow foreign companies to buy their way in. Some consumer protection regulation 'is more onerous than it needs to be. Business has already begun to indicate a need to re-examine national regulation to ensure that the regulatory environment is the minimum necessary'. Environmental regulations, it complained, 'can cause an excessive increase in the cost' of supplying services 'and become in themselves barriers to trade'.[29]

Among the priorities for the new trade talks, Stephen Byers, the Secretary of State for Trade and Industry, announced, was 'reducing the burden on business and barriers to trade represented by industrial standards and technical regulations'.[30] A public information document produced by his department celebrated the World Trade Organization's assault on the US Clean Air Act (the United States was forced to reduce its pollution standards in order to allow dirty fuels from Brazil and Venezuela to enter the American market) as 'a considerable achievement'.[31] Another paper published by the Department of Trade and Industry suggested that companies should face only 'voluntary codes' for protecting the environment, and then only when it suits 'their own business reasons'.[32] When the European Union defied the WTO by banning imports of hormone-contaminated beef from the United States, only

319

one country tried to undermine the common position: the United Kingdom.

The British government presented the liberalization of trade in all sectors and the removal of the regulations which might slow it or modify it as not only necessary but also inevitable. 'Resistance,' Tony Blair warned, 'is easy to demand, but won't work.'[33] He was wrong. The demonstrations in Seattle, during which tens of thousands of people from all over the world campaigned against the threats the new talks presented to the environment and democracy, helped to create opportunities for developing countries to contest the proposals put forward by the First World. The protests exposed some of the differences between the European Union and the United States, forced governments to explain their policies to their people and, in doing so, to change them. The talks collapsed. This was, however, by no means the end of such designs.

*

The lobby groups promoting the interests of big business had already discovered that they did not need the World Trade Organization to force open markets and bring down regulatory standards. They could achieve these objectives by attacking regulations within existing trade blocs, expanding those blocs and then connecting them to others, with the final objective of forging a single global market. They had been working towards this end in Europe for years.

The European Round Table of Industrialists, or ERT, is an association of the chief executives of forty-six of the biggest companies in Europe. According to Pehr Gyllenhammar, the Chief Executive of Volvo and the ERT's first Chairman, it was founded, in 1983, because 'Europe is really doing nothing. It's time for the business leaders to enter this vacuum and seize the initiative.'[34]

In April 1983, 'with the active support of Etienne Davignon and François-Xavier Ortoli, then Members of the European Commission',[35] Gyllenhammar assembled the Chief Executives of ICI, Unilever, Nestlé, Philips, Fiat and ten other major corporations. Their purpose was to link the European Community's economics, so that their companies could reach 'the scale necessary to resist pressure from non-European competitors'.[36] If regulations in Western Europe were harmonized to create a single market, big companies could become bigger, as they could produce the same product by the same means throughout the community. In January 1985, one of the ERT's members, Wisse Dekker, the Chief Executive of Philips, presented a paper to the European Commission containing detailed plans for the establishment of a single European market.[37]

As the researcher Maria Green Cowles has documented, the ERT worked closely with the President of the European Commission, Jacques Delors, to turn these plans into reality by 1992.[38] Dekker and other Round Table executives began threatening national governments that if they did not lend their approval to the integration scheme, big business would move its operations elsewhere, making much of the European workforce redundant. The European Council swiftly complied, by commissioning, in March 1985, Lord Cockfield to produce the White Paper which would soon become the basis for the Single European Act.[39] The European Round Table became the Act's enforcer, lobbying and pressurizing governments and working closely with the commission to speed up its implementation. 'The ERT,' the Round Table recorded, 'felt it was necessary to keep a watch on the established timetable ... Every six months, ERT Members met the leading officials in the country holding the EU presidency to encourage action on the 1992 programme.'[40] The ERT, Jacques Delors later noted, was 'one of the main driving forces behind the Single Market'.[41]

European Monetary Union was advanced by means of a similar strategy. The European Round Table of Industrialists, working with the German Chancellor and the French President, established, in 1987, a subsidiary called the Association for the Monetary Union of Europe. It was chaired by Wisse Dekker of Philips, who was, by then, also the Chairman of the ERT. Working within the commission, which provided it with financial support, and in close liaison with the French and German governments, the association proposed some of the key EMU initiatives. One of its roles, it told its members, was 'protecting major companies from any suspicion about special advantages that they could gain from EMU at the expense of the public or of small businesses'.[42]

Having unified the European market, big business would need the means of shifting its goods around the trade zone cheaply and swiftly. It required, in other words, a massive, publicly funded network of transport corridors to link the far-flung provinces of its new empire. In 1984, Pehr Gyllenhammar published a paper called *Missing Links*, which demanded a tunnel under the English Channel, a roadbridge connecting Germany to Scandinavia, a European high-speed train system and a new, Europe-wide roadbuilding programme.[43] Though all his schemes aroused sustained local and national opposition, as people contested the destruction of homes and wild places, he got everything he asked for. The obligation to keep developing the ERT's 'Trans-European Networks' was written into the Maastricht Treaty.

But the European Round Table of Industrialists also wanted to change the very nature of government. 'Too many job opportunities in Europe's network of businesses,' the ERT complained, 'are lost because of obstacles set up by European traditions and over-prescriptive legislative systems.'[44] Europe requires, it insisted, 'a minimal regulatory system with the maximum of flexibility'.[45] 'Government and business need to share information, goals and cultures, and to pull together as a team.'[46]

Here too, the Round Table appears to have encountered some success. 'The ERT', its Web site boasts, 'has contacts with the Commission, the Council of Ministers and the European Parliament. Every six months the ERT meets with the government that holds the EU presidency to discuss priorities. At national level, each Member has personal contacts with his own national government and parliament.'[47] Interviewed in 1993, the Secretary-General of the ERT, Keith Richardson, boasted that 'Access means being able to phone Helmut Kohl and recommend that he read a report ... Access also means John Major phoning ... to thank the ERT for its viewpoints, or having lunch with the Swedish Prime Minister just prior to the Swedish decision to apply for EC membership.'[48]

In 1994, the ERT told the commission that it should 'establish a European Competitiveness Advisory Group ... as a method for maintaining a continuing dialogue between industry and government'. It 'should have no more than twelve members and include industrialists, academics and trade union representatives'.[49] Two weeks later, the European Council instructed the president of the commission to set up a Competitiveness Advisory Group. It had thirteen members, and included industrialists, academics and trade union representatives. Three of them were also members of the ERT, several of the others were corporate chief executives. The unionists, Keith Richardson later explained, were there to give the 'CAG reports . . . extra weight'.[50] The group immediately began to produce documents shadowing ERT policies, calling, for example, for more funding for Trans-European Road Networks, 'faster privatization and liberalisation' and greater flexibility in working hours and wages.[51]

The Round Table has singled out the British government for special commendation, as it has been implementing the ERT's recommendations further and faster than any other European state.[52] The Round Table was, it records, especially pleased with the Labour government's support for the Single Market Action Plan, which the ERT had helped to engineer and guide, and its enthusiasm for European enlargement. Until July 1999, the British minister responsible for implementing these policies was Lord Simon. Before he became a minister, Lord Simon was Vice-Chairman of the European Round Table of Industrialists.

*

Slowly, the ERT's plans are falling into place. They began with a demand for the closer integration of the existing members of the European Union. This was soon followed by lobbying to increase the size of the union. European enlargement, the ERT argued, provided an opportunity to solve several of the 'problems' it perceived in central and eastern Europe.[53] It would force new members to reduce their taxes, remove the 'restrictions on the purchasing of land by foreign companies' and combat the 'dominance of national players' (local companies) in those countries.[54] To prepare themselves for entry, central and eastern European nations must 'ensure that programmes to privatize and liberalise local infrastructure continue without delay'.[55]

The ERT mapped out the sequence of steps the European Union should follow in bringing new members into the fold. At the European Summit in Helsinki in December 1999, which took place just six days after the collapse of the World Trade Organization talks, the heads of government announced the next phase of enlargement. Their schedule mirrored the recommendations mapped out by the ERT.

But this was merely the latest in a series of steps towards a far grander plan to enable big business to get bigger. In May 1997, just three weeks after taking office, Tony Blair approved a project hatched years before by the European Trade Commissioner Sir Leon Brittan and a number of corporate lobby groups. The United States and the European Union, he agreed, would start to establish a single, transatlantic market. Any product or practice approved in one place would become acceptable in both. The lowest standards in either trading bloc, in other words, would be applied universally. If, for example, the US government decided that injecting cattle with growth hormones is safe, Europe would have to adopt that as its regulatory standard. This meant that European people would have to accept American laws, even though they could not exercise influence over the legislators who passed them. The French government later objected in the strongest terms, describing the proposal as 'indecent' and 'absurd'.[56] The plan was dropped.

But one year after the first attempt, at the next EU–US summit, in May 1998, an almost identical scheme, though slower and subtler than the first one, was approved by Bill Clinton, Jacques Santer and, as President of the European

Council, Tony Blair. The Transatlantic Economic Partnership would, like the plan it replaced, work towards the 'mutual recognition and approval' of regulations throughout the trade zone. Its architects have clearly learnt from the failure of the first plan and the overwhelmingly hostile reaction to the Multilateral Agreement on Investment. Instead of attempting to introduce these seismic changes all at once, they are harmonizing the rules one by one, with no fixed timetable and no publicity. Quiet as the process is, however, its consequences could scarcely be more momentous. As the research organization Corporate Europe Observatory has documented, slowly, imperceptibly, the regulations protecting human health, human rights and the environment are being contested and, where possible, dismantled on both sides of the Atlantic.

It should not be entirely surprising to learn that among the early targets of the Transatlantic Economic Partnership are European laws restricting the use of biotechnology. In July 1998, David Aaron, the US Under-Secretary of Trade, told Congress that 'the EU approval process for the products of biotechnology is ... overly political.' His complaint, he announced, would 'be taken up in the Biotech Group of the Transatlantic Economic Partnership.'[57] The partnership would be used, the US Agricultural Attaché in Brussels announced, to force Europe to import the maize varieties it had thus far failed to approve.[58] Other targets included the European Union's data protection laws: the United States would seek to pull them down in favour of its own weaker rules.[59] The US Grocery Manufacturers' Association would seek to use the Transatlantic Economic Partnership, its spokeswoman told the July 1998 US Congressional hearing, to attack the European Union's 'very restrictive' food additive laws, its eco-labelling schemes and its recycling programmes.[60]

*

These plans, for a single market incorporating Europe and North America, are often attributed to the former European Trade Commissioner Sir Leon Brittan, now Lord Brittan of Spennithorne. Brittan and the commission played important parts, but the drama was written and directed by another body, a gathering of around a hundred chief executives from Europe and the United States called the Transatlantic Business Dialogue.

The Business Dialogue, whose members run such companies as Philips, ICI, Unilever, Siemens, Boeing, Ford, Procter and Gamble and TimeWarner, was established in 1995 on the advice of both the European Commission and the US Department of Commerce. Its purpose, according to the US Under-Secretary of Commerce, was 'to identify those barriers to trade or opportunities for liberalization on which both business communities [the US and the EU] could agree as targets for government action. We should put the business "horse" before the government "cart".'[61]

This is certainly how the power in this relationship appears to be disposed. The role of business, the Transatlantic Business Dialogue's European Chair explained in March 1999, is 'to formulate proposals, then submit them to governments for implementation'.[62] The TABD will, it announced, 'insist on implementation of all deliverables and expect satisfactory and positive answers from Administrations'.[63] To this end, it has set deadlines for government action.

Though the Transatlantic Business Dialogue has no

official status and is not mentioned in any of the European treaties, governments and the European Commission appear to consider themselves obliged to defer to it. An internal Commission working document reveals that 'Follow-up to the TABD recommendations is a high priority task. Vice-president Sir Leon Brittan and Commissioner Dr. Bangemann have therefore decided to personally oversee the process and will be in direct regular contact with the TABD co-chairmen on this matter.'[64] In a letter dated 8 March 1999, Brittan promised the TABD co-chairman Jérôme Monod his 'full personal support for the TABD process as well as on the continuing co-operation of my officials. Clearly the value of TABD lies to a great extent in successful implementation of the decisions you take, although of course not all decisions can be immediately given effect.'[65] The US Commerce Secretary William Daley recorded that: 'The TABD said it [trade liberalization] was important; we heard them and acted.'[66]

The Transatlantic Business Dialogue has demanded that governments in Europe or the United States should subject any law they might propose to a 'trade impact statement' to assess whether it will help or hinder the aims of multinational companies.[67] It fought Europe's plans to phase out some of the chemicals which damage the ozone layer.[68] It was partly responsible for the European Union's suspension of a proposed ban on the use of animals for testing cosmetics. It foresees, according to its former co-chairman, 'a new commercial century', in which market forces 'will overwhelm the ability of our social, political, and economic institutions to cope with them'. The TABD, he announced, was 'building the institutions to handle this change'.[69]

In 1999, the European commissioners for trade and

enterprise, the US Commerce Secretary and the Director General of the World Trade Organization attended the Transatlantic Business Dialogue's annual conference. They were briefed on the line they should take at the world trade talks in Seattle. The governments and officials did precisely as they were asked. 'It is difficult,' the US Under-Secretary of Commerce commented, 'to overstate the effect the TABD has had on trade liberalisation ... in fact virtually every market-opening move undertaken by the United States and the EU in the last couple of years has been suggested by the TABD.'[70]

*

The masterplan is now falling into place. The Transatlantic Business Dialogue will, it asserts, 'develop a worldwide network of bilateral agreements with identical conformity procedures'.[71] The Transatlantic Economic Partnership, in other words, is just the first of such schemes. A greatly expanded Europe will form part of a single trading bloc with the US, Canada and Mexico, whose markets have already been integrated by means of the North American Free Trade Agreement. NAFTA will grow, the US government hopes, to engulf all the Americas and the Caribbean. The US senate has already passed a bill, misleadingly entitled the Africa Growth and Opportunity Act, forcing African countries to accept NAFTA terms, on pain of losing all aid, investment and terms of trade. Russia and most of Asia are being dragged into line by the International Monetary Fund. By means of an audacious coup executed by the International Chamber of Commerce, even the United Nations appears to have been coopted into helping implement this scheme.[72]

Before long, in other words, only a minority of nations

will lie outside a single, legally harmonized global market, and they will swiftly find themselves obliged to join. By the time a new world trade agreement has been negotiated, it will be irrelevant, for the WTO's job will already have been done. Nowhere on earth will robust laws protecting the environment or human rights be allowed to survive. Elected representatives will, if these plans for a new world order succeed, be reduced to the agents of a global government: built, coordinated and run by corporate chief executives.

CHAPTER ELEVEN

A Troublemakers' Charter

If I had sought to be comprehensive, this book would have been very long and even more boring. I have been able to examine only a few of the areas of public life into which corporations have intruded, and I'm sorry to find that I have neither the time nor the space to handle many others. But, before concluding, I would like to mention a few of those I have been unable to cover in depth.

The most important of my omissions, I feel, is the corporate takeover of schools. According to the European Round Table of Industrialists, 'The provision of education is a market opportunity and should be treated as such.'[1] The British government seems to agree.

Most of the ideas now being tested in the United Kingdom were first developed in the United States. Schooling there is a commodity, widely traded on the stock market, and worth around $650bn. There are many ways of making money from education, but the most widespread is the use of school as an advertising medium. It is a lucrative business. Children are easily swayed by advertising, and in school they are, of course, a captive market. 'The kids we're reaching,' one marketing executive has observed, 'are consumers in training.'[2]

While playgrounds, gyms, corridors and even exercise book covers are used as billboards, the principal means by which most advertisers reach children in American schools is through sponsoring teaching packs and television programmes. Schools, especially the poorer ones, take them, as they are often desperately short of resources. But, while nominally free, many carry hidden costs.

The US Consumers' Union studied sponsored teaching packs distributed to schools by some of America's biggest corporations.[3] Nearly 80 per cent of the packs, it found, 'contained biased or incomplete information, promoting a viewpoint that favors consumption of the sponsor's product or service'. A pack produced by Procter and Gamble, for example, suggested that the clear-cut felling of forests 'mimics nature's way of getting rid of trees'.[4] Disposable nappies, whose manufacture consumes large quantities of wood pulp and which pose major waste-disposal problems, were, it claimed, more environmentally friendly than cloth nappies. The company forgot to add that it is one of the world's biggest manufacturers of disposable nappies. An education pack produced by the American Coal Foundation maintained that 'the earth could benefit rather than be harmed from increased carbon dioxide'.[5] The 'Kids Get Going With Breakfast' teaching pack, sponsored by Kelloggs, teaches children to beware of foods with high fat contents, but omits to warn them to look out for sugar and salt.[6] The 'Critical Thinking About Critical Issues: Freedom of the Press' pack, produced by Mobil Corporation, 'confuses freedom of the Press', the Consumers' Association notes, 'with free enter prise, suggesting that the First Amendment guarantees free-market capitalism'.[7]

Forty per cent of American secondary schools, generally the poorest, have signed deals with a broadcasting company called Channel One Communications. Channel One gives televisions, video recorders and satellite dishes to schools, in exchange for a guarantee that its programmes will be shown to 80 per cent of the pupils nearly every day. It broadcasts a twelve-minute news programme, containing two minutes of advertisements. Advertisers pay up to $200,000 for a thirty-second commercial. It is a good investment, for unlike the ads on their televisions at home, these ones have to be watched. The advertisements promote sweets and fatty foods, clothes, music and trainers. They undermine, some teachers complain, their efforts to encourage children to eat healthily, and subject the poorer pupils to commercial pressures to which they cannot respond. Children in schools with Channel One, American researchers found, were more likely to accept the propositions 'I want what I see advertised', 'designer labels make a difference' and 'a nice car is more important than school'.[8]

British children have been inoculated with similar ideas. Here too teaching packs have been distributed whose educational value is open to question. A contribution from Cadbury's, for example, explained to children, 'Chocolate is a wholesome food that tastes really good. It is fun to eat at any time of the day and gives you energy and important nutrients that your body needs to work properly.'[9] British Nuclear Fuels explained the mishaps in the nuclear industry with the information 'Accidents happen all the time. Can you think of some accidents that have happened in school, at home, or locally?'[10] When WHSmith gave £1m worth of promotional materials to schools, David Blunkett, the Secretary of State for Education, publicly thanked them, earning the lucky company a three-minute feature on the BBC's *Nine O'Clock News*. This is worth, I am told, the equivalent of well over £1m spent on advertising.

McDonald's has produced packs which ask children to find the names of the company's products in a word puzzle, to choose matching images of its french fries and milk shakes, and to compose a song entitled 'Old McDonald had a Store'.[11] A leaked copy of the company's *Operations Manual* reveals that 'Schools offer excellent opportunities. Not only are they a high traffic [sales] generator, but students are some of the best customers you could have.'[12] In 1998, billboards appeared in British schools for the first time, accompanied by financial contributions from a company called Imagination for School Media Marketing. The costs of providing free e-mail accounts for all schoolchildren, generously supplied by the Internet company Excite Inc, will be recouped through on-screen advertising.

But since the mid-1990s, companies have been lobbying for still greater access. According to the European Round Table of Industrialists, 'All too often the education process itself is entrusted to people who appear to have no dialogue with, nor understanding of, industry and the path of progress . . . A profound reform of education systems in Europe is needed.'[13] The round table suggested that 'partnerships should be formed between schools and local business'.[14] The British government has supplied precisely what it requested. In 1998 it launched what it called a 'partnership between businesses, parents, schools and LEAs [Local Education Authorities]'.[15]

Britain's Education Action Zones (EAZs) are clusters of schools whose standards are lower than they should be, which apply to the government for special treatment. If selected, their management is handed over to an 'action forum', on which all the 'partners' are represented. EAZs are not allowed to form unless businesses are involved. The corporations give the schools extra money or payments in kind, which are supplemented by matching funds from the government. They also help to run the zone. Education Action Zones, the government announced in 1998, 'are the test bed for the education system of the twenty-first century'.[16]

The money, for schools which are chronically under-resourced, is welcome, but many parents and teachers fear that its receipt is accompanied by a new set of problems. Among the action zone partners are a number of Britain's most controversial companies.

The London Borough of Lambeth's Education Action Zone is run not by the local authority but by the oil company Shell, which has been fiercely criticized by human rights and environment campaigners. The EAZ in Wythenshawe, Manchester, is run by Manchester Airport, which encountered furious local and national resistance when it built a second runway through one of the region's most striking landscapes. The weapons manufacturer British Aerospace helps to run zones in Hull, Plymouth and Teesside; Tesco is guiding the development of schoolchildren in Herefordshire; and ICI, a company with one of Britain's most egregious pollution records, is helping to shape young minds in Blackburn. Cadbury Schweppes, which has, as detailed above, circulated partisan educational materials in Britain, sits on an action forum in Birmingham, while

Kellogg's, which has attracted similar opprobrium in the United States, helps to run education in Salford and Trafford. McDonald's is managing schools in Dudley, Teesside and North Somerset.

In return for their financial contributions, the munificent companies can reap both public relations benefits – as their good works become known to parents and teachers – and potential recruits, as they can guide educational policies better to meet their employment needs. This role has been made explicit in some zones. Lambeth's EAZ, for example, aims to 'increase understanding and experience of employer culture'.[17] Some parents fear that one result will be that children come to identify with these companies, accepting that they are upright and ethical, whatever the firms' records and intentions may be.

Some of the corporations involved in EAZs are hoping for still closer unions with schools. In the United States, over 1,000 state schools have already been contracted out to private companies. The consequences for education have been, in some cases, disastrous, as the needs of shareholders conflict with those of the children. The two companies which appear to be represented on more EAZs in Britain than any others are British Telecom, which is hoping to expand its involvement in information technology for schools, and a firm called Nord Anglia, whose core business is 'education management'.

Education management in Britain looks as if it is about to become big business. In February 1999, King's Manor School in Guildford, Surrey, became the first state school in Britain whose administration was handed over to a private company. One month later, the government announced that it would contract out educational services to private companies in Hackney, east London. In November 1999, the Department for Education and Employment named a consultancy company as its 'preferred bidder' to run the schools in the London Borough of Islington. Nord Anglia predicts that 200 state schools will be wholly managed by private companies in Britain within five years.[18] While the companies involved so far have good track records, there are inherent conflicts between corporate needs and educational needs. Not the least of these is that the companies running schools will come under pressure from their shareholders to select out pupils who do badly, in order to raise their ratings and win more contracts.

*

School is not the only means of reaching our 'consumers in training'. In Britain the advertising industry, another sector whose activities I would like to have covered in more detail, is powerful and poorly regulated. British children, as a result, are exposed to more advertisements than any others in the EU. While Sweden, Norway, Belgium and Austria all ban direct advertising to children on television, children's TV in Britain shows an average of seventeen advertisements per hour. British advertisers now spend over £150m on selling toys and games, six times more (in absolute terms) than they spent in 1992.[19] Soft drinks, confectionery and fast food command still greater sums. McDonald's alone spent £22m on TV advertising in 1997.[20] When it tried to sue two campaigners for libel, the judge ruled that the campaigners' claim that the company's activities 'exploit children by using them, as more susceptible subjects of advertising, to pressurise their parents into going to McDonald's' was 'justified' and 'true'.[21] Several agencies, including some of the biggest, such as Saatchi and Saatchi and McCann-Erickson, have opened special children's divisions. Stephen Colegrave of Saatchi and Saatchi has explained the logic of targeting children. 'Children are much easier to reach with advertising. They pick up on it fast and quite often we can exploit that relationship and get them pestering their parents.'[22]

The Independent Television Commission's code on advertising to children could scarcely be clearer. 'No method of advertising', it insists, 'may be employed which takes advantage of the natural credulity and sense of loyalty of children.' 'Advertisements must not exhort children to purchase' or 'ask their parents or others to make enquiries or purchases'. 'No advertisement may lead children to believe that if they do not have or use the product or service advertised they will be inferior ... or liable to contempt or ridicule.' The rules, in other words, are a precise description of the scope and purpose of children's advertising. It is hard to see how any current advert aimed at children would slip through the net, were the regulations applied. But both the Independent Television Commission and the Advertising Standards Authority are weakly constituted and reluctant to use their limited powers. Both authorities, for example, ban the encouragement of 'pester power', but, according to *Marketing Week* magazine, this bane of all parents – much of it driven by advertising – was worth £8.4bn a year in the UK in 1998.[23]

This could be one of the reasons why spending on children's toys and clothes has trebled, in real terms, in thirty years. Poorer families complain that the bombardment of messages is impossible to resist. One mother interviewed by Friends of the Earth in 1998 reported, 'You can't keep up with what they want. It's one toy after another, they play with them for a week, a month and they're rubbish, they want another toy. Adverts make them think they can have everything they want.'[24] Another observed, 'He just wants everything. I can't explain that I can't afford it. I have to buy what he wants.'[25] Advertising executives are unsympathetic. 'If parents have become so wimpish that they can't stand up to their children and are putting the blame on advertising, that's a sorry state of affairs,' according to the Director-General of the Incorporated Society of British Advertisers, John Hooper.[26] Standing up to your children might be easy when you have a salary like Mr Hooper's and can buy them most of what they want. It is surely far harder when you are struggling to make ends meet and your children are made to feel like second-class citizens because they arrive at school without the latest sportswear.

When Sweden assumes the European presidency in 2001, it will attempt to relieve these inordinate pressures, by introducing new restrictions on children's advertising throughout the European Union. British advertising agencies have been mobilizing to stop them. They are also attempting to overturn the ban on advertising toys on Greek TV and the French ban on advertising alcohol.[27]

Sanctions against advertisers who break codes of practice in Britain are ineffective. The Advertising Standards Authority (ASA) has no statutory powers. It can report persistent offenders to the Office of Fair Trading, but it is reluctant to use this deterrent. It usually requests that the offending company withdraw an advertisement it finds to be misleading or untrue.[28] As the ASA works slowly, this is often easy for companies to do: the rulings are frequently made long after the advert has ceased to be published. Were the ASA permitted to fine companies, or force them to publish retractions at their own expense, it might command some respect among advertisers, but in the absence of effective sanctions, many firms produce deliberately offensive or mis-leading campaigns in order to provoke controversy. There is also concern that the Advertising Standards Authority, which is funded by the advertising industry, has come to identify itself with its paymasters. When the Consumers' Association challenged its effectiveness, Caroline Crawford, the ASA's Director of Communications, claimed: 'Advertising causes very few problems for consumers and the industry is per-forming extremely well.'[29] The government has made it clear that it has no intention of doing anything about this. Self-regulation, it believes, is working.

But while encouraging people to buy is easy for British corporations, whether or not their advertisements are accu-rate, using advertisements to encourage people not to buy is next to impossible. The regulation of advertising in Britain ensures that we are allowed to hear only what is good about a product or activity, and expressly forbidden to hear what is bad.

Broadcast promotions are governed by the Independent Television Commission's code, which insists that 'no adver-tisement may show partiality as respects matters of political or industrial controversy or relating to current public pol-icy'.[30] This regulation does not appear to apply to corporate campaigns presenting partial accounts of controversial busi-ness activities, such as those commissioned by the nuclear and oil industries. It does, however, apply to pressure groups.

In 1999, the campaigning organization People for the Ethical Treatment of Animals commissioned an advert to be broadcast on Sky Sport during National Fishing Week, in which it was to relay the shocking intelligence that fish feel pain when they are hooked. The advertisement was banned by the ITC, on the basis that it was 'political'. Interestingly, a few months before, the National Society for the Prevention of Cruelty to Children had run a campaign on national television campaigning against child abuse. This was judged to be non-political. One thing distinguishes the politics of the two campaigns. No one sells child-abusing kits, or organizes a National Child Catching Week. The NSPCC ad, in other words, offends no legitimate vested interests.

Most pressure groups no longer bother to try to advertise, after a series of rulings in the mid-1990s. In 1994, the Radio Authority blocked a radio recruitment campaign by Amnesty International, on the basis that Amnesty is a political organization. In 1995, the Advertising Standards Authority told Friends of the Earth to withdraw a cinema ad warning that mahogany logging destroys rainforests, on the grounds that 'expert opinion . . . is divided' (experts funded by the industry deny that there's a problem).[31] In 1997, Christian Aid's television advert calling for an end to Third World debt was stopped because the organization's 'objects are . . . of a political nature'.[32]

The Independent Television Commission's prohibition, its guidelines continue, 'precludes . . . campaigning for the purposes of influencing legislation'.[33] What this appears to mean is campaigning for the purposes of changing legislation. Advertisements whose aim is to create the impression that all is well with an industry are an essential component of the lobbying process against, for example, a reduction in public funds for nuclear power, or the tougher regulation of oil production. If the influence you seek to exert is to prevent political change, your advert is acceptable. 'Political', the rulings of the regulatory authorities appear to suggest, means offensive to the status quo.

The ITC itself is not without affiliations. Its Chairman, Sir Robin Biggam, is also a non-executive director of British Aerospace, which sells anti-personnel weapons to Turkey. Some of them have been used to attack Kurdish separatists. In 1999, the ITC revoked the broadcasting licence of Med TV, the Kurdish satellite station based in Britain, after Turkish government complaints that it provided a forum for Kurdish separatists.

*

The Labour government has sustained the central project bequeathed by its predecessor, namely to 'repeal daily any wholesome act established against the rich, and provide more piercing statutes daily, to chain up and restrain the poor'.[34] For the past fifteen years, people seeking to challenge corporate power have been increasingly regulated. The 1986 Public Order Act restricted the right to demonstrate. The 1992 Trade Union Act criminalized many previously legal union activities, among them such grave threats to public order as carrying insulting banners. The 1994 Criminal Justice Act empowered the police to break up most public protests. The 1996 Security Service Act and 1997 Police Act included in their definition of serious crime 'conduct by a large number of persons in pursuit of a common purpose': peaceful protesters were thus exposed to state-endorsed bugging, burglary and arbitrary searches. MPs warned the government that the 1997 anti-stalking act could be used against non-violent demonstrators. The warnings were ignored, with the result that several campaigners have been served with injunctions or arrested for protests outside company premises.

The Terrorism Bill, debated in Parliament in 2000, expands the definition of terrorism to include 'the use or threat, for the purpose of advancing a political, religious or ideological cause, of action which ... involves serious violence against any person or property'. Anyone found in possession of 'information' which might indicate a 'reasonable suspicion' that it could be used for such purposes is identified by the bill as a terrorist. This definition would reclassify, for example, both the activists tearing up genetically engineered crops and the sympathizers receiving their literature. As the MP Alan Simpson has pointed out, were the new law applied even-handedly, dozens of Members of Parliament would have to be jailed as terrorists.

Business, on the other hand, has been released from many of its obligations. When Labour came to power, David Clark, the Chancellor of the Duchy of Lancaster, indicated that he would drop the Conservative policy of removing as many restrictions on business as possible. He replaced the Conservative government's Deregulation Unit with a Better Regulation Unit. 'A fair, safe and prosperous society,' he explained, 'depends on good regulation. People look to the government to ensure benefits such as fair terms of employment, a cleaner environment and safer products. In many cases statutory regulations are the only or best way to pursue such aims.'[35] Nigel Griffiths, the Minister for Consumer Affairs, appeared to share his views. In May 1998, to the fury of corporate lobbyists, he refused to water down Britain's implementation of the European Union's consumer protection directive. In July 1998, both ministers were sacked.

David Clark had been obliged to appoint as Chair of the Better Regulation Taskforce Lord Haskins, who is the head of the wholesaling company Northern Foods. He was also a member of the Hampel Committee on corporate governance, which did nothing to disguise its contempt for regulatory burdens on business. The report he helped to compile for the committee declared, 'The emphasis on accountability has tended to obscure a board's first responsibility ... to enhance the prosperity of the business over time.'[36] Unsurprisingly, his taskforce argued that there should be fewer rules for British business. It suggested that state regulation be replaced by self-regulation, economic incentives and codes of practice, such as those 'operated by the Advertising Standards Authority'.[37]

By September 1998, the government had entirely reversed its initial policy. There would, it announced, be fewer government inspectors, enforcing fewer regulations. The inspectors would cease to be industry police, and become advisers instead. In June 1999, Stephen Byers, the Secretary of State for Trade and Industry, told the British Chambers of Commerce that the government 'will be applying the following key principles to our work from now on: ... a presumption against regulation. Regulation will only be introduced where absolutely necessary and where all other avenues have been pursued.'[38] Regulations would 'automatically lapse' after a certain date. Enforcement, he promised, would be 'business-friendly'.[39]

In April 1999, the Better Regulation Unit was replaced by the Regulatory Impact Unit. Rather than balancing the interests of the public and corporations, as David Clark had proposed to do, the new unit would 'help Government reduce the cumulative burden of regulation' and ensure 'greater consultation with industry'.[40] It would, it promised, seek out any regulations it deemed unnecessary and eliminate them.

The business-friendly press campaigns stoutly against regulation – or red tape, as its opponents always call it – and it is true that some rules have fallen too heavily on small businesses in Britain. But regulation is all that prevents companies from dumping their costs onto society. If corporations are allowed to encourage smoking by advertising cigarettes, for example, more people are likely to contract smoking-related diseases. If car manufacturers are not prevented from attaching bull bars to the front of their vehicles, then more of the children hit by cars will die. If pollution control measures are abandoned, the environment will be destroyed. Deregulation, in other words, can become a subsidy for careless or greedy companies. Its effects are felt most keenly by workers in hazardous industries.

In 1996, the government's Health and Safety Executive instructed its inspectors to reduce their prosecutions of companies putting their workers at risk. The Conservatives had already repeatedly cut the executive's budget, and this new advice resulted in a 25 per cent decline in health and safety enforcement notices in 1997. Perhaps unsurprisingly, the change was accompanied by a 20 per cent increase in deaths and serious injuries in the workplace: the first time the figures had risen for decades.[41] There appears to be, in other words, a direct relationship between the vigour with which companies are prosecuted for endangering their employees and the number of people killed, maimed, blinded or disabled. If companies are treated gently, workers are treated harshly.

In Britain, money is officially more valuable than human

life. The directors of British companies are individually responsible for keeping the price of their shares as high as they can. If they neglect this 'fiduciary duty', they can be prosecuted and imprisoned. If, on the other hand, they neglect to protect their workforce, with the result that an employee is killed, they remain, in practice, immune from prosecution. The company, if it is unlucky, will suffer an inconsequential fine, which will not touch the lives of the directors.

Around 360 people are killed at work every year in Great Britain. Research by the law professor Gary Slapper suggests that around eighty of these deaths should result in prosecutions for corporate manslaughter.[42] But only two companies, both of them tiny, have ever been convicted of this crime. The problem is that while corporations have acquired many of the rights of human beings, they have managed to shed many of the corresponding responsibilities. A company can be convicted of manslaughter only if a director or senior manager can be singled out as directly responsible for the death. If responsibility is shared by the board as a whole, the firm, bizarrely, is innocent of reckless or intentional killing.

The problem is compounded, as I have suggested, by the notorious reluctance of the government's Health and Safety Executive (HSE) to prosecute anyone for anything. The Centre for Corporate Accountability calculates that of the 47,000 major injuries in the workplace reported between 1996 and 1998, the HSE investigated just 11 per cent.[43] Of these investigations, only 10 per cent resulted in a prosecution. The police, by contrast, investigate all incidents, outside the workplace, which cause serious injury. Interestingly, the executive is five times more likely to examine injuries on farms than in the mining industry, which might suggest that it is rather braver when dealing with small companies than it is when dealing with large ones. And though the HSE's own studies suggest that 70 per cent of *deaths* in the workplace result from 'management failure', it prosecutes in only 19 per cent of cases.[44] Even when it does secure a conviction, the penalties are slight. In Britain, a human life is now worth an average of £18,000: it is often cheaper for companies to kill their workers than to improve their safety records. The truth, unpopular with business leaders, is that red tape saves lives, while deregulation kills.

In 1996, the Law Commission reported that the corporate killing laws were in urgent need of reform. In 1997, two weeks after the Southall rail crash, in which seven people died, the Home Secretary told the Labour Party conference that he would introduce 'laws which provide for conviction of directors of companies where it's claimed that as a result of dreadful negligence by the company as a whole, people have lost their lives'.[45] It took two and a half years for Mr Straw to launch a consultation document on corporate killing. Even so, while the government proposes that companies could be convicted of corporate manslaughter whether or not an executive has been singled out for blame, it suggests that the directors of grossly negligent companies should be subject to no greater penalty than disqualification.

Unable to discharge its duty, the Health and Safety Executive has attempted, instead, to stifle its critics. In March 1998 a confidential memo was leaked from its Open Government Unit.[46] It warned recipients that four individuals were 'becoming persistent in their enquiries to HSE'. The note continued, 'We wish to monitor those who appear to have an interest in a range of HSE's activities and who may be looking to exploit replies received in ways unfavourable to HSE . . . any contact with these people should be reported to the Open Government Unit.'[47] The four people it named were all highly respected professionals, with an expert interest in health and safety issues. They were distinguished from others who might have been 'persistent in their enquiries', however, in that they had all been critical of the HSE's failures to prosecute.

When the agency's novel approach to open government was questioned in parliament, the Health and Safety Minister, Angela Eagle, offered an intriguing interpretation. 'The purpose of the memorandum is to ensure that the named enquirers get all the information to which they are entitled in a consistent, fully explained and usable form.'[48] Ms Eagle agreed to deposit a copy of the note in the House of Commons library, but, in accordance with the principles of open government, she carefully blotted out all the names. As a result, MPs were unable to see that the recipients of the memo included the HSE's Director-General.

*

If governments are not prepared to regulate, they must, as Lord Haskins suggested, use 'economic incentives' to amend corporate behaviour. Compliance, in other words, must be bought. There are already plenty of means by which money is transferred from the state to corporations.

Corporations have learnt that by threatening to move elsewhere, precipitating the loss of thousands of jobs, they can ensure not only that the regulations they dislike are removed, but also that governments will pay vast amounts of money to persuade them to stay. By playing nations or regions off against each other, the companies can effectively auction their services, securing hundreds of millions of pounds of taxpayers' money which might otherwise have been spent, for example, on hospitals or schools. State benefits for individuals might be diminishing, but the corporate welfare state is booming.

In 1997, British Aerospace, a company little known for its poverty, insisted that it needed £120m from the government if it were to build a new jet in Britain rather than overseas. At first, the government resisted. Officials at the Treasury pointed out that aid was wholly unnecessary: the company could finance the new model itself. But by the end of 1998, it caved in, and handed British Aerospace the money it was demanding. In March 2000 the government generously threw in a further £530m, to help the destitute company build another new model. In 1997, another distressed corporation, Rolls-Royce, won £200m to build a jet engine in Britain. Scores of smaller donations have been made to such good causes as Ford, Rupert Murdoch's Sky TV and the lottery company Camelot. When Labour came to power, it hinted that it would stop handing out money to corporations. But its three largest deals alone, when averaged across the three years in which they were concluded, represent an increase of 130 per cent on the favours distributed by the Conservatives during their last five years in office. Critics have suggested that if individuals sought to extract money by similar means, they would be charged with blackmail.

While taxpayers' money is being given to corporations, corporations are required to contribute ever decreasing amounts of tax. Even before the Labour government came to power, corporation tax in Britain was the lowest of any major industrialized country. The Conservatives had reduced it from 52 per cent to 33 per cent. In 1997, the Labour government cut it by a further 2 per cent. In 1999, it cut the tax again, to 30 per cent. The Chancellor, Gordon Brown, boasted that this was 'now the lowest rate in the history of British corporation tax, the lowest rate of any major country in Europe and the lowest rate of any major industrialised country anywhere, including Japan and the United States'.[49]

In March 2000, Gordon Brown cut the capital gains tax levied on higher rate taxpayers from 40 per cent to 10 per cent, half the level in the United States. He also abolished the 'withholding tax' on bond sales by British financial corporations. This annulment cost the Exchequer £300m and infuriated other European governments, which had been trying to introduce a standard rate throughout the EU. The biggest lorries on Britain's roads – but only the biggest – would also be exempted from much of the duty they had to pay.

Yet, while these corporate taxes have withered, personal taxation in Britain, as the Conservatives have pointed out, rose by some eight pence in the pound during the first three years of Labour's term in office. This reflects a long-term trend. Corporation taxes in the United States, the *Economist* magazine reports, rendered one-third of total federal tax revenues before the Second World War. Now they account for just 12 per cent, a quarter of the amount delivered by personal tax.[50] More mobile than ever before, big businesses can bully governments into relieving them of their responsibilities. If a state won't cut the taxes it levies, they threaten to disinvest, and move to somewhere which will. The highly paid, like the corporations which employ them, can also play one state off against another, driving down the top rates of income tax. The tax burden, as a result, has shifted to those who can't get away: the poor and middle-incomed.

To some corporations operating in Britain, taxation levels are irrelevant, for they manage to pay nothing. According to the *Economist*, News Corporation, Rupert Murdoch's main British holding company, made £1.4bn in profits in the twelve years to 1999. But, as a result of legal tax avoidance measures, it has paid no net British corporation tax.[51]

While businesses devise ever more ingenious means of escaping taxation, they also lobby to ensure that the rest of us pay our dues. In October 1999, the Confederation of British Industry told the government that it should not reduce taxes on consumers, but should spend its surplus money, instead, on public infrastructure (this would, incidentally, provide more revenue for corporations, especially those hoping to secure more contracts under the Private Finance Initiative). In the same statement, however, it suggested that corporation tax should continue to be reduced.[52] The corporate takeover of Britain is to be financed not by the corporations, but by you and me.

*

When aristocrats enjoyed inordinate power in Britain, they insisted that they were the only ones who had the wisdom and expertise needed to run the country. Today business people make the same claim. Governments as well as newspapers appear to have convinced themselves of this proposition, and it has led, among other interesting phenomena, to the curious spectacle of government seeking a mandate from the corporations. The flow of power prescribed by the democratic model has been reversed. Big business has become the leviathan of the third millennium, the monster before which our representatives feel obliged to prostrate themselves. The people we have appointed as the guardians of our liberties have delivered us into its maw. Some of the measures required to tame this creature are narrow and specific.

The Private Finance Initiative, for example, must be scrapped. Hospitals, schools, prisons and transport systems will respond to the wider public interest only when they are publicly managed. The planning system must be reformed, granting objectors the right to appeal against developments which have not been foreseen in local plans and forbidding developers to hand money to the councils assessing their proposals. The Department of the Environment must stop promoting the industries it is supposed to regulate. The government needs to detach itself from the grip of the supermarkets, and find the courage to break up the largest chains. Some of the most damaging out-of-town stores could be either closed altogether or turned into covered farmers' markets, in which local producers could sell directly to consumers.

Now that the Prime Minister acknowledges 'legitimate public concern' about genetic engineering,[53] the government should reassess its farming policies, bolstering those parts of the market in which demand is unmet, while withdrawing support from those parts decisively rejected by consumers. The patenting of genes must be repealed. We also need a new approach to the funding of our universities, with clear guidelines regulating the use of corporate money, to prevent the stifling of research results and other constraints on academic freedom. It is surely not beyond the means of a government which has secured a significant budget surplus and speaks with such conviction of its commitment to the 'knowledge economy' to bring the state funding of university research up to or even above the global average. It should clean out the research councils, encouraging them to support work of the kind which might lead to major breakthroughs in understanding, and close down the deeply flawed Foresight programme. The corporate intrusion into schools should be stopped dead. A government which wanted to protect the workforce, consumers and the environment would be seeking carefully to re-regulate the businesses threatening public health and safety.

The legal advantages corporations enjoy over people should be withdrawn. They should, for example, no longer be able to sue for libel. Britain's libel laws are the most draconian in the world. As they are formidably expensive to apply, they favour those with the deepest pockets. The burden of proof rests on the defendants: they are guilty until proven innocent. However poor the defendants might be, they are not entitled to legal aid. So journalists, editors, publishers, printers, broadcasters, even newsagents and bookshops, engage in self-censorship, avoiding hazardous subjects. As a result, the corporations are able to prevent exposure of their activities and silence dissent. In America, the judiciary has ensured that 'public figures', the corporations among them, shouldn't be allowed to sue for libel, on the grounds that this would stifle free speech.

Other measures require a wider reassessment of public policy. While certain powers have been devolved to regional and local government, for example, powers must also be devolved *from* local government to ordinary people. In theory, community planning events, in which everyone with an interest in the neighbourhood assembles to decide jointly how their area should develop, provide the means of ensuring that the needs of society as a whole are met by development, rather than only those of the developers. Chapter 3 shows how these events can go terribly wrong. But were they conducted fairly, within a legally recognized framework, and were their results given statutory weight in planning decisions, they would become a powerful means by which people could reclaim control over their own lives, forcing companies to respect their wishes.

We should also, perhaps, start to engage in the politics of scale, seeking to reduce the size of businesses, so that they become more amenable to the persuasions of governments, citizens and consumers. Mergers and takeovers should be, wherever possible, resisted. Perhaps we should consider establishing a size limit for corporations, forcing them to divest parts of their business if they become too big.

But most importantly, when a corporation has proved to be a menace to society, the state must be empowered to destroy it. We should reintroduce, in other words, that ancient safeguard against corporate government, the restrictive corporate charter. In 1720, after corporations had exceeded their powers in Britain, the government introduced an act which provided that all commercial undertakings 'tending to the common grievance, prejudice and inconvenience of His Majesty's subjects' would be rendered void.[54] Corporations which broke the terms of their charters could be wound up. Big business, once again, must be forced to apply for a licence to trade, which would be revoked as soon as its terms are breached.

*

None of these measures are likely to be either workable or lasting if businesses are able to escape our enhanced standards by moving to countries with looser regulations and more attractive incentives. Big business has seized so much of the economy that when large corporations leave, the economic consequences can be disastrous. By bidding against each other to attract companies, countries undermine each other's standards and expose their populations to predatory practices. We need, in other words, global trade agreements which set harmonized minimum standards, rather than only harmonized maximum standards.

Multinational firms must be forced to conform to the international rules binding those states which have joined the United Nations. They should be legally obliged, for example, to protect their employees from accident and neglect wherever they operate, and to withhold from harming consumers or the wider community and damaging the environment. They should be subject to human rights laws, enforceable anywhere on earth, whose neglect would result in prosecution at international tribunals.

Global taxation measures – harmonizing corporate taxes, preventing companies from shifting their money to tax havens, and levying a tariff on all international currency transactions – would forestall one of the world's gravest impending problems: the erosion of the tax base as states offer ever more generous terms to the ultra-rich in order to attract their money. These would not be easy either to implement or to enforce, not least because they would hand a formidable advantage to countries playing outside the rules. Whether we intervene or not, however, corporate taxes will converge worldwide, but downwards, rather than upwards. It is possible to conceive of a system of sanctions against tax havens, rather like the sanctions imposed today upon countries seeking to protect their markets. Perhaps there should also be a worldwide cap on executive pay, tackling inequality by ensuring that managers and directors cannot be given more than a certain multiple – eight or ten perhaps – of the salary of the lowest paid member of their workforce, including sub-contractors. If bosses wanted to raise their wages, they would have to raise everyone else's as well.

But corporations will never be subjected to meaningful international rules while the negotiation of global agreements is opaque and undemocratic. We need to democratize international decision-making, so that it remains within the public domain, rather than being removed to the murky world of corporate lawyers and unaccountable committees. This might involve, for example, prior parliamentary approval of all national negotiating positions. We should consider holding referenda on the most important international decisions, just as the government proposes a referendum on whether or not to enter the European single currency.

*

All this, of course, looks wildly optimistic and unrealistic. While corporations are being granted ever greater freedoms, how on earth could we contemplate such sweeping restrictions? What could possibly prompt governments to reverse their policies and confront the very faction of which they are most afraid? Where are the powers which could make these propositions viable? Well, dear reader, they lie with you.

The corporations are powerful only because we have allowed them to be. In theory, it is we, not they, who mandate the state. But we have neglected our duty of citizenship, and they have taken advantage of our neglect to seize the reins of government. Their power is an artefact of our acquiescence.

Governments will reassert their control over corporations, in other words, only when people reassert their control over governments. If political participation could break the bars of totalitarian state communism, it can certainly force elected governments to hold corporations to account.

This will happen only through the peaceful mobilization of millions of people in nations all over the world. Globalization, in other words, must be matched with internationalism: campaigning, worldwide, for better means of government.

We have little power as consumers. Consumer democracy is an illusion, not least because some have more votes than others. Those with the most power in the market are disinclined to use it to change the system which has rewarded them so well. There are, moreover, few parts of the economy from which we can withdraw our custom: we might dispute the merits of the Private Finance Initiative, for example, but if we fall ill we have to go to hospital. At present, many people have no choice but to shop at supermarkets or to eat food containing the products of genetic engineering.

Nor is there a political system which, if we were only to embrace it, would solve all our problems. There is no utopia, no perfect state. Political arrival is the prerequisite of tyranny, as the architects of heaven always end up designing a hell. Rather, democracy is sustained not by the system which prescribes it, whatever that might be, but by the challenges to that system. A political system is only as good as the capacity of its critics to attack it. They are the people who enforce the checks and balances which prevent any faction – the corporations, the aristocracy, the armed forces, even, for that matter, trades unions or environment groups – from wielding excessive power.

Our strength, in other words, lies in our citizenship, in our ability to engage in democratic politics, to use exposure, enfranchisement and dissent to prise our representatives out of the arms of the powers they have embraced. We must, in other words, cause trouble. We must put the demo back into democracy.

Legitimate protest takes many forms, including parliamentary opposition, lobbying by constituents and pressure groups, campaigning journalism and adamantly non-violent direct action. It should not be confined to parliamentary politics or even to strictly legal channels. Parliament is incompletely representative. It tends to concentrate on the concerns of target voters and powerful institutions, rather than on those of the poor, the vulnerable or the unborn. Elections are blunt instruments, generally won or lost on a small number of issues: tax, for example, or the economy. They do not allow us to refine our demands. Their results can be fine-tuned only by means of more persistent political activity. While corporate lobbyists infiltrate every particle of government, it is absurd to suggest, as some do, that the extra-parliamentary politics which seeks to counteract their influence is undemocratic.

The legal framework on which parliament builds, moreover, pre-dates democracy. It was designed to protect those who drafted it – the titled, propertied, literate few – from the rightful claims of those they had dispossessed. Possession remains nine-tenths of the law, and as corporations seek to expand their domain, seizing resources which once belonged to all of us, the law dilates to accommodate their demands.

Troublemaking is the means by which both our dispossession and the laws enforcing it are challenged. It is a costly nuisance, a drain on public resources, an impediment to the smooth functioning of government. It is also the sole guarantor of liberty. It forces our representatives to listen to those they have failed to represent. It inoculates the political agenda with new ideas and new perspectives. Without it, political systems sclerotize and succumb to corruption. As the freed slave and anti-slavery campaigner Frederick Douglass wrote in 1857, 'Those who profess to favor freedom, and yet deprecate agitation, are men who want crops without plowing up the ground. They want rain without thunder and lightning ... Power concedes nothing without a demand. It never did and it never will.'[55]

There are signs that agitation is already beginning to extract a few concessions. Both the superstores and the biotechnology companies have had to adjust some of their practices in response to popular protest. The World Trade Organization has been forced to take note of some of the concerns of developing countries, after their sustained objections and the demonstrations in Seattle. The initial attempts to approve a flawed Multilateral Agreement on Investment were abandoned after the revelation of its contents precipitated a public outcry in many parts of the world.

Some trading relationships are also beginning to shift. While governments have been attempting to engineer a single, harmonized global trading system, throughout Europe and the United States citizens' groups are breaking the market up. Organic box schemes and local farmers' markets have begun to restore some balance to commercial encounters, reducing the scale of business until the power of producers and consumers is roughly equivalent, reintroducing accountability to the food chain, curbing the environmental impacts of production and transport. In some sectors, such as farming, forestry and fishing, some companies have been obliged to seek a licence to trade, submitting their products to independent certification by bodies such as the Soil Association and the Forest Steward-ship Council. Though the power of consumers is, as I have suggested, limited, such constraints are likely to spread to other sectors. While governments are ever more reluctant to regulate, citizens seem to be able to force corporations to shoulder a few of their responsibilities.

It would be a mistake, however, to assume that big business will be easily subjugated. The corporations' grip on the state is firm, and most of the citizens' movements resisting it are, as yet, weak. Those seeking to contain corporate power will be forced to confront not only the corporations themselves but also the states which have succumbed to their dominion. They will suffer privations, vilification and, as the law is further distorted to accommo-date business demands, even imprisonment. But the struggle for freedom was ever thus.

No one else will fight this battle for us. There will be no messiah, no conquering hero to deliver us from the corpor-ate leviathan. Most of our representatives have been either coopted or crushed. Only one thing can reverse the corpor-ate takeover of Britain. It's you.

Notes

Introduction

1 Jonathon Lord, Westminster City Council, personal communication, February 2000.

2 Mediasign Marketing Ltd, Publicity pack, undated; Claire Gardener, Mediasign, pers. comm., December 1998.

3 The Police Act, 1996. Chapter 16, 93(1).

4 Sue Worthington, City of London Police, pers. comm., March 2000.

5 <http://www.cleveland.police.uk/>, November 1998.

6 Paul Lillington, Avon and Somerset Police, pers. comm., March 2000.

7 *Herald*, 9 October 1998.

8 *Daily Dome*, 5 January 2000. Millennium Experience in association with Associated London Metro Ltd, London.

9 Tony Blair, 28 September 1999, speech to the Labour Party Conference.

10 The CornerHouse, February 2000, *Dams Incorporated: The Record of Twelve European Dam Building Companies*. The Swedish Society for Nature Conservation.

11 *World at One*, BBC Radio 4, 28 September 1999.

12 Department of Trade and Industry, 1996, *Protecting Business*

Information I (*Understanding the Risks*) and II (*Keeping it Confidential*), sent to me by the DTI, February 1998.

13 Abraham Lincoln, 21 November 1864, letter to Col. William F. Elkins.

14 Peter Mandelson, Secretary of State for Trade and Industry, 2 November 1998, speech to the Confederation of British Industry's annual conference.

15 Tony Blair, 11 November 1997, speech to the Confederation of British Industry's annual conference.

16 Peter Mandelson, as note 14.

17 Tony Blair, May 1998, foreword to the *Fairness at Work* white paper, Department of Trade and Industry.

18 Daniel Bennett, March 1999, *The Creation and Development of English Commercial Corporations and the Abolition of Democratic Control over their Behaviour*, Programme on Corporations, Law and Democracy, <http://www.corporatewatch.org/pages/dan_corp.html>.

19 *Observer*, 8 November 1998.

20 Peter Mandelson and Roger Liddle, 1996, *Can Britain Survive?*, cited in the *Observer*, 2 August 1998.

21 Adam Smith, 1776, *An Inquiry into the Nature and Causes of the Wealth of Nations*, Chapter 7, Part 2.

22 *Financial Times*, 23 December 1999.

23 As note 22.

Chapter One: The Skye Bridge Mystery

1 Robbie the Pict, 1997, *The Cludgie Stane of Destiny: The Truth behind its Return*: Scottish Exchequer Press, Isle of Skye.

2 House of Commons Committee of Public Accounts, 1998, Forty-second Report, *The Skye Bridge*. The Stationery Office, London.

3 <http://www.miller.co.uk>, February 1999.

4 £6m is the figure cited in the tender document by Scottish

Office Roads Directorate/JMP Consultants, 1989, *A Bridge to Skye – Information for Prospective Tenderers* (Scottish Office document RD15), and in the Scottish Office report of the public inquiry into the Skye Bridge Crossing (May 1992), section 8, paragraph 31. The Miller Web site (as note 3) suggests that the cost may have been £7m. An earlier report by JMP Consultants (1988, *Report to the Highland Council: Skye Bridge Revised Traffic and Economic Feasibility Report* (Scottish Office document RD12)) suggests that the total cost of land and approach roads should have been £1,640,600.

5 Skye and Kyle Against Tolls, 1997, *Project Report 1*; Skye and Kyle Against Tolls press release, 16 October 1998, *Eilean Ban Hand-Over: Who Got the Missing £200,000?*; House of Commons Committee of Public Accounts, 1998, as note 2, Minutes of Evidence, p. 18.

6 House of Commons Committee of Public Accounts, 1998, as note 2, Minutes of Evidence, p. 6.

7 House of Commons *Hansard*, 14 January 1999, Column 471.

8 National Audit Office, 1997, *The Skye Bridge (HC 5)*. The Stationery Office, London.

9 As note 8; Skye and Kyle Against Tolls, 1997, *Project Report 1*.

10 *House of Commons Committee of Public Accounts, 1998*, as note 2, Minutes of Evidence, pp. 9, 16.

11 As note 10, p. 9.

12 As note 10, p. 13. Also, <http://www.miller.co.uk>, February 1999.

13 Calum MacDonald, 9 February 1999, House of Commons *Hansard*, Column 171.

14 *House of Commons Committee of Public Accounts*, 1998, as note 2.

15 Letter from Robbie the Pict to the Managing Director, Skye Bridge Company, 24 March 1997.

16 Memorandum of Agreement between the Secretary of State for Scotland, Skye Bridge Tolls Ltd, The Miller Group Ltd,

Miller Civil Engineering Ltd, Dyckerhoff & Widmann AG and Miller-Dywidag Joint Venture, March 1990. Referred to by the court as 'Crown Production 16'.

17 House of Commons *Hansard*, Parliamentary Answer to Question no. 43194, 16 June 1998.

18 *Herald*, 7 May 1998.

19 As note 18.

20 Skye and Kyle Against Tolls press release, 12 January 1999, *'Fatal Flaw' in the Toll Bridge Legislation*.

21 *West Highland Free Press*, 3 October 1997.

22 *Herald*, 13 October 1999.

23 *West Highland Free Press*, 29 January 1999.

24 *Herald*, 27 August 1999.

25 JMP Consultants Ltd and Quayle Munro Ltd, for the Scottish Office Roads Directorate, March 1990, *Skye Crossing: Invitation to Tender. Volume 1: Administrative, Contractual, Legislative and Financial Aspects*, DA2–2/2.

26 *Herald*, 16 January 1998, 21 January 1998.

27 *Herald*, 16 January 1998.

28 *San Francisco Chronicle*, 13 November 1998.

29 *Herald*, 29 April 1998.

30 *San Francisco Chronicle*, 22 October 1998.

31 <http://www.miller.co.uk>, February 1999.

32 Skye and Kyle Against Tolls, 1997, *Project Report 2*.

33 European Investment Bank statute, article 18(1), cited in Skye and Kyle Against Tolls, 1997, *Project Report 2*.

34 Article 130 of the Treaty of Rome, cited in Skye and Kyle Against Tolls, 1997, *Project Report 2*.

35 As note 32.

36 As note 32.

37 House of Commons *Hansard*, 14 January 1999, Column 472.

38 The Scottish Office, May 1992, *Report of the Public Inquiry into the Skye Bridge Crossing*, section 3, paragraph 121.

39 As note 38.

40 JMP Consultants' Report to the Highland Council, 1985/86, *A*

Bridge to Skye (Feasibility Study), Volume One (Scottish Office document RD11); JMP Consultants Report to the Highland Council, 1988, *Skye Bridge Revised Traffic and Economic Feasibility Report* (Scottish Office document RD12).

41 *West Highland Free Press,* 20 October 1995, 15 December 1995; Brian Wilson, 16 October 1995, statement to the *Herald.*

42 *West Highland Free Press,* 2 February 1996.

43 *West Highland Free Press,* 16 October 1998.

44 *West Highland Free Press,* 23 October 1998.

45 *West Highland Free Press,* 25 April 1997.

46 *West Highland Free Press,* 27 June 1997.

47 As note 46.

48 E.g. Henry McLeish, 21 July 1998, House of Commons Standing Committee (pt 13); Donald Dewar, 4 July 1997, House of Commons *Hansard* columns 288–290.

49 *Scotland on Sunday,* 4 January 1998.

50 Letter from Henry McLeish MP to Geoffrey Robinson MP, 11 February 1998.

51 House of Commons Committee of Public Accounts, 1998, as note 2.

52 *Construction News,* 15 January 1998.

53 *Herald,* 28 July 1999 and 30 July 1999.

Chapter Two: Hospital Cases – The Corporate Takeover of the National Health Service

1 David Loughton, quoted in the *Coventry Evening Telegraph,* 30 June 1998.

2 Speech to the 1996 Unison Conference, reported in *Hospital Development,* August 1996, vol. 27, no. 7.

3 *Financial Times,* 16 March 2000.

4 *Guardian,* 4 July 1997.

5 House of Commons *Hansard,* 6 July 1998, Column 388.

6 Allyson Pollock, Jean Shaoul and Declan Gaffney, July 1998,

The Walsgrave Hospitals PFI Development: A Report to the Coventry and Warwickshire Health Authorities.

7 As note 6.
8 From a report commissioned by the Coventry Health Authority, cited in Allyson Pollock, Jean Shaoul and Declan Gaffney, July 1998, as note 6.
9 Jean Shaoul, 22 December 1998, *Labour's Backdoor Privatisation of Essential Public Services*, <http://socialequality.com/news/1998/dec1998/brit-d22.shtml>.
10 Coventry and Warwickshire Health Authorities, December 1998, *Consultation Document on New Hospital Facilities in Coventry.*
11 Allyson Pollock, Jean Shaoul and Declan Gaffney, July 1998, as note 6.
12 As note 10.
13 Coventry Health Authority Executive Team, 20 April 1999, Report to the Coventry Health Authority Meeting of 23 April 1999, *Outcome of the Consultation 'A New Hospital for Coventry'.*
14 As note 13.
15 As note 13.
16 As note 10.
17 Coventry Community Health Council Survey, cited in Coventry Health Authority, 16 March 1999, *Consultation on New Hospital Facilities in Coventry.*
18 Allyson Pollock, June 1998, *Notes on PFI* (commissioned by the British Medical Association).
19 *Financial Times*, 24 April 1997.
20 As note 19.
21 Study by Newchurch and Company, cited by Allyson Pollock, June 1998, as note 18, and *Financial Times*, 5 June 1998.
22 *British Medical Journal*, 17 July 1999, vol. 319.
23 Declan Gaffney and Allyson Pollock, 1999, *Downsizing for the 21st century: A Report to Unison Northern Region on the North Durham Acute Hospitals PFI Scheme.* Unison, London.

24 Public Services Privatisation Research Unit, 1997, *Private Finance Initiative: Dangers, Realities, Alternatives.* PSPRU, London.

25 As note 24.

26 As note 24.

27 *Financial Times,* 10 February 2000.

28 *Building,* 21 March 1997.

29 *Sunday Mail,* 10 January 1999.

30 Cited in the *Herald,* 19 January 1999.

31 *Independent,* 9 January 1999.

32 Declan Gaffney and Allyson Pollock, December 1997, *Can the NHS Afford the Private Finance Initiative?.* British Medical Association, London.

33 As note 32.

34 *Hospital Development,* October 1996, vol. 27, no. 9.

35 As note 32.

36 As note 32.

37 *Government Opportunities,* August 1997, vol. 3, no. 2.

38 *Financial Times,* 21 April 1997.

39 Arthur Andersen and Enterprise LSE, 17 January 2000, *Value for Money Drivers in the Private Finance Initiative* (commissioned by the Treasury Taskforce). <http://www.treasury-projects-taskforce.gov.uk/>.

40 *Financial Times,* 11 January 1997.

41 *Government Opportunities,* April 1997, vol. 2, no. 10.

42 National Audit Office, 28 January 1998, *The Private Finance Initiative: The First Four Design, Build, Finance and Operate Roads Contracts (HC476).* The Stationery Office, London.

43 Transport 2000, 22 March 1997, *DBFO Update for South West TAR Meeting.*

44 Emma Must, Transport 2000, pers. comm.

45 As note 24.

46 *Guardian,* 4 June 1998.

47 Jack Straw's speech to the Prison Officers' Association, 19 May 1998.

48 *Prison Privatisation Report International,* October 1996.

49 HM Prison Service, cited by the Select Committee on Public Accounts, 15 July 1998, *Fifty-Seventh Report: The PFI Contracts for Bridgend and Fazakerley Prisons.*

50 *Guardian,* 26 August 1998.

51 House of Commons *Hansard,* 12 February 1998; *Prison Privatisation Report International,* March 1998.

52 *Prison Privatisation Report International,* June 1998.

53 *Prison Privatisation Report International,* April 1998.

54 *Prison Privatisation Report International,* September 1998.

55 *Guardian,* 29 January 1999.

56 *Observer,* 31 January 1999.

57 *Observer,* 26 September 1999.

58 Cited in the *Guardian,* 30 June 1999.

59 Chantrey Vellacott DFK, 1999, *Economics Report,* cited by Declan Gaffney, Allyson Pollock, David Price, Jean Shaoul, 10 July 1999, 'PFI in the NHS – is there an Economic Case?', *British Medical Journal,* vol. 319.

60 *Financial Times,* 11 December 1997.

61 Department of the Environment Property Holdings, *Private Finance in Government Accommodation.* Stationery Office, London. Cited by Derek Kerr, spring 1998, 'The PFI miracle', *Capital & Class,* vol. 64.

62 *Financial Times,* 18 June 1997.

63 Derek Kerr, spring 1998, as note 61.

64 Sir Malcolm Bates, 23 June 1997. His recommendations are published at <http://www.treasury-projects-taskforce.gov.uk/intro/bates.htm>.

65 *Building,* 30 May 1997.

66 *Government Opportunities,* November 1997, vol. 6, no. 5, and *Financial Times,* 23 September 1997.

67 *The Bates Report,* as note 64.

68 *The Times,* 27 May 1997.

69 *The Bates Report,* as note 64.

70 *Building,* 29 November 1996.

71 Later cited in the *Guardian,* 26 January 1998.

72 *Guardian*, 26 January 1998.

73 *Financial Times*, 11 January 1997.

74 West Midlands Friends of the Earth, 10 May 1996, *Birmingham Northern Relief Road: Economic Briefing*.

75 As note 74.

76 *North Warwickshire Gazette*, 1 October 1994.

77 E.g. open letter to John Prescott from West Midlands residents, <http://www.venus.co.uk/weed/roads/r98/>.

78 Treasury Taskforce, Private Finance, 1997, *Partnerships for Prosperity: The Private Finance Initiative*.

79 Jack Straw's speech to the Prison Officers' Association, 21 May 1996.

80 *Prison Privatisation Report International*, May 1997.

81 As note 80.

82 Jack Straw's speech to the Prison Officers' Association, 19 May 1998.

83 *Financial Times*, 14 November 1997.

Chapter Three: Breaking Point – The Smashing of Southampton

1 Southampton Network Regeneration Partnership, 1995, *Southampton's Bid*.

2 Paul Jenks, 1995, Foreword to Southampton Network Regeneration Partnership, as note 1.

3 Southampton Regeneration Partnership, undated, *Putting New Life into the City: An Introduction*.

4 *Local Government Chronicle*, 12 July 1996.

5 Southampton Network Regeneration Partnership, 1995, as note 1.

6 Community/Urban Design Assistance Team, 1985, *St Mary Street, Southampton*.

7 Gerald Eve Ltd, 1998, *Fast Forward: St Mary's Urban Village Action Plan*. Southampton Regeneration Partnership, English Partnerships, Urban Villages Forum.

8 Community/Urban Design Assistance Team, 1985, *St Mary Street, Southampton*.

9 Gerald Eve Ltd, 1998, as note 7.

10 Southampton Network Regeneration Partnership, 1995, as note 1.

11 Cited by Siobhan Ryan, 11 August 1997, open letter to the Environment and Services Committee, Southampton City Council.

12 Steve Oliver, Neighbourhood Initiatives Foundation, 12 September 1996, letter to John Graylands of Hyde Housing Association and Southampton Regeneration Partnership.

13 Southampton City Council, July 1997, *Draft West Itchen Neighbourhoods Regeneration Plan*.

14 Southampton City Council, September 1997, *West Itchen Neighbourhoods Regeneration Plan: Summary of Consultation Draft and Questionnaire*.

15 Southampton City Council, July 1997, as note 13.

16 Report of Head of Planning and Development Management, Southampton City Council, to the Strategy and Resources Committee, 7 July 1997.

17 *Southampton Advertiser*, 14 August 1997.

18 DTZ Pieda Consulting, undated, *St Mary's Business Survey and Property Ownership Study*.

19 John Thomson and Partners, 1997, *Re-Drawing the Map Together: Southampton's Community Planning Weekend, 22–25 November 1996*.

20 Gerald Eve Ltd, 1998, as note 7.

21 Simon Milner, Gerald Eve Urban Initiatives, April 1999, pers. comm.

22 As note 21.

23 Southampton Network Regeneration Partnership, 1995, as note 1.

24 Southampton City Council and Imry (Southampton) Ltd, August 1997, *West Quay*.

25 *Property Week*, 17 October 1997.

26 As note 24.
27 As note 24.
28 As note 24.
29 Southampton City Council, *SRB1 – Year Two Financial Summary 1996/97.*
30 John Arnold and Paul Jenks, October 1998. Taped interview.

Chapter Four: How to Buy Planning Permission – The Department of the Environment's Conflicts of Interest

1 From research by Dr Ian Roberts, Director of the Child Health Monitoring Unit at the Institute for Child Health, Great Ormond Street Hospital.
2 Linda Wade, February 2000, pers. comm.
3 Anti-Red Route Campaign, notes from a meeting of 27 January 2000 between ARRC members and legal services officer, Royal Borough of Kensington and Chelsea.
4 The Labour Party, 1994, *In Trust for Tomorrow: Report of the Labour Party Policy Commission on the Environment.* The Labour Party, London.
5 Council for the Protection of Rural England, December 1998, *Departure Applications and Call-ins.*
6 Department of the Environment, Transport and the Regions, 23 August 1999, press release no. 843.
7 Oxford City Council, circulated on 25 June 1996, *Leisure Development Adjacent to Ice Rink, Oxpens Road,* joint report of the Director of Property and Leisure Services and the Director of Central Services, marked 'Not for Publication'.
8 Stewart Bates, Regional Development Director, Safeway Stores PLC, 6 June 1995, letter to the Chief Executive, Western Isles Island Council.
9 Brian Stewart, Chief Executive, Western Isles Island Council, 7 June 1995, letter to Stewart Bates, Safeway Stores PLC.

10 *Newbury Weekly News*, 19 February 1998 and 2 July 1998, and Janet Griffin and Chris Baker, pers. comm.

11 Stella Manzie, 4 March 1998, letter to the *Newbury Weekly News*.

12 *Newbury Weekly News*, 19 February 1998.

13 As note 11.

14 *Newbury Weekly News*, 5 March 1998.

15 *Newbury Weekly News*, 12 March 1998 and 2 July 1998.

16 As note 15.

17 Minutes of Environment Committee meeting, West Berkshire Council, 30 June 1998.

18 Jim Sherry, West Berkshire Council, July 1998, *Payment of Council's Costs by Developers*.

19 As note 18.

20 Department of the Environment, Transport and the Regions, *Annual Report*, 1996.

21 Department of the Environment, Transport and the Regions, December 1996, *The Construction Sponsorship Directorate*.

22 As note 20.

23 As note 20.

24 Patrick Harrison, press officer, Department of the Environment, Transport and the Regions, 27 March 1997, pers. comm.

25 As note 20.

26 Sir Ian Dixon, 1998, contribution to *Forty Heads on One Peacock: Reflections on Ten Years of CIC*. The Construction Industry Council, London.

27 Construction Industry Board, Working Group 7, 1996, *Constructing a Better Image*. Thomas Telford, London.

28 Construction Industry Board, 3 March 1997, press release.

29 Tony Baldry, 1998, contribution to *Forty Heads on One Peacock*, as note 26.

30 *Building*, 22 August 1997.

31 As note 30.

32 *Building*, 11 July 1997.

33 *Building Design*, 24 November 1997.

34 *Building*, 12 September 1997.

35 Department of the Environment, Transport and the Regions, *Annual Report*, 1998.

36 As note 27.

37 As note 27.

38 As note 27.

39 As note 27.

40 *Building*, 26 September 1997.

41 *Contract Journal*, 25 June 1997.

42 National Construction Week, 15 April 1999, press release no. CCL99/103.

43 National Construction Week, 1999, *National Construction Week Organiser's Pack*.

44 *Construction Monitor*, 19 September 1997: Department of the Environment, Transport and the Regions.

45 Construction Industry Council, *Annual Review 1997/8*.

46 *Building*, 25 May 1997.

47 *Building*, 24 October 1997.

48 *Building*, 9 October 1998.

49 *Yorkshire Post*, 16 June 1998.

50 *Contract Journal*, 28 May 1997.

51 *Contract Journal*, 18 March 1998.

52 *Building*, 17 April 1998.

53 Alan Francis, Regional Development Officer, RADAR, May and July 1999, pers. comm.

54 *Contract Journal*, 26 August 1998.

55 *Contract Journal*, 12 August 1998.

56 As note 55.

57 *Observer*, 5 July 1998.

58 *Estates Gazette*, 24 February 1996.

59 As note 58.

60 Department of the Environment, Transport and the Regions, 3 November 1998, press release no. 926, *Revolution in Rethinking Construction Underway – John Prescott*.

61 Department of the Environment, Transport and the Regions, November 1998, *Rethinking Construction – The Movement for Innovation. Proposed Demonstration Projects.*

62 Department of the Environment, Transport and the Regions, 27 September 1999, press release no. 939: *Raynsford Proposes UK Construction Scheme to Aid Turkish Reconstruction.*

63 *Building*, 29 October 1999.

64 *Construction Monitor*, 21 September 1998, Department of the Environment, Transport and the Regions.

65 *Construction Monitor*, 26 October 1998, Department of the Environment, Transport and the Regions.

66 *Construction Monitor*, 22 February 1999, Department of the Environment, Transport and the Regions.

67 Michael Meacher, 21 April 1999, written answer to Parliamentary Question no. 81121.

68 <http://www.bcbforum.demon.co.uk/>, April 2000.

69 Department of the Environment, Transport and the Regions, 12 May 1998, press release no. 362, *Richard Caborn Pledges a Better Deal for the Environment on Quarrying.*

70 Department of the Environment, Transport and the Regions, January 1994, *Sustainable Development: the UK Strategy.* The Stationery Office, London. This is still used by the DETR as a policy statement.

71 Department of the Environment, Transport and the Regions, 27 January 1999, press release, *Nick Raynsford Encourages Industry Commitment to Sustainable Construction.*

72 E.g. DETR missions to Jordan and Egypt (October 1997), Poland (January 1998), Philippines (March 1998).

73 Department of the Environment, Transport and the Regions, *Annual Report 1998.*

74 Department of the Environment, Transport and the Regions, 26 June 1997, press release no. 242, *Construction Minister Backs British Exports.*

75 E.g. *Sunday Times*, 18 January 1998; *Western Morning News*, 15 May 1998.

76 *Building Design*, 19 September 1997.

77 *Birmingham Post*, 25 November 1997.

78 *Planning*, 13 February 1998.

79 Mr Prescott's announcement was cited in the Chancellor's Pre-Budget Statement, 9 November 1999.

80 Department of the Environment, Transport and the Regions consultation paper, 1998, *Modernising Planning: Streamlining the Processing of Major Infrastructure Projects and Other Projects of National Significance*.

81 Department of the Environment, Transport and the Regions, January 1999, *The Economic Consequences of Planning to the Business Sector*.

82 Department of the Environment, Transport and the Regions, 23 April 1999, *Modernising Planning: A Progress Report*.

Chapter Five: Economic Cleansing – How the Superstores Conquered Britain

1 Chapman Warren, May 1997, *Retail Assessment*. Prepared on Behalf of London and Cardiff Properties Ltd and Brunswick Holdings PLC.

2 Department of Town Planning, University of Wales College, Cardiff, June 1990, *Retail Potential in Mid Wales* (commissioned by the Development Board for Rural Wales).

3 Verdict, cited in the *Guardian*, 20 December 1999.

4 Keynote Ltd, 1997, *Retailing in the UK*.

5 Research by Verdict, cited in Department of the Environment, Transport and the Regions, October 1998, *The Impact of Large Foodstores on Market Towns and District Centres*. The Stationery Office, London.

6 Keynote Ltd, 1998, *Supermarkets and Superstores*.

7 As note 4.

8 Department of the Environment, Transport and the Regions,

October 1998, *The Impact of Large Foodstores on Market Towns and District Centres*. The Stationery Office, London.

9 As note 1.

10 Department of the Environment, Transport and the Regions, October 1998, as note 8.

11 As note 10.

12 Jonathon Guscott, Planning Officer, Brecon National Park Authority, 18 May 1999.

13 As note 1.

14 As note 12.

15 As note 1.

16 Sam Porter, Paul Raistrick, January 1998, *The Impact of Out-of-Centre Food Superstores on Local Retail Employment*, the National Retail Planning Forum, c/o Corporate Analysis, Boots Company plc, Nottingham.

17 As note 16.

18 Letter from Emma Hallett, New Economics Foundation, April 1998.

19 Government Statistical Service, *National Travel Survey, 1989/ 91; National Travel Survey, 1994/96*.

20 Hugh Raven, Tim Lang and Caroline Dumonteil, 1995, *Off Our Trolleys?*, Institute for Public Policy Research, London.

21 *Observer*, 26 July 1998.

22 As note 21.

23 Department of the Environment, Transport and the Regions, 1998, *A New Deal for Transport: Better for Everyone*. The Stationery Office, London.

24 John Breach, 29 July 1998, press release, *Pollution: Time to Turn the Smoglight on the Multiples, and Gasp*. The British Independent Fruit Growers' Association.

25 Angela Paxton, 1994, *The Food Miles Report: The Dangers of Long Distance Food Transport*. The SAFE Alliance, London.

26 *Freight* magazine, December 1999, April 1998, March 1998. The Freight Transport Association; *Global Transport*, Spring 1997.

27 *Guardian*, 9 February 1999.

28   *Mail on Sunday*, 12 May 1996.

29   *Guardian*, 28 October 1993.

30   *Observer*, 2 August 1998.

31   *Financial Times*, 20 January 2000.

32   Corporate Intelligence on Retailing, cited in the *Observer*, 27 September 1998.

33   Tesco, Summer 1998, *Clubcard* Magazine.

34   Caroline Cranbrook, 1997, *The Rural Economy and Supermarkets*. Great Glemham Farms, Suffolk.

35   *Grower*, 23 October 1997, cited in Shayne Mitchell, 1998, *Checking Out the Supermarkets: Competition in Retailing*. Published by Colin Breed MP, House of Commons.

36   British Independent Fruit Growers' Association, 11 November 1999, press release, *Supply of Groceries from Multiple Stores: Monopoly Inquiry. British Independent Fruit Growers' Association Gives Oral Evidence*.

37   *Panorama*, 23 November 1998.

38   John Cleland, Director of Produce, Meat, Poultry and Fish, Asda, 13 October 1998, letter to suppliers.

39   Safeway, 5 November 1999, *Good News from Safeway*.

40   *Panorama*, 23 November 1998.

41   As note 40.

42   *Daily Mail*, 23 August 1999.

43   Paul Dobson, Michael Waterson and Alex Chu, September 1998, *The Welfare Consequences of the Exercise of Buyer Power*, Office of Fair Trading, Research Paper 16.

44   John Breach, April 1998, *Regulation of Major Multiple Retailers (MMRs)*. British Independent Fruit Growers' Association.

45   *Scotsman*, 14 March 1998.

46   Christian Aid, 1999, *Taking Stock: How the Supermarkets Stack up on Ethical Trading*.

47   As note 46.

48   *Observer*, 20 June 1999.

49   As note 43.

50   E.g. Mike Godliman, Verdict, cited in the *Independent on*

Sunday, 15 August 1999; survey by A. C. Neilsen, cited in the *Sunday Times*, 1 November 1998; investigation by the *Sunday Times*, 22 August 1998, 30 August 1998, 22 November 1998; Paul Dobson, Michael Waterson and Alex Chu, as note 43; Keynote Ltd, 1996, *Supermarkets and Superstores*.

51 Citizen Organising Foundation, 20 December 1998, *How the Poor Pay More at Christmas*.

52 As note 43.

53 Monopolies and Mergers Commission, 1981, *Discounts to Retailers*. The Stationery Office, London.

54 Office of Fair Trading, 1985, *Competition and Retailing*. The Stationery Office, London.

55 *Independent Retail News*, 24 May 1996 and 6 June 1997.

56 Shayne Mitchell, 1998. *Checking Out the Supermarkets: Competition in Retailing*. Published by Colin Breed MP, House of Commons.

57 John Bridgeman, quoted in the *Grocer*, 1 August 1998.

58 *Grocer*, 8 August 1998.

59 *SuperMarketing*, 25 September 1998.

60 *SuperMarketing*, 7 August 1998.

61 *Times*, 20 October 1999.

62 *Independent*, 8 December 1999.

63 Competition Commission, 31 January 2000, *Summary for Consultation of Issues Raised*, <http://www.competition-commission.gov.uk/04issues.htm>.

64 Ian MacDougall, Williams de Broe, quoted in the *Guardian*, 2 February 2000.

65 Ann Brooks, local resident, 13 April 1999, pers. comm.; Tim Byng, Head of Property Services, Cheltenham Borough Council, 28 June 1999, pers. comm.; Hugh Denham, Council for the Protection of Rural England, 28 June 1999, pers. comm.; Council for the Protection of Rural England, 25 November 1998, press release: *Countryside Charity Calls for Action to End Planning Loopholes*.

66 *Extra* (Romsey's local paper), 10 September 1998; Bridget

Yallup, Romsey Awareness Group, 2 August 1998, pers. comm.

67 *Independent on Sunday*, 10 August 1997.

68 *SuperMarketing*, 3 March 1995.

69 *Journal of Planning and Environment Law*, July 1995; *The Times Law Reports*, 13 May 1995; *SuperMarketing*, 3 March 1995.

70 *Observer*, 6 February 2000.

71 *Estates Gazette*, 4 October 1997.

72 *Guardian*, 10 May 1997.

73 Andrea Barlow, Asda, quoted in *SuperMarketing*, 24 December 1997.

74 *Estates Gazette*, 6 December 1997.

75 Simon Gibbs (Planning Inspector), 22 April 1998, *Appeals by Tesco Stores Ltd and Railtrack plc: Report of Public Inquiry*.

76 Department of the Environment, Transport and the Regions, 1996, Planning Policy Guidance 6: *Town Centres and Retail Developments*.

77 *Observer*, 17 October 1999, 10 October 1999.

78 As note 77.

79 House of Commons *Hansard*, 4 June 1997, Column 390.

80 Office of Fair Trading, 8 April 1999, press release, *Bridgeman Refers Supermarkets*.

81 House of Commons Environment, Transport and Regional Affairs Select Committee, 11 January 2000, *Second Report on the Environmental Effects of Supermarket Competition*, <www.parliament.uk/commons/selcom/etrahome>.

82 Ann Robinson, BRC Director General, in *Annual Review 1998*. The British Retail Consortium.

83 The British Retail Consortium, *Annual Review 1998*.

84 As note 83.

85 As note 83.

86 As note 82.

87 T. Marsden and N. Wrigley, 1995, 'Regulation, retailing and consumption', *Planning & Environment*, vol. 27.

88 *Sunday Times*, 4 October 1998.

Chapter Six: **The Fat Cats Directory**

1 *Financial Times*, 20 March 1998.

2 *Independent*, 21 May 1997.

3 *Private Eye*, 30 October 1998.

4 The Countryside Agency, <http://194.196.160.72/news/roway1. htm>, April 2000.

5 Urban Task Force, 1999, *Towards an Urban Renaissance*: Department of the Environment, Transport and the Regions.

6 *Observer*, 12 September 1999.

7 *Lloyd's List*, 26 November 1996.

8 Department of Trade and Industry, 13 February 1998, press release, *EU Ministers meet in Cambridge to improve the Single Market*; *Sunday Telegraph*, 3 August 1997; House of Commons *Hansard*, 23 July 1997, Column 986.

9 *Guardian*, 5 September 1997; *Observer*, 3 August 1997; *Independent*, 17 February 1997; *Spur*, June 1997, The World Development Movement; *Private Eye*, 30 October 1998.

10 *Observer*, 21 December 1997.

11 *Guardian*, 8 May 1999.

12 ENDS Report no. 246, July 1995; *Environment Business*, 13 September 1995.

13 *New Scientist*, 4 April 1998.

14 ENDS Report no. 297, October 1999.

15 *Guardian*, 8 February 1999.

16 <http://www.environment-agency.gov.uk/files/shame.htm>, as at April 1999.

17 Friends of the Earth, 2 September 1998, press release, *FoE Calls on Environment Agency Chief to Resign*.

18 <http://www.environment-agency.gov.uk/files/shame.htm>, April 1999.

19 Friends of the Earth, 1 April 1998, press release, *FoE Fingers Filthy Factory – ICI*.

20 <http://www.environment-agency.gov.uk/files/shame.htm>, April 2000.

21 SMMT Response to review of UK National Air Quality Strategy, April 1999, <http://www.smmt.co.uk/briefing_papers/files/AirQuality.doc>.

22 *The Times*, 26 October 1996.

23 Mick Hamer, 1987, *Wheels within wheels: a study of the road lobby*. Routledge & Kegan Paul, London.

24 *SchNEWS*, 22 January 1998 and 3 April 1998. Published by Justice?, Brighton; *Private Eye*, 19 February 1999.

25 *Private Eye*, 6 March 1998.

26 Better Regulation Taskforce, May 1998, *Consumer Affairs*.

27 *Private Eye*, 8 August 1997.

28 *Observer*, 29 November 1998, 21 March 1999.

29 *Observer*, 16 May 1999; *SchNEWS*, 30 April 1999. Justice?, Brighton.

30 Export Group for the Constructional Industries, August 1999, memorandum submitted to the House of Commons Select Committee on Trade and Industry.

31 *Private Eye*, 22 January 1999.

32 <http://www.bbsrc.ac.uk>, January 2000.

33 <http://www.bioindustry.org/>, April 2000.

34 *Food Magazine* 43, Oct/Dec 1998, the Food Commission, London.

35 As note 34.

36 Department of the Environment, Transport and the Regions, 1998, *A New Deal for Transport: Better for Everyone*. The Stationery Office, London.

37 The CornerHouse, February 2000, *Dams Incorporated: The Record of Twelve European Dam Building Companies*. The Swedish Society for Nature Conservation; *Observer*, 5 December, 1999.

38 <http://www.environment-agency.gov.uk/files/shame.htm>, April 2000.

Chapter Seven: **Monsanto's Magic Potion**

1 rBST Internal Review Team, Health Protection Branch, Health Canada, 1998, *rBST (Nutrilac) 'Gaps Analysis' Report.*

2 As note 1.

3 R. Casorso, 1 March 1990, *Review of rBST*, cited in rBST Internal Review Team, as note 1.

4 Erik Millstone, University of Sussex, 5 June 1997, letter to John Verrall.

5 Erik Millstone, Eric Brunner and Ian White, 20 October 1994, *Nature*, vol. 371.

6 Ian Alexander, 27 August 1997, E-mail to Ruth Swinimer et al., subject: *Telephone call from Monsanto U.S.*

7 John Verrall, 1998, *Report on the Manipulation of Codex Alimentarius* (for Jacques Santer, President of the European Commission).

8 World Trade Organisation, 18 August 1997, *EC Measures Concerning Meat and Meat Products (Hormones): Complaint by Canada*. Report of the Panel, section VI.49.

9 Len Ritter, 1997, 'Report of a Panel on the Relationship between Public Exposure to Pesticides and Cancer for the Ad Hoc Panel on Pesticides and Cancer, Canadian Network of Toxicology Centres, Guelph, Ontario, Canada', *Cancer*, vol. 80.

10 JECFA, List of participants at the 50th meeting of the Joint FAO/WHO Expert Committee on Food Additives, Rome, 17–26 February 1998.

11 David Kowalczyk, 23 March 1998, fax to Ian Alexander.

12 rBST Internal Review Team, as note 1.

13 *Globe and Mail News*, 27 October 1998.

14 Health Canada, cited in *Rachel's Environment and Health Weekly*, 22 October 1998, no. 621.

15 *Toronto Star*, 21 September 1998; *Lancet*, 23 January 1999.

16 Shiv Chopra, 1 October 1999, letter to Senator Noel Kinsella.

17   Margaret Haydon, Shiv Chopra et al., 17 September 1999, letter to André Lachance, Bureau of Veterinary Drugs.

18   *Rachel's Environment and Health Weekly*, 17 March 1994, no. 381.

19   Cited in Office of Consumer Affairs, US Food and Drug Administration, 1997, *Backgrounder: Bovine Growth Hormone or Bovine Somatotropin*.

20   Judith Juskevich and Greg Guyer, 24 August 1990, 'Bovine Growth Hormone: Human Food Safety Evaluation', *Science*, vol. 249.

21   rBST Internal Review Team, as note 1.

22   Department of Consumer Affairs, City of New York, review no. 194. Cited in John Verrall, 1998, as note 7.

23   John Scheid, spokesman, FDA, quoted in Jeff Kamen, March 1999, 'Formula for Disaster: an Investigative Report on Genetically Engineered Bovine Growth Hormone in Milk and Consequences for your Health', *Penthouse Magazine*.

24   E.g. Samuel Epstein, 1996, 'Unlabeled Milk from Cows Treated with Biosynthetic Growth Hormones: A Case of Regulatory Abdication', *International Journal of Health Services*, vol. 26, No. 1; T. B. Mepham et al., 19 November 1994, 'Safety of milk from cows treated with bovine somatotropin', *Lancet*, vol. 344; Judith C. Juskevich and C. Greg Guyer, 'Bovine Growth Hormone: Human Food Safety Evaluation', *Science*, vol. 249 (1990); William H. Daughaday and David M. Barbano, 'Bovine Somatotropin Supplementation of Dairy Cows: is the Milk Safe?', *Journal of the American Medical Association*, vol. 264, no. 8 (22 August 1990); C. G. Prosser et al., 'Increased Secretion of Insulin-like Growth Factor-1 into Milk of Cows Treated with Recombinantly Derived Bovine Growth Hormone', *Journal of Dairy Science*, vol. 56 (1989).

25   C. J. Xian et al., 1995, 'Degradation of IGF-I in the Adult Rat Gastrointestinal Tract is Limited by a Specific Antiserum or the Dietary Protein Casein', *Journal of Endocrinology*, vol. 146; Toshikiro Kimura et al., November 1997, 'Gastrointestinal

Absorption of Recombinant Human Insulin-Like Growth Factor-I in Rats', *Journal of Pharmacology and Experimental Therapeutics*, vol. 283, no. 2. See also: R. K. Rao et al., February 1998, 'Luminal Stability of Insulin-Like Growth Factors I and II in Developing Rat Gastrointestinal Tract', *Journal of Pediatric Gastroenterology and Nutrition*, vol. 26, no. 2; A. F. Philipps, May 1997, 'Growth of Artificially Fed Infant Rats: Effect of Supplementation with Insulin-like Growth Factor I', *American Journal of Physiology*, vol. 272, no. 5; Douglas Burrin et al., May 1996, 'Orally Administered IGF-I Increases Intestinal Mucosal Growth in Formula-fed Neonatal Pigs', *American Journal of Physiology*, vol. 270, no. 5 part 2.

26   Samuel S. Epstein, 1996, 'Unlabeled Milk from Cows Treated with Biosynthetic Growth Hormones: A Case of Regulatory Abdication', *International Journal of Health Services*, vol. 26, no. 1.

27   M. N. Pollak, H. T. Huynh and P. Lefebvre, 1992, 'Tamoxifen reduces insulin-like growth factor 1 (IGF-1)', *Breast Cancer Research and Treatment*, vol. 22.

28   June M. Chan et al., 23 January 1998, 'Plasma Insulin-Like Growth Factor-I and Prostate Cancer Risk: A Prospective Study', *Science*, vol. 279.

29   Susan E. Hankinson et al., 9 May 1998, 'Circulating concentrations of insulin-like growth factor I and risk of breast cancer', *Lancet*, vol. 351, no. 9113.

30   *Rachel's Environment and Health Weekly*, 17 March 1994, no. 381.

31   *St. Louis Post-Dispatch*, 23 January 1999.

32   *Guardian*, 20 February 1999.

33   Walter Hobgood, Vice-President, Monsanto, 18 February 1994, letter to retail grocers.

34   Jeff Kamen, March 1999, as note 23.

35   Richard Burroughs, quoted in Jeff Kamen, March 1999, as note 23.

36   Michael Taylor, 10 February 1994, 'Interim Guidance on the

Voluntary Labeling of Milk and Milk Products From Cows That Have Not Been Treated With Recombinant Bovine Somatotropin', *Federal Register*, vol. 59 no. 28, cited in *Rachel's Environment and Health Weekly*, 17 March 1994, no. 381.

37 As note 7; The Edmonds Institute, 1998, *FDA: Monsanto's Washington Branch Office*, <http://www.edmonds-institute.org/door.html>.

38 As note 7

39 As note 7.

40 US General Accounting Office, cited in John Verrall, as note 7.

41 Executive Branch, US Federal Government, January 1994, *BST: Executive Summary*. Cited by Robert Cohen, <http://www.antidairycoalition.com>.

42 Robert Cohen, 19 July 1998, *Antidairy Coalition Newsletter*, <http://www.antidairycoalition.com>.

43 The Edmonds Institute, 1998, as note 37.

44 *St. Louis Post-Dispatch*, 27 December 1998.

45 From papers obtained from the FDA in a lawsuit pursued by the Alliance for Bio-Integrity. Cited in Alliance for Bio-Integrity press release, 24 June 1999, *FDA Documents Show They Ignored GMO Safety Warnings From Their Own Scientists*, <http://www.bio-integrity.org>.

46 House of Commons *Hansard*, 3 November 1998, answer to Parliamentary Question no. 57703.

47 *Observer*, 27 February 2000.

48 *St. Louis Post-Dispatch*, 27 December 1998.

49 As note 48.

50 *Dail Report*, 5 October 1999, Noel Dempsey's response to Question no. 18728/99.

51 *Sunday Telegraph*, 11 July 1999.

52 *International Trade Reporter*, 30 June 1999, vol. 16, no. 26.

53 *Reuters*, 20 May 1999.

54 *Dow Jones News*, 29 June 1999.

55 *Reuters*, 27 August 1999.

56 *FWN*, 21 July 1999.

57 *Guardian*, 3 December 1999.

58 *Observer*, 20 June 1999.

59 As note 58.

60 Veterinary Medicines Directorate, Ministry of Agriculture Fisheries and Food, January 1997, *Bovine Somatotropin (BST)*, CP(INF)97/17.

61 Food and Agriculture Organization of the United Nations/ World Health Organization Joint Expert Committee on Food Additives, 50th Meeting, Rome, 17–26 February 1998, *Summary and Conclusions*, <http://www.who.int/pcs/jecfa/ summary_50.htm>.

62 The Greens in the European Parliament, 16 April 1999, press release, *EU Scientific Experts Point to Human Health Risks from rBST Use.*

63 As note 62.

64 As note 7.

65 JECFA, 1998, 50 Meeting, Summary and Conclusions. Quoted in John Verrall, as note 7.

66 As note 7.

67 Minutes of the Bureau of Veterinary Drugs Ad Hoc BST Advisory Committee, 9 October 1997.

68 Ian Alexander, 18 November 1997, Email to Ruth Swinimer, Donald Landry and Mansen Yong, subject: *Conversation with Monsanto.*

69 David Kowalczyk, Director, Regulatory Affairs, Protiva, Monsanto, 5 December 1997. Letter to Ian Alexander.

70 As note 7.

71 Scientific Committee on Animal Health and Animal Welfare, 10 March 1999, *The Animal Welfare Aspects of the Use of Bovine Somatotrophin: Conclusions and Recommendations*, <http://europa.eu.int/comm/dg24/health/sc/scah/ out21_en.html>.

72 Scientific Committee on Veterinary Measures Relating to Public Health, 15–16 March 1999, *Report on Public Health*

Aspects of the Use of Bovine Somatotrophin, <http://
europa.eu.int/comm/dg24/health/sc/scv/out19_en.html>.

Chapter Eight: A Padlock on the Food Chain

1 Robert Fraley, *Farm Journal,* cited by the Rural Advancement
Fund International, September 1996: *The Life Industry,* <http:/
/rafi.org/web/>.
2 *Evening Standard,* 23 February 1999.
3 Rural Advancement Fund International, 1998, *Are Patents Out
of Control?: Human Rights and Predatory Patents,* <http://
rafi.org/web/action-patents.shtml#patents>.
4 J. Enyart, June 1990, *A GATT Intellectual Property Code.* Les
Nouvelles, pp. 54–6.
5 Monsanto, 1996, *Roundup Ready® Gene Agreement,* coded
SEM(97)8-../ljd.
6 George Poste, quoted in *Seedling,* March 1997: Genetic
Resources Action International, <http://www.grain.org/
publications/mar97/mar972.htm>.
7 Department of Trade and Industry, February 1996, *Proposal
for a Directive of the European Council and Parliament on the
Legal Protection of Biotechnological Inventions: Compliance Cost
Assessment,* COM (95)66L.
8 Gareth Evans, Consultant in Medical Genetics, St Mary's
Hospital, Manchester, 1 July 1997, letter to MEPs. Cited in
the CornerHouse, September 1997, *No Patents on Life: A
Briefing on the Proposed EU Directive on the Legal Protection of
Biotechnological Inventions.*
9 Andrew Read, Department of Medical Genetics, St Mary's
Hospital, 20 November 1997, letter to Tessa Jowell, Minister
of State for Health.
10 Gareth Evans, Consultant in Medical Genetics, St Mary's
Hospital, Manchester, on behalf of the Clinical Genetics Service, 15 July 1997, letter to MEPs.

11 Howard Dalton et al., 20 February 1997, 'Patent Threat to Research', letter to *Nature*, vol. 385.

12 The European Commission, 1997, *Directive on the legal protection of biotechnological inventions*, Article 5, paragraph 2.

13 As note 10.

14 Alastair Kent, quoted in the *Independent*, 17 November 1993.

15 Genetic Interest Group, February 1995, evidence to House of Commons Inquiry, quoted by Ricarda Steinbrecher, Women's Environment Network, *Opposition to Patenting*.

16 Alastair Kent, March 1997, *Patents for Life*.

17 Roberta Tweedy, Director, the Neurofibromatosis Association, 31 March 1998, deposition to the European Parliament, *The European Biotechnology Directive*.

18 Roberta Tweedy, 2 August 1997, letter to the *Independent*.

19 Bernadette Moran, Development Officer, Huntingdon's Disease Association of Ireland, undated, letter to MEPs.

20 British Society for Human Genetics, undated, *Patenting of Human Gene Sequences and the EU Draft Directive*.

21 European Campaign on Biotechnology Patents, March 1998, *The European Biotech Patents Directive*.

22 Simon Gentry, Director of External Affairs, SmithKline Beecham, 6 May 1998, pers. comm.

23 As note 22.

24 Simon Gentry, 1997, Genetic Interest Group *Annual Report*.

25 As note 22.

26 *Guardian*, 17 January 2000.

27 *Financial Times*, 15 March 2000.

28 Early Day Motion no. 904, 27 March 1995, *Patenting of Life*.

29 Invest in Britain Bureau, 1998, *What is Happening in the Biotechnology Field?*, <http://www.dti.gov.uk/ibb>.

30 *Guardian*, 4 June 1998.

31 Jack Cunningham, May 1998, quoted on the BBC Web site, 30 August 1998, <http://news.bbc.co.uk/hi/english/health/newsid_161000/161173.stm>.

32 Lennart Hardell and Mikael Eriksson, 15 March 1999, 'A

Case-Control Study of Non-Hodgkin Lymphoma and Exposure to Pesticides', *Cancer*, vol. 85, no.6.

33 William Pease et al., 1993, *Preventing Pesticide-related Illness in California Agriculture*: School of Public Health, University of California, Berkeley; J. C. Robinson et al., 1994, *Pesticides in the Home and Community: Health risks and policy alternatives*. School of Public Health, University of California, Berkeley, cited in Pesticide Action Network North America, 10 January 1997, press release: *Monsanto Agrees to Change Ads*, <http://www.panna.org/panna>.

34 Lord Donoughue, 21 July 1999, House of Lords *Hansard*, Column 968.

35 As note 34.

36 *Daily Mail*, 13 February 1999.

37 As note 36.

38 *Observer*, 4 July 1999.

39 Peter Kilfoyle, 16 June 1999, reply to Parliamentary Question no. 85962, House of Commons *Hansard*.

40 John Battle, 13 July 1999, reply to Parliamentary Question no. 88953.

41 The Cabinet Office, 19 February 1999, *GM Foods: Policy and Presentational Issues*.

42 As note 41.

43 Paul Britton, the Cabinet Office, 11 May 1999, letter to several ministerial private secretaries and 10 Downing Street.

44 As note 43.

45 Jack Cunningham, 21 May 1999, House of Commons *Hansard*, Columns 1371 to 1384.

46 Jack Cunningham, 23 June 1999, reply to Parliamentary Question no. 86783. House of Commons *Hansard*.

47 As note 46.

48 As note 45.

49 *Daily Express*, 23 July 1999.

50 *Observer*, 21 February 1999.

51 *Observer*, 23 May 1999.

52 Lord Sainsbury, *Observer*, 26 September 1999.

53 Carnegie Institution of Washington, 15 December 1997, press release, *Christopher Stone Elected Carnegie Trustee.*

54 Stephen Byers, 25 February 1999, reply to Parliamentary Question no. 73134, House of Commons *Hansard.*

55 Foresight Programme, Department of Trade and Industry, March 1998, *Food Chain Group Report.*

56 As note 55.

57 *Independent*, 8 March 1999.

58 Sir Robert May, 16 February 1999, *Today* Programme, BBC Radio 4.

59 Stephen Byers, 19 April 1999, reply to Parliamentary Question no. 70440, House of Commons *Hansard.*

60 Jeff Rooker, 4 February 1999, House of Commons *Hansard*, Column 1065.

61 *Observer*, 12 September 1999.

62 Friends of the Earth, 15 December 1998, press release, *Lord Sainsbury (Biotech Backer) Chairs Public Consultation on GMOs for the Government.*

63 *Daily Mail*, 13 September 1999.

64 Department of Trade and Industry, 16 April 1999, press release no. P/99/325, *Sainsbury Announces Biotechnology Clusters Team.*

65 Department of Trade and Industry, 5 August 1999, press release no. P/99/683, *Lord Sainsbury Unveils 10-point Action Plan for Biotechnology Clusters.*

66 As note 65.

67 Jeff Rooker, 19 April 1999, reply to Parliamentary Question no. 80791, House of Commons *Hansard.*

68 *Telegraph*, 29 January 1999.

69 Department of Trade and Industry, April 1999, *Demonstrator Project Support, BIO-WISE News* Issue 2, <http://www.dti.gov.uk/biowise>.

70 *Professional Engineering*, 23 July 1997.

71 *PA News*, 17 January 1999.

72 Mr Prescott's announcement was cited in the Chancellor's Pre-Budget Statement, 9 November 1999.

73 The Invest in Britain Bureau, Department of Trade and Industry, <http://www.dti.gov.uk/ibb>.

74 Department of Trade and Industry, 1999, *BioGuide*, <http://www.dti.gov.uk>.

75 The Invest in Britain Bureau, as note 73.

76 As note 73.

77 As note 73.

78 Friends of the Earth, 9 July 1998, press release: *FoE Calls for Government Genetic Advisors to be Sacked.*

79 Alan Gray, quoted in the *Sunday Times*, 5 September 1999.

80 As note 79.

81 *Independent*, 13 February 1999.

82 Janet Bainbridge, quoted in *Splice* magazine, August/September 1998, vol. 4, no. 6. The Genetics Forum.

83 Tony Blair, *Independent on Sunday*, 27 February 2000.

Chapter Nine: Silent Science – The Corporate Takeover of the Universities

1 Robin Grove-White, external examiner, University of Edinburgh, 16 October 1996, *Examiner's report.*

2 University of Edinburgh, 24 April 1996, press release, *The Centre for Human Ecology.*

3 Robert Robertson, The Resource Use Institute Ltd, 14 April 1993, Letter to Ulrich Loening, Director of the Centre for Human Ecology.

4 Ian Wilson, Marine Development Ltd, 10 April 1993, letter to Malcolm Slesser, Honorary Fellow, the Centre for Human Ecology.

5 Douglas Faulkner, D. Faulkner and Associates, 21 October 1996, letter to Ulrich Loening, who remained Director of the independent Centre for Human Ecology.

6 Sir Stuart Sutherland, 24 April 1996, University of Edinburgh press release, *Academic Freedom, Teaching Responsibilities and Mr Chris Brand.*

7 Office of Science and Technology, 1993, White Paper, *Realising Our Potential, a Strategy for Science, Engineering and Technology.* Stationery Office, London.

8 As note 7.

9 <http://www.foresight.gov.uk/about.html>.

10 Ian Taylor, Autumn 1995. *A change for the better? Science & Public Affairs.*

11 Department of Trade and Industry, London, 1998, White Paper, *Our Competitive Future: Building the Knowledge Driven Economy*, <http://www.dti.gov.uk/comp/competitive/wh_int1.htm>.

12 E.g. Department of Trade and Industry, <http://dtiinfo1.dti.gov.uk/ost/forwardlook99/states/hefcdeni/text.htm>, May 2000.

13 Save British Science, 9 November, 1999. Cited by the BBC, <http://news2.thls.bbc.co.uk/hi/english/sci/tech/newsid_511000/511305.stm>.

14 The Committee of Vice-Chancellors and Principals of the Universities of the UK, December 1999, *Spending Review 2000 – the UK submission of CVCP: Investing in Universities and Colleges for Global Success.*

15 The Committee of Vice-Chancellors and Principals of the Universities of the UK, quoted in the *Times*, 15 December 1998.

16 Professor Sir Alec Broers, Vice-Chancellor, Cambridge University, 8 November 1999. Quoted in Cambridge University press release, *Cambridge and MIT: Torchbearers to UK's Enterprise Future – World's Top Two Research and Business Giants Join Forces for an International Enterprise Partnership.*

17 Cambridge University, 8 November 1999, as note 16.

18 As note 16.

19 *Sunday Telegraph*, 15 November 1998.

20 As note 19.

21 *Times*, 13 November 1996.

22 As note 21.

23 Greg Muttitt and Chris Grimshaw, 2000, *Degrees of Involvement: An examination of the relationship between the upstream oil and gas industry and UK higher education institutions*. CorporateWatch.

24 The Geology and Petroleum Geology Department, University of Aberdeen, Department of Geology & Petroleum Geology, 'Staff directory', <http://www.abdn.ac.uk/geology/staff/staff-dir.htm>, October 1998, cited in Greg Muttitt and Chris Grimshaw, 2000, as note 23.

25 As note 23.

26 David Whyte, 30 May 1998, *Power, Corruption and Lies: the World According to the UK Oil and Gas Industry*, paper presented to the OILC National Conference, Patio Hotel, Aberdeen.

27 As note 26.

28 Henry Stelfox et al., 8 January 1998, *Conflict of Interest in the Debate over Calcium-Channel Antagonists. New England Journal of Medicine*, vol. 338, no. 2.

29 As note 28.

30 At <http://www.bbsrc.ac.uk>, 21 January 2000.

31 As note 30.

32 Biotechnology and Biological Sciences Research Council, 13 October 1999, press release, *BBSRC concern about GM paper in The Lancet*.

33 BBSRC, 30 September 1999, press release, *GM pollen findings are 'not new'*.

34 BBSRC, 7 June 1999, press release, *BBSRC regrets destruction of GM crop*.

35 BBSRC, 13 January 1999, press release, *£15 million to find out which genes do what*.

36 BBSRC, 15 July 1999, press release, *Consolidation of the*

Institute of Arable Crops Research (IACR) will boost research into sustainable agriculture.

37 BBSRC, 13 October 1999, press release, *Over £11M cash injection for research in genomics.*

38 BBSRC, Business and Innovation Unit, <http://www.bbsrc. ac.uk/opennet/structur/biig/bigbiu.html>, May 2000.

39 BBSRC, Industry Fellowships Scheme, <http://www.cc.bbsrc. ac.uk/opennet/structur/biig/ifs.html>, May 2000.

40 BBSRC, Business and Innovation Unit, <http://www.bbsrc. ac.uk/opennet/structur/biig/bigbiu.html>, May 2000.

41 BBSRC staff contract, leaked to GeneWatch and quoted by Norfolk Genetic Information Network, 18 February 1999, press release: *Scientists gagged on GM foods by public funding body with big links to industry.*

42 Health and Safety Executive, quoted in *Private Eye*, 22 January 1999.

43 Department of Trade and Industry, Foresight for Food and Drink: Alcoholic Drinks, <http://193.82.159.123/documents/ fsze00004/fsze0000410.html>, January 2000.

44 As note 43.

45 Department of Trade and Industry, Foresight for Food and Drink: Fruit and Vegetables, <http://193.82.159.123/docu-ments/fsze00007/fsze000075.html>, January 2000.

46 Department of Trade and Industry, Foresight for Food and Drink: Dairy, <http://193.82.159.123/documents/fsze00006/ fsze000068.html>, May 2000.

47 Department of Trade and Industry, Foresight for Food and Drink: Meat, <http://www.foresight.gov.uk>, January 2000.

48 As note 47.

49 Foresight Programme, Department of Trade and Industry, March 1998, *Food Chain Group Report.*

50 As note 49.

51 Department of Trade and Industry, *The Food Chain Group – Shaping the Future of the Food Industry*, <http:// www.foresight.gov.uk>, January 2000.

52　As note 51.

53　Department of Trade and Industry, *Winning through Foresight: Action for Food & Drink*, <http://193.82.159.123/documents/fsze00002/fsze000023.html>, January 2000.

54　As note 53.

55　Department of Trade and Industry, *A review of the role of Agriculture, Horticulture and Forestry in the UK Economy*, <http://193.82.159.123/documents/fsza00003/fsza000032.html>, December 1999.

56　Department of Trade and Industry, Foresight for Agriculture, Horticulture & Forestry, <http://193.82.159.123/documents/fsza00007/fsza000073.html>, January 2000.

57　Department of Trade and Industry, *Progress Through Partnership: 15 – Retail & Distribution*, <http://193.82.159.123/retail/retail2005.html>, January 2000.

58　As note 57.

59　<http://www.ufiltd.co.uk>, December 1999.

60　Department of Trade and Industry, 15 December 1998, press release no. P/98/1029, *Lord Sainsbury Announces Public Consultation on Biosciences*.

61　Department of Health, July 1999, White Paper, *Saving Lives: Our Healthier Nation*. The Stationery Office, London.

62　As note 61.

63　As note 61.

64　Friends of the Earth, 29 September 1999, press release, *GM Crops: Genetic Pollution Proved: GM Pollen Found Miles from Trial Site*.

65　Dick van Steenis, spring 1999, *CorporateWatch* magazine, no. 8.

Chapter Ten: **Government in Exile – The Corporate Bid for World Domination**

1　Renato Ruggerio, Director-General, the World Trade Organization, December 1996, speech to the World Trade Organization's Singapore Ministerial meeting.

2 E.g. letter from Michael Jampel, International Investment Policy Section, Department of Trade and Industry, 25 September 1997, to Tony Gosling; letter from Andrew Smith MP, 31 March 1998, to Sarah Wild.

3 Organisation of Economic Cooperation and Development, 1997, *Multilateral Agreement on Investment (Draft Negotiating Text)*.

4 Organisation of Economic Cooperation and Development, 1997, *Multilateral Agreement on Investment (Draft Negotiating Text)*, quoted by Friends of the Earth US, 19 February 1997, fact sheet, *The OECD Multilateral Agreement on Investment (MAI)*.

5 Organisation of Economic Co-operation and Development Web site, <http://www.oecd.org/daf/cmis/cime/mnetext.htm>, May 2000.

6 Corporate Europe Observatory, February 1998, *Maigalomania: Citizens and the Environment Sacrificed to Corporate Investment Agenda*, Corporate Europe Observatory, Brussels.

7 International Chamber of Commerce Commission on International Trade and Investment Policy, 30 April 1996, document 103/179, cited in Corporate Europe Observatory, February 1998, as note 6.

8 Jerome Monod, Pehr Gyllenhammar and Wisse Dekker, September 1991, *Reshaping Europe: A Report from the European Round Table of Industrialists*, ERT, Brussels.

9 As note 8.

10 Global Trade Watch, December 1998, *NAFTA at Five: A Report Card*, <http://www.citizen.org/pctrade/nafta/reports/5years.htm>.

11 US Labor Department NAFTA–TAA data, up to 19 November 1998. Cited in Global Trade Watch, December 1998, as note 10.

12 INEGI, *Manufacturing Industry Productivity, Various Countries January 1993–September 1998*. Cited in Global Trade Watch, December 1998, as note 10.

13 Jose Maria Imaz, January 1997, *NAFTA Damages Small Businesses, El Barzon*, Mexico City. Cited in Global Trade Watch, December 1998, as note 10.

14 House of Commons Environmental Audit Committee, 8 February 1999, *The Multilateral Agreement on Investment (MAI)*.

15 Department of Trade and Industry, 26 November 1998, press release no. P/98/944, *Brian Wilson Welcomes 'Constructive Discussion' on Future of International Investment Rules*.

16 Department of Trade and Industry, 24 November 1998, press release no. P/98/932, *Brian Wilson Reaffirms Benefits of Investment Liberalisation for Developing Countries*.

17 European Commission Directorate General I (External Relations), 15 December 1998, *WTO New Round: Trade and Investment*. Note for the Attention of the 113 Committee.

18 As note 17.

19 As note 17.

20 As note 17.

21 UNCTAD, 1995, *Translating Uruguay Round Special Provisions for Least Developed Countries into Concrete Action: Issues and Policy requirements*, report to the Ad Hoc Working Group on Trading Opportunities in the New International Trading Context. Cited by Oxfam, November 1999, Position Paper, *Loaded Against the Poor: World Trade Organisation*.

22 E.g. New England Burma Roundtable, 5 November 1998, *US Court Revokes Massachusetts Burma Law*, and 22 June 1999, *Federal Appeals Court Rules Against MA Burma Law*.

23 <http://www.uscsi.org>, November 1999, cited in David Price, Allyson Pollock and Jean Shaoul, 27 November 1999, 'How the World Trade Organisation is Shaping Domestic Policies in Health Care', *Lancet*, vol. 354.

24 Coalition of Service Industries, *Services 2000, USTR Register Submission*. Response to *Federal Register* Notice of 19 August 1998 [FR Doc 98=n22279], cited by Susan George, July 1999, 'State Sovereignty Under Threat: Globalising Designs of the

WTO', *Le Monde Diplomatique*, <http://www.monde-diplomatique.fr/en/1999/07/?c=05george>.

25 Charlene Barchefsky, cited by Susan George, as note 24.

26 World Trade Organisation Secretariat, 18 September 1998, document no. S/C/W/50, *Health and Social Services*, cited by John Hilary, November 1999, *GATS 2000 and the Public Health Sector: The US Services Industry Finds a Friend*, Briefing for the World Development Movement.

27 The World Development Movement, 22 November 1999, *The World Trade Organisation: Update on pre-Seattle Negotiations*.

28 Department of Trade and Industry, 1999, *Liberalising Trade in Services: A Consultative Document on the 'GATS 2000' negotiations in the World Trade Organisation and Forthcoming Bilateral Negotiations*.

29 As note 28.

30 Stephen Byers, 14 June 1999, Speech to the Keidanren, Tokyo. The same phrase is used in Department of Trade and Industry, 1 February 1999, press release no. P/99/84, *Wilson Voices Support for Multilateral Trading System*; and by Richard Caborn, Minister for Trade, 15 September 1999, *Customs and Trade Facilitation*, speech to the Commonwealth Symposium, London.

31 Department of Trade and Industry, May 1999, *The UK and the World Trade Organisation: An Introduction to the Next Round*. Stationery Office, London.

32 Department of Trade and Industry, June 1999, *International Investment: the Next Steps*.

33 Tony Blair, 19 May 1998, Speech to World Trade Organisation, Geneva.

34 Pehr Gyllenhammar, 1983, quoted on the European Round Table's Web site at <http://www.ert.be/5_achiev/origens.htm>, September 1997.

35 As note 34.

36 As note 34.

37 At <http://www.ert.be/5_achiev/achievem.htm>, September 1997.

38 Maria Green Cowles, December 1995, 'Setting the Agenda for a New Europe: The ERT and EC 1992', *Journal of Common Market Studies*, vol. 33. no. 4.

39 As note 38.

40 <http://www.ert.be/5_achiev/achievem.htm>, September 1997.

41 Jacques Delors, March 1993, quoted by the European Round Table of Industrialists, <http://www.ert.be/5_achiev/achievem.htm>, September 1997.

42 Association for the Monetary Union of Europe, *Annual Report 1995*, quoted in Corporate Europe Observatory, May 1997, *Europe, Inc.: Dangerous Liaisons Between EU Institutions and Industry*, Corporate Europe Observatory, Amsterdam

43 European Round Table of Industrialists, 1984, *Missing Links*, ERT, Brussels.

44 European Round Table of Industrialists, November 1998, *Job Creation and Competitiveness through Innovation*, ERT, Brussels.

45 European Round Table Web site, <http://www.ert.be/2_activ/future.htm>, September 1997.

46 As note 44.

47 European Round Table of Industrialists' Web site, <http://www.ert.be/pc/enc03.htm>, May 2000.

48 Keith Richardson, quoted in J. Hallen and R. Thoren, April 1993, 'Det Hanger pa Kontakterna', *Metallarbetaren*, vol. 4.

49 European Round Table of Industrialists, May 1994, *European Competitiveness: The Way to Growth and Jobs*. ERT, Brussels.

50 Keith Richardson, 21 February 1997, interviewed in Corporate Europe Observatory, May 1997, as note 42.

51 Corporate Europe Observatory, May 1997, as note 42.

52 As note 44.

53 The European Round Table of Industrialists, 1998, *The East–West Win–Win Business Experience*, ERT, Brussels.

54 As note 53.

55 As note 53.

56 Reuters, 11 May 1998.

57 David Aaron, Under-Secretary of Commerce for International Trade, 28 July 1998, Statement to the House Committee on Ways and Means Subcommittee on Trade.

58 James Murphy, Assistant US Trade Representative for Agricultural Affairs, 3 March 1999, Statement to the House Agriculture Committee, Subcommittee on Risk Management, Research and Specialty Crops.

59 David Aaron, Under-Secretary of Commerce for International Trade, cited in *Corporate Europe Observer*, October 1998, vol. 2.

60 Mary Sophos, Senior Vice President, Government Affairs, The Grocery Manufacturers of America, 28 July 1998, statement to the House Committee on Ways and Means, Subcommittee on Trade.

61 Timothy Hauser, Acting Under Secretary of Commerce for International Trade, 23 July 1997, Statement to the House Committee on Ways and Means, Subcommittee on Trade. Cited by Corporate Europe Observatory, 25 October 1999, Briefing Paper, *Transatlantic Business Dialogue (TABD): Putting the Business Horse before the Government Cart*, Corporate Europe Observatory, Amsterdam.

62 Jérôme Monod, 18 March 1999, statement to the REX Committee, European Parliament, cited by Corporate Europe Observatory, 25 October 1999, as note 61.

63 Transatlantic Business Dialogue, 18 March 1999, *History – Organisation*, cited by Corporate Europe Observatory, 25 October 1999, as note 61.

64 European Commission Services, 22 September 1998, TABD Implementation Table, 1998, Working Document, cited by Corporate Europe Observatory, 25 October 1999, as note 61.

65 Leon Brittan, 8 March 1999, letter to Jérôme Monod, cited by Corporate Europe Observatory, 25 October 1999, as note 61.

66 William Daley, 13 June 1997, US Department of Commerce press release, *US and EU Reach Agreement on Mutual Recognition of Product Testing and Approval Requirements*.

67 Transatlantic Business Dialogue, March 1999, Conclusions of the TABD Chief Executives' Conference, Berlin. Cited in Corporate Europe Observatory, 1999, *Doing Business in Berlin: Transatlantic Business Dialogue (TABD) Annual Conference 1999*.

68 As note 67.

69 Dana Mead, Co-chairman of the Transatlantic Business Dialogue, March 1999, *Leadership challenges for the Third Millennium*, *Chief Executive* magazine, cited by Corporate Europe Observatory, 25 October 1999, as note 61.

70 Timothy Hauser, acting Under Secretary of Commerce for International Trade, 23 July 1997, Statement to the House Committee on Ways and Means, Subcommittee on Trade. Cited by Corporate Europe Observatory, 25 October 1999, as note 61.

71 Horst Langer, Transatlantic Business Dialogue, 10 March 1998, 'Transatlantic Business Dialogue (TABD) – A Step Toward Better Economic Relations', speech to the European-American Chamber of Commerce, New York. Cited by Olivier Hoedeman, October 1998, *The Transatlantic Economic Partnership (TEP)*, Corporate Europe Observatory, Amsterdam.

72 See *Corporate Takeover of the United Nations Continues. Corporate Europe Observatory*, 27 April 1998, vol. 1.

Chapter Eleven: **A Troublemakers' Charter**

1 European Round Table of Industrialists, November 1998, *Job Creation and Competitiveness through Innovation*, ERT, Brussels.

2 Joseph Fenton, Donnelly Marketing, cited in Consumers' Union, 1999, *Captive Kids: A Report on Commercial Pressures*

on Kids at School, <http://www.igc.org/consunion/other/captivekids/>.

3 Consumers' Union, 1999, as note 2.

4 Consumers' Union, 1999, as note 2.

5 Consumers' Union, 1999, as note 2.

6 Consumers' Union, 1999, as note 2.

7 Consumers' Union, 1999, as note 2.

8 *Observer*, 5 April 1998.

9 *Daily Telegraph*, 24 May 1996.

10 *Times Educational Supplement*, 14 June 1996.

11 *Times Educational Supplement*, 19 February 1999.

12 McDonald's *Operations Manual*, quoted by Dave Morris, spring 1999, 'Inviting the McWolf into the Fold', *Corporate Watch*, vol. 8.

13 European Round Table of Industrialists, November 1998, *Job Creation and Competitiveness through Innovation*, ERT, Brussels.

14 European Round Table of Industrialists, 1995, *Education for Europeans: Towards the Learning Society*, ERT, Brussels.

15 Department for Education and Employment, 23 June 1998, press release no. 318/98, *£75 million Boosts Radical Education Action Zones to Raise Standards*.

16 Stephen Byers, quoted in the *Times Educational Supplement*, 26 June 1998.

17 Lambeth Education Action Zone, cited by Bernard Regan, 2000, *Education For Sale?*, <http://www.ett.org.uk/art50_3_br.html>.

18 *Sunday Times*, 7 February 1999.

19 Mintel Market Intelligence, July 1997, *Toys and Games*.

20 *Guardian*, 19 December 1998.

21 Mr Justice Bell, 19 June 1997, High Court of Justice, Queen's Bench Division, No. 1990-M-NO. 5724: *McDonald's Corporation and McDonald's Restaurants Ltd v. Helen Steel and David Morris*.

22 Stephen Colegrave, quoted in the *Guardian*, 22 November 1999.

23 *Marketing Week*, cited in the *Financial Times*, 27 October 1998.

24 Friends of the Earth, 28 November 1998, press release, *Parents Protest at Pester Power: Survey Shows Parents Angry as Kids Bombarded With TV Ads.*

25 As note 24.

26 *Campaign*, 18 July 1997.

27 The Advertising Information Group, March 1999, *Notices* no. 34, <http://www.aig.org/notices/no34/comm34.html>.

28 See Louise Gitter, November 1996, 'Misleading Health Information in Advertising', *Consumer Policy Review*, vol. 6, no. 6, and Benet Middleton and David Rodwell, May 1998, 'Regulating Advertising – Time to Get Tough?', *Consumer Policy Review*, vol. 8, no. 3.

29 *Campaign*, 20 June 1997.

30 Independent Television Commission, 1997, *Code of Advertising Standards and Practice.*

31 Letter from Rachael Dougherty, Advertising Standards Authority, 28 July 1995, to Blake Lee-Harwood, Friends of the Earth.

32 *Times*, 16 December 1997.

33 Independent Television Commission, 1997, *Code of Advertising Standards and Practice.*

34 *Coriolanus*, Act 1, Scene 1.

35 David Clark, Better Regulation Unit, mission statement, <http://www.cabinet-office.gov.uk/regulation>, June 1997.

36 *The Hampel Report on Corporate Governance*, cited in *The Times*, 5 February 1998.

37 Christopher Haskins, 1998, foreword to *Principles of Good Regulation*, Better Regulation Task Force, <http://www.cabinet-office.gov.uk/regulation/1998/task_force/principles.htm>.

38 Stephen Byers, 3 June 1999, speech to the British Chambers of Commerce, <http://www.dti.gov.uk/Minspeech/byers040699.htm>.

39 As note 38.

40 <http://193.128.244.178/regulation/index.htm>, May 2000.

41 *Guardian*, 29 July 1997.

42 Gary Slapper, 1999, *Blood in the Bank: Social and Legal Aspects of Death at Work*, Ashgate, Dartmouth.

43 Select Committee on Environment, Transport and Regional Affairs, 1999, *Memorandum by The Centre for Corporate Accountability (HSE 20)*.

44 As note 43.

45 *Guardian*, 3 October 1997.

46 Health and Safety Executive, Working Party on Freedom of Information, Open Government Unit, 18 December 1997, *Memorandum on Persistent Inquirers for Information, Special Monitoring*.

47 As note 46.

48 Angela Eagle, 12 May 1998, response to Parliamentary Question no. 41601, House of Commons *Hansard*.

49 Gordon Brown, 1 November 1999, speech to the CBI Conference, <http://www.treasury.gov.uk/press/1999/p179_99.html>.

50 *Economist*, 31 May 1997.

51 *Economist*, 29 January 2000.

52 *Observer*, 31 October 1999

53 Tony Blair, 27 February 2000, *Independent on Sunday*.

54 The Bubble Act, section 18, 1720. Cited by Daniel Bennett, March 1999, *The creation and development of English commercial corporations and the abolition of democratic control over their behaviour*, Programme on Corporations, Law and Democracy, <http://www.corporatewatch.org/pages/dan_corp.html>.

55 Frederick Douglass, 4 August 1857, *North Star*.

Index

JOHN SERGEANT

Give Me Ten Seconds

PAN BOOKS

Today he is the Political Editor of ITN, but for thirty years John Sergeant worked for the BBC, latterly as Chief Political Correspondent. *Give Me Ten Seconds* is his riveting, frequently hilarious and often touching autobiography. In it, he takes us from his rather curious childhood to his early years as a reporter on the *Liverpool Post*, and thence to the BBC. Memorably handbagged by Mrs Thatcher on the steps of the Paris Embassy following her failure to retain the leadership of the Conservative Party, Sergeant has been the man on the spot at most of the major news stories of the last twenty years. His mordant wit, keen sense of the absurd and acute powers of analysis pervade the book. He has a wealth of funny anecdotes featuring the key political figures of our time and his understanding of the labyrinthine workings of Westminster – and Broadcasting House – is second to none.

'An all-time rip-roaring read'
Independent on Sunday

'This intriguing autobiography covers the author's broadcasting life and snapshots from an extraordinary family history Sergeant is neither self-deprecating nor boastful . . . as moving as John Mortimer's memoirs, The Summer of Dormouse'
The Times

'Excellent'
Daily Telegraph

MICHAEL MOORE

Adventures in a TV Nation

PAN BOOKS

A collection of classic stories of controversy, hypocrisy and down-right ridiculousness. Michael Moore has many hysterical things to say about deserving targets of all political persuasions from the anaemic left to the giddy right. Hailed as 'brilliant' and 'subversive' on both sides of the Atlantic, Moore champions the issues which concern us all. Only in *TV Nation* will you witness the unthinkable and the simply wish-fulfilling: Mexican and African Americans gate-crashing a Ku Klux Klan rally to regale them with love songs and install a kissing booth; the home of the director of the largest car alarm company in America being woken to the tuneful chorus of a dozen car alarms at 6 a.m.

If you have ever felt powerless or at the mercy of the system, *Adventures in a TV Nation* is guaranteed to lift your spirits.

MICHAEL MOORE

Downsize This!

PAN BOOKS

From the creator of the hit BBC TV show *TV Nation*, the most popular documentary of all time, the Emmy award-winning *Roger And Me*, and the stupendously successful *Stupid White Men*, comes a new edition of his classic book for all you disillusioned, political abstainees who are working longer hours for less pay and have had enough.

Michael Moore has established himself as someone who just won't shut up, go away, or otherwise do what political and corporate fat cats would like him to do.

Nothing but the truth is sacred in this hilarious screed on the state of the USA. With chapter headings such as 'Why Doesn't General Motors Sell Crack?' setting the tone for a biting indictment of American corporate politics, Moore's take no prisoners attitude is brutally funny, insightful, irrepressible. The issues raised are universal. Michael Moore lifts the veil on the people who set themselves up as our role models and exposes them.

OTHER BOOKS

AVAILABLE FROM PAN MACMILLAN

MICHAEL MOORE
DOWNSIZE THIS!   0 330 41915 3   £7.99
ADVENTURES IN A TV NATION   0 330 41914 5   £7.99

JOHN SERGEANT
GIVE ME TEN SECONDS   0 330 48490 7   £7.99

JOHN SIMPSON
A MAD WORLD, MY MASTERS   0 330 35567 8   £7.99
STRANGE PLACES,
    QUESTIONABLE PEOPLE   0 330 35566 X   £7.99

All Pan Macmillan titles can be ordered from our website,
www.panmacmillan.com, or from your local bookshop
and are also available by post from:

Bookpost, PO Box 29, Douglas, Isle of Man IM99 1BQ
Credit cards accepted. For details:
Telephone: +44(0)1624 677237
Fax: +44(0)1624 677237
E-mail: bookshop@enterprise.net
www.bookpost.co.uk

Free postage and packing in the United Kingdom

Prices shown above were correct at the time of going to press.
Pan Macmillan reserve the right to show new retail prices on covers
which may differ from those previously advertised in the text
or elsewhere.